THE SENSE OF HISTORY
IN GREEK AND
SHAKESPEAREAN DRAMA

THE SENSE OF HISTORY
IN GREEK AND
SHAKESPEAREAN DRAMA

By TOM F. DRIVER

COLUMBIA UNIVERSITY PRESS

NEW YORK 1960

PUBLISHED IN GREAT BRITAIN, INDIA, AND PAKISTAN
BY THE OXFORD UNIVERSITY PRESS
LONDON, BOMBAY, AND KARACHI
LIBRARY OF CONGRESS CATALOG CARD NUMBER: 59-15146
MANUFACTURED IN GREAT BRITAIN

For Anne

What is the basis of dramatic art?
"Historic art."
Nothing can be more reasonable. Poetry
has been compared with painting; very good,
but a better comparison would be between
poetry and history.

DIDEROT

PREFACE

Not only in literature, but also in virtually every other intellectual pursuit, our age is evincing its interest in problems of time. The subject is so omnipresent, its ramifications so multifarious, that one can imagine our appearing to some distant observer very much like fish who have decided to solve the riddle of water.

However futile the task, we have our reasons for attempting it. There are terrors in our day which blanket the future with uncertainty. The order of time in which our fathers believed—inevitable progress—has been destroyed, and it is incumbent upon us to discover another. Hence, the contemporary concern with the philosophy of history.

In this atmosphere, it seemed likely that a study of cultural assumptions regarding history in Shakespeare and the Greeks would be valuable. Being a student of literature, I hoped such a study would throw light on the question of dramatic form, enlarging our understanding of dramatists whom we seem destined to love more than to comprehend. If, at the same time, the study contributed to a more general understanding of man in his historical situation, so much the better.

While writing on so grand and complex a subject, I have kept in mind the warning contained in the censure which Esteban pronounced in *Fuente Ovejuna*: "They pretend to be as learned as theologians the way they mix up the past and the future—but if you ask them anything about the immediate present they are completely at a loss." It has been my trustful assumption that knowledge of what our greatest dramatists expressed about the past and the future would be of value in the present.

The book is divided into three parts. The first begins by sketching the background in terms of both drama and history, answering the question why one should consider drama and history together. From there I turn to the separate understandings of time and history held by the classical Greeks and in the Judaeo-Christian stream. Although the scope of the work did not permit this part of the investigation to utilize original sources, I believe it affords sound conclusions based upon the research of others.

The second part is an unavoidable digression made necessary by the lack of any widespread agreement about the meaning of the phrase "dramatic form." Since my purpose is to show that it is the form of the plays, more than their subject matter, which bears the mark of the presuppositions about time, it was obligatory to inform the reader of what I think is involved when one speaks of dramatic form.

The third part is an examination, in some detail, of four Greek and four Shakespearean plays in the light of the material in Part I, using the method of comparison and contrast. In every case but one I have tried to juxtapose plays which show some similarity in theme or subject matter, in order that the differences in form might be thrown into higher relief. In the case of *Macbeth* and the *Oedipus Tyrannus* I chose two very compact plays in which the question of structure is paramount. The Appendix gives further reasons for having selected the particular plays in question.

The biblical quotations in my text are from the *Revised Standard Version*. As I was nowhere making a point of the influence of the language of the English Bible on Shakespeare, it seemed best to use the most accurate modern translation. The Shakespearean quotations are from *The Complete Plays and Poems of William Shakespeare*, ed. by William A. Neilson and Charles J. Hill (Cambridge, Mass., 1942). The text of *The Persians* used is edited by Gilbert Murray, *Asechyli, Septem Quae Supersunt Tragoediae* (Oxford, 1952). Elsewhere, quotations from the Greek tragedians are from the Loeb Classical Library editions. Unless otherwise noted, the translations are my own.

In the preparation of this work I have been greatly assisted by Professors S. F. Johnson, Oscar James Campbell, Moses Hadas, and James Muilenburg, for whose guidance and friendship I am very grateful. I wish to acknowledge special indebtedness to Professors Hadas and Johnson, and to Mr. Gerritt Lansing and Mr. Henry Wiggins of the Columbia University Press, who have been instrumental in bringing the book into print. The manuscript was faithfully edited by Miss Anita Weiner. My obligation to other scholars and teachers is partly acknowledged in the footnotes; but the reader will perceive, better than I, my debt to many who remain unnamed.

TOM F. DRIVER

Union Theological Seminary
New York, 1959

CONTENTS

PART I: INTRODUCTION

I

DRAMA AND HISTORY

It was Aristotle himself who first found it desirable to examine the relation between drama and history. What Aristotle—or, more correctly, dramatic practice before him—joined could not easily be put asunder.

In 1605, Francis Bacon, eager to defend poetry against its critics, could assert: "Poetry is . . . nothing else but *Fained Historie*." [1] Florio in 1591 had complained that none of the plays of the English stage were "right comedies . . . nor right tragedies . . . [but] representations of histories without any decorum." [2] Sir Philip Sidney wrote (1595): "And even *Historiographers*, although their lippes sound of things done, and veritie be written in their foreheads, have been glad to borrow both fashion and perchance weight of the Poets." [3] As for more recent times, the comment of Eric Bentley on Friedrich Hebbel reveals a strong current in modern thought:

Hebbel is the first great dramatic critic and practitioner to show the explicit influence of that historical imagination which is one of the great novelties of modern times. . . . Those who think of history and tragedy as necessarily antithetic would assert that Hebbel wrote dramatic histories and not tragedies. For history is his very mode of vision. [4]

That playwrights have been attracted to history as subject matter for representation on the stage is well known. [5] Aeschylus has left us one

---

[1] *Of the Proficiencies and Advancement of Learning*, Book II, fols. 17 and 18, quoted in Lily B. Campbell, *Shakespeare's Histories* p. 101. For a full discussion, see chapter, "History Versus Poetry in Renaissance England", pp. 85–105.

[2] *First Fruits*, quoted by Thomas R. Lounsbury in *Shakespeare as a Dramatic Artist*, p. 12.

[3] "The Defence of Poesie," in *The Complete Works of Sir Philip Sidney*, ed. by Albert Feuillerat, III, 5.

[4] *The Playwright as Thinker*, pp. 28–29.

[5] Cf. Irving Ribner, *The English History Play in the Age of Shakespeare*, Chap. 1.

out-and-out history play in *The Persians*, and there is evidence that others were written by his contemporaries. The Roman *fabulae prae-textae*, although their number was small and only the *Octavia* survives, employed historical subjects.[6] The Renaissance was fascinated by the romance of representing past events on the stage, as Florio lamented.

In the modern theater, history has appeared as an alluring subject wherever romanticism has been a strong force, in spite of the fact that romanticism in the long run tends to destroy historical thinking. When Dumas *père* said in 1831 that "life is not interesting, but history is," he was at the farthest pole from Diderot's assertion in 1758 that history is the basis of dramatic art. The latter regarded history as an avenue of entrance into real human existence in time and social relationships: history embraced the present moment, its limits and possibilities. Diderot was interested in history because he was, or fancied himself to be, a realist. Dumas regarded history as an avenue of escape from the uninteresting reality of present life. "History," the then and there, the glorious, was interesting; life, the here and now, the evident, was not. Few better comparisons could be found to illustrate drama's continual interest in history, and also the highly equivocal character of "history" as a term. When the drama is related to history, what is it, in fact, related to? And how deep does the concern of the dramatic for the historic go?

The connections between drama and history lie much deeper than might be thought from the mere observation that historical material frequently finds its way onto the stage. That in itself would be natural enough; for what could be more obvious than that the playwright in search of material should turn to stories already set forth about things that have happened? If Bandello has written *novelle* that go well on the stage, why not have a look at Holinshed or Plutarch, who also have set down interesting narratives? Considered in this light, history is simply one of a number of possible sources for plot and character.

However, if the inquiry be pushed further—if it be carried to the point where it becomes necessary for an Aristotle to distinguish between poetry and history, or for a Diderot to declare historic art to be

---

[6] E. C. Chickering, *An Introduction to Octavia Praetexta*, p. 15. Titles and/or fragments of eleven *fabulae praetextae* remain in addition to the *Octavia*. See Frank J. Miller, *The Tragedies of Seneca*, pp. 417–20, who points out that this is a very small number compared with the total number of titles, fragments, and plays known. He attributes the lack of quantity and significance in the genre not to Roman lack of patriotism or historical subjects, but to too great dependence upon the Greek dramatists.

the very basis of dramatic art—then a more subtle problem presents itself. Here we have to look into the meaning of "history" and to inquire about the nature of the drama itself.

To the modern scientific mind the difference between history as documented fact and drama as fictional or semi-fictional tale makes their distinction necessary. Nevertheless, in older usage the language preserved the wisdom that any coherent history was a story, was (in the root meaning) a fabrication, something made. Narrative, taken alone, is certainly not a peculiar attribute of drama. It belongs equally to the romance, to the novel, or to narrative poetry. Drama, however, is distinguished from these literary forms by its special, complex relationship to the reality we call time. As a *narrative* art, along with the others just mentioned, it addresses itself to the telling of events which take place in the past, present, or future; and by its use of language it may refer consciously to the phenomenon of passing time. But as a *performing* art, along with music and the dance, it has its very existence in time. The fully realized drama is itself a temporal act. The latter point is one which has not often been stressed. As Eric Bentley has put it:

Analyses of the structure of plays seldom fail to tell us where the climax lies, where the exposition is completed, and how the play ends, but they often omit a more obtrusive factor—the *principle of motion*, the way in which a play copes with its medium, with time-sequence.[7]

That the drama is so closely bound up with time—not only dealing with it as idea, or presenting it as narrative, but also utilizing it as a constituent factor in its performance—means that the drama can never be a subject of purely literary study. It has to be known in relation to the stage, to the theater for which it was conceived. The notion of "theater," when carried to its fullest, corresponds to a more general notion of the total physical and temporal setting in which human action is conceived as taking place.[8] The act of performing the play in the theater, therefore, becomes a miniature reflection of historical action generally, since it is a significant action taking place within the limits imposed by the conventions of the theater. This will be particularly true in those dramatic periods, such as the Greek and Elizabethan, where the theater was frankly accepted as the locus of the action and

[7] *In Search of Theatre*, p. 332.

[8] A general indebtedness to Francis Fergusson's *The Idea of a Theatre*, should be recognized here. Professor Fergusson has shown the importance of the notion of the cosmos as theater for the great periods of dramatic creativity. See especially pp. 128–30.

where there was not, as in recent times, an attempt to black out both audience and theater, leaving only the illusion-world brightly lit. (Even the latter practice has its ideational presuppositions, owing as it does so much to the spirit of the laboratory, invoked by Zola, and to an age which until quite recently has appeared determined to find truth in the detailed study of isolated phenomena, divorced from the configurations of historical events and from the social fabric.)

The theater, then, tends to reflect the assumptions of its age regarding time and history because it is on the one hand a narrative of temporal events, and on the other hand an enactment taking place within a moment of time. Since events taking place inside an assumed frame of reference are its subject matter, and the temporal re-enactment of those events is its medium, it becomes a miniature history in itself.

Recent philosophical attention to the nature and method of historical writing has brought to the fore certain aspects of the historical enterprise which show how clearly it belongs to the field of the humanities, in contrast to earlier, simpler understandings of history as purely an empirical science. The philosophical implications of the historical endeavor have been examined, as well as its kinship with literature; and these studies have shown that history, like literature and philosophy, is a construct of the mind, in addition to whatever may be said of it as scientific investigation. That is, as an investigation it may be, and should be, as scientific as possible—in the reliance upon documentary, archaeological, and other evidence—but as a reconstruction of the past it inevitably brings into play the imagination as a formative element.

Although the *Oxford English Dictionary* lists nine different senses of the word "history," these may be reduced essentially to three. The root meaning in Greek, apparently, was investigation or inquiry. The term ἱστορία, which has that meaning, is traced to the root ἰδ, which means "to know." Therefore, ἱστορία was a "finding out." [9] The earliest Greek history writing was characterized by the spirit of empirical investigation. Herodotus adopted as his explicit method the interrogation of eye witnesses to the events he wished to describe.[10] It is the scientific understanding of history which has reappeared as the

[9] "the word ἱστορίη shows its Ionian origin, and always connoted physical research too, which was originally its true meaning." Werner Jaeger, *Paideia: The Ideals of Greek Culture*, I, 379.

[10] R. G. Collingwood, *The Idea of History*, pp. 24–25.

hallmark of modern historiography, taking its lead from the call for
objectivity, accuracy, and unbiased investigation set forth in the nineteenth century by B. G. Niebuhr and Leopold von Ranke.

By the time the Romans had borrowed the word from the Greeks
and it had passed into Latin as *historia*, the primary meaning had
changed to that of a *narrative* of past events, which in turn led to its
being used to denote any narrative, so that it came to mean merely an
account, a tale, or a story. The word "story" itself is, of course, derived
from it. This change is extremely important. It represents a shift from
emphasis upon the enterprise of discovering truth, in more or less
pragmatic ways, to emphasis upon the accomplished result, the literary
(or oral) form into which the inquiry is finally cast. Although this new
emphasis strikes us as peculiarly Roman, rather than Greek, it had begun to appear before Rome's ascendancy. No doubt the conjunction
of rhetoric with history, which began perhaps in Thucydides, was
partly responsible.

The ambiguity of the term passed over into English and became
one of the reasons why "drama" and "history" are so often linked
together. They are both narrative; and they may be true or fictional.
Thus Shakespeare in the Induction to *The Taming of the Shrew* can
have his characters say:

> Your honour's players . . .
> Are come to play a pleasant comedy; . . .
> It is a kind of history   (ii. 131–44)

without implying necessarily that the "history" is a true story. At the
same time, the other connotation of the word means that the idea of
factuality is never completely absent, so that the dramatist who calls
his play a history is inviting his audience to make believe, to pretend
that this is a story which happened "once upon a time."

The use of the word "history" to refer primarily to a narrative or
account of something led, in turn, to its third basic meaning. The shift
from emphasis on inquiry to emphasis on narrative reflected an awareness that some form, some cohesive unity might be said to exist in the
very events described. This awareness could not help but lead to the
eventual application of the word, not to the enterprise of discovery,
and not to the narrative of events, but to the very events themselves.
Thus we get the word in its modern sense, as when we speak of "the
study of history." The assumption here is that the history of a nation,

a person, an idea, or a biological form, exists already, and that the scholar sets himself to discover what that history is. In this view, the facts themselves are history.

From the original Greek meaning, through the later Greek and Latin, to the modern view of history as a subject of study, a course of development may be discerned. There is first a separation between the objects studied and the endeavor by means of which the study is carried on. "History" refers only to the latter. Then there is a concern for the form in which the telling of the inquiry is set out, parallel with a feeling that the object of study itself has a form and cohesiveness. Then there is an identification of form with the object studied. The third attitude may share with the first a scientific spirit of investigation, but there lies within it a deposit from the second which assumes a pattern and structure in events, and this assumed structure comes to be called history.

The foregoing analysis of the term "history" should make it clear that a different conception regarding man's orientation in the world of time and events is presupposed in each of the three meanings we have noted. These conceptions, which until recent times were not often consciously reflected upon, represent what we may call the historical consciousness. It should be clear that where the term "history" refers to an inquiry or process of investigation rather than to the object of study there is no "history" in the modern sense. There is, therefore, a radically different historical consciousness. A man who lives where there is no organized history to be studied—but only various occurrences and a certain lore of the past—must have a quite different view of himself in relation to the flow of time from the man who lives where "history" is already conceived of as a reality, as having a certain form, to which he may address himself.

If we may distinguish between ἱστορία as "inquiry," and *historia* as "account" or "tale," then the change from one to the other reflects an awareness on the part of Rome which the classical period in Greece did not have—namely, that the events of time, past and present, could be thought of as possessing a form comparable to the form of a narrative. However slowly this awareness may have developed, it must be clear to anyone who compares the *Aeneid* with the Homeric epics that Vergil writes for people who are prepared to assume an identity between the story of Rome and the history of the known world.[11]

[11] See Chap. II, pp. 35–37 of this book.

It is this preconception of time and the content of time which informs the historical consciousness of a given age and the most representative of its writers, painters, and other artists. And it is this historical consciousness which, I suggest, bears a close relation to the art of the drama.

It should be borne in mind, then, that when one speaks of the relation of drama to history he is referring not only to the idea of narrative, but also—and more importantly—to one or more of several conceptions of time. If history is thought of as simply "everything that has happened"—which is more or less the encyclopedic idea, but essentially an unhistorical view—then of course the drama, like everything else, is related to it, but in so general a way as to have no particular significance. If, on the other hand, history is regarded as, say, a dialectical movement in the Hegelian sense, a specific and pregnant idea of time is manifest; and it is then possible to build a theory of dramatic structure upon it, as, for instance, Marian Galloway has done in a recent book on playwriting technique.[12] One should be wary of making too much of a particular philosophical theory, and even more wary of applying that theory to dramatic works written in periods before the theory emerged. However, if it can be discovered that a certain general conception of history was assumed within a given age, then there is reason to suspect that the drama of that age will reflect that conception in its structure. That variant structures are evident in the Greek and the Shakespearean drama, and that the assumptions regarding time and history in their respective ages go far to account for them is the thesis presented here.

The modern philosopher of history rediscovers the two early meanings of history as "inquiry" and as "account" or "story." The result is that he sees historical thinking to be the perception of meanings and patterns in the flow of events. Inasmuch as these meanings and patterns are thought of as belonging to the world of time—in contrast to essentially timeless patterns such as those of mathematics or aesthetics —they may be said to partake of the dramatic.

I have been helped to see the various components of what is here called "history" by R. G. Collingwood's influential work, *The Idea of History*. The essential problem which occupies Collingwood's attention

---

[12] *Constructing a Play.* See pp. 20–25, where the reader is also referred to the source— Hegel, *The Philosophy of Fine Art.* Hegel's own theory of tragedy rested squarely upon his understanding of time.

in the book is the relation of the historian to the evidence with which he deals, and to the events which are revealed to him through that evidence. Collingwood perceives that the relation of the historian to evidence and events is not at all the same as that of the natural scientist to the phenomena which the latter must collect, classify, and propound hypotheses to explain. The historian is always confronted with the problem of authenticity if his evidence is documentary and with the problem of relevance to his inquiry in any case. Thus his endeavor from the outset involves many judgments and decisions of a type not raised for the natural scientist.

Yet the complexity regarding evidence is but a prelude to that regarding the historian's relation to the past event itself, and it is on the latter point that Collingwood makes certain observations which are pertinent to our present analysis. His own words will be the most concise:

The historian, investigating any event in the past, makes a distinction between what may be called the outside and the inside of an event. By the outside of the event I mean everything belonging to it which can be described in terms of bodies and their movements: the passage of Caesar, accompanied by certain men, across a river called the Rubicon at one date, or the spilling of his blood on the floor of the senate-house at another. By the inside of the event I mean that in it which can only be described in terms of thought: Caesar's defiance of Republican law, or the clash of constitutional policy between himself and his assassins. The historian is never concerned with either of these to the exclusion of the other. He is investigating not mere events (where by a mere event I mean one which has only an outside and no inside) but actions, and *an action is the unity of the outside and inside of an event.* He is interested in the crossing of the Rubicon only in its relation to Republican law, and in the spilling of Caesar's blood only in its relation to a constitutional conflict. His work may begin by discovering the outside of an event, but it can never end there; he must always remember that the event was an action, and that his main task is to think himself into this action, to discern the thought of its agent.[13]

For my present purposes, the significant element lies in the words I have italicized. History is not simply "what happened," unless that phrase be taken to imply the total meaning of the event.[14]

[13] *Idea of History,* p. 213. Italics are mine.

[14] Unfortunately, Collingwood's love of thought for its own sake leads him almost immediately to upset the balance which he had expressed in the assertion that the historian is never concerned with either the outside or the inside of the event, the one to the exclusion of the other. Two pages later he has become so carried away with emphasizing the inside that he

Collingwood comes even closer to dramatic thinking when he considers the historian's task of re-enacting past experience. In line with his assertion that the historian is concerned with the inside as well as the outside of the occurrences he studies, Collingwood says that the historian must rethink, in order to rediscover, the thoughts of the past. That is to say, he must re-enter by imaginative process the situation in which the original agent was compelled to act, and he must reproduce in his own mind the process of decision by which that agent came to his own specific resolutions and deeds ". . . But how does the historian discern the thoughts which he is trying to rediscover? There is only one way in which it can be done: by rethinking them in his own mind." [15] Having so stated the matter, Collingwood is then drawn almost involuntarily into the further observation that historical thinking involves re-enactment. The paragraph from which we have just quoted ends with this sentence: "The history of thought, and therefore all history, is the re-enactment of past thought in the historian's own mind." A subsequent section of the book (the arrangement is his editor's) is devoted to "History as Re-Enactment of Past Experience."

No one will have difficulty in perceiving the close parallels to the drama which are here set up in Collingwood's "idea of history." To be sure, his tendency to reduce history to the history of thought goes too far. Yet the stress is valuable because it prevents history being taken as merely a collection of "facts," and it establishes the possibility of entering again into the past (or drawing the past into the present), and so guarantees the organic, living character of what we call history. Now if we hold that the historian is always concerned both with the inside and the outside of events, and if we simultaneously broaden the idea of re-enactment to include not only imaginative rethinking but also the re-doing of the event, we are in the realm of drama. For the task of the dramatist is to perceive not only the external event which he would narrate, but also its internal meaning, its appearance to those who participated in it; and he must re-create out of his imaginative sympathy the feelings, desires, and judgments of those who acted in the history which thus emerges under his pen. The actual theater performance, without which the drama is incomplete, is the

---

makes his famous assertion, "All history is the history of thought." We need not concur in the latter statement to be able to appreciate the correctness in the former perception of history as a discovery of inner meanings conjoined to outer circumstances and occurrences.

[15] *Idea of History*, p. 215.

extension of the dramatist's imagination, which is then shared by director, actor, and ultimately by the audience. In these circumstances re-enactment is carried to the fullest, as the history is re-projected in physical terms in a social situation, carried beyond the historian's study to the communal arena once more.

The reader may be inclined to grant the validity of these observations with regard to historical drama (he knows that Shakespeare tells us not only that Bolingbroke deposed Richard II, but also what each of them may be imagined to have said and thought on that occasion); but he may feel that historical drama is after all only a small portion of dramatic literature, that therefore the history-drama analogies should not be pressed too far. In that case, let me turn to Collingwood again:

> If it is by historical thinking that we rethink and so re-discover the thought of Hammurabi or Solon, it is in the same way that we discover the thought of a friend who writes us a letter, or a stranger who crosses the street. . . . It is only by historical thinking that I can discover what I thought ten years ago . . . or what I thought five minutes ago. . . . In this sense all knowledge of mind is historical.[16]

That is to say, the historical idea is present wherever, be it past or present, an event is to be considered in both its subjective and objective aspects, wherever a willing agent is involved. The basic dichotomy thus established is not between history and literature (commonly separated because one is fact, the other fiction) but between history and nature—or, thinking of the scholarly disciplines which study them, history and natural science.

> In the case of nature, this distinction between the outside and the inside of an event does not arise. The events of nature are mere events, not the acts of agents whose thought the scientist endeavours to trace. . . . When a scientist asks, "Why did that piece of litmus paper turn pink?" he means, "On what occasions do pieces of litmus paper turn pink?" When an historian asks, "Why did Brutus stab Caesar?" he means, "What did Brutus think which made him decide to stab Caesar?" The cause of the event, for him, means the thought in the mind of the person by whose agency the event came about: and this is not something other than the event, it is the inside of the event itself.[17]

The dramatist is thus allied with the historian, as over against the natural scientist in his intention to present human events in their dual aspects of objective occurrence and volitional action. Were history

---

[16] *Idea of History*, p. 219.   [17] *Ibid.*, pp. 214–15.

regarded as a mere collection of facts in sequence, the relation to drama would be obscure; for then drama as history would have to be seen as nothing but the staged presentation of past happenings, presumably to inform or refresh the mind as to what went on. Very little drama has done that, and no important drama has attempted it. All great drama has been concerned to show the feelings, desires, and judgments of men in the events of which they themselves form a part.

Later in this work I shall attempt to show that the Hellenic culture was concerned with nature far more than with history—with the way things universally occur, with the forms and structures of reality, in contrast to the way in which man's unique decisions create new situations in which other unique decisions are called for. Nevertheless, we shall have to point out that in its dramatic character the Greek drama ran counter to the prevailing philosophical views; for to be dramatic it had to examine not only the μοῖρα, which determined the outside of the events, it had also to rethink and re-enact the thoughts and decisions of its heroes. To the extent that those decisions appeared as real, the drama partook of the historic, in Collingwood's sense. Much of the greatness of the Greek drama arises from the tension thus resulting from "historical" elements forcing their way into "natural" presuppositions.

We have been examining one point of affinity between historical thinking and dramatic thinking—namely, the concern of both for the inner as well as the outer side of action. Another point of affinity lies in the necessity for both to perceive patterns of significance and meaning in a sequence of events.

The dramatist and the historian, since both are storytellers, must choose from the data at their disposal the particular events which are significant for the total work and must know, or at least feel, what the principle of coherence and significance is. If the dramatist begins with a plot ready-made (whether of his own invention or another's), the question is already decided. But if he begins with material that must be reduced to dramatic form or altered to suit his purpose (novel, chronicle, old play or what-have-you), his first task is to select and organize. In order to fulfill that task, he must have in mind (or "in his bones") a principle which will impart meaning and form to the whole.

This problem confronts the novelist, the short-story writer, and the poet; but it is particularly acute for the dramatist because a play's compactness and necessity for presentation before an audience force its author to pay more attention to selection and structure. The audience must receive a dominant impression at one sitting and at first hearing. The drama cannot escape the requirement of making sense under the discipline of time.

The historian, too, must select and organize from the material at his disposal. To do so, he also must have a principle, something according to which his many events may be related. Like the dramatist, he most often does not invent such a principle or pattern himself, though occasionally a Marx or a Toynbee will attempt to do so. The historian, like the dramatist, usually sets out to tell better a story which has first been told by poet, tradition, or ancient record.

Gustav Freytag, in *Technique of the Drama* (pp. 15–16), has a very explicit statement of the selecting and shaping activities of both the dramatist and the historian, similar to that presented here. He follows it with one equally explicit regarding the difference between poet and historian:

But he [the historian] is distinguished from the poet by this, that he seeks conscientiously to understand what has actually occurred, exactly as it was presented to view, and that the inner connection which he seeks is produced by the laws of nature which we revere as divine, eternal, incomprehensible. To the historian, the event itself, with its significance for the human mind, seems of most importance. To the poet, the highest value lies in his own invention, and out of fondness for this, he, at his convenience, changes the actual incident [p. 16].

That, of course, is true if taken as an expression of the poet's freedom; but it is necessary to say that the poet's own invention is not an ultimate value *per se*. Invention is the poetic means of achieving significance. The bulk of drama has not been given over to fantasy. It has striven to imitate action in a recognizable world; and it is in the latter aim that the parallel between the dramatist and the historian is found.

It does not particularly matter whether the historian or the dramatist is original in his selectivity and interpretation. What is important is that the material with which each is concerned requires selection and interpretation at some point in its development. The historian may choose to elaborate a universal history, in which case he must omit vastly more from the record than he includes, adopting the most meaningful principle of inclusion and relevance. Or he may choose to write the history of one nation, one tribe, one period, or the like, in which case his initial problem is to determine what constitutes a proper unit of study, so that the limits of his inquiry are not merely arbitrary. In every case, he is faced with the necessity for perceiving some type of structural unity. This unity is never objectively "there." It is chosen by the historian, or assumed by his culture. Such choice or assumption I call the discovery of patterns and meanings in history. These patterns and meanings are not the same in every age and among all peoples. In Chapters II and III, I shall outline some of the major differences between the historical (or, as it happens, ahistorical) assumptions of classical Greek culture and those of the Hebraic-Christian tradition.

Like the historian, the dramatist deals with events which have occurred, or are assumed to have occurred, in time and space. He must arrange those events into an order, involving emphasis and subordination. He must decide upon or assume a certain role for time to play in the unfolding of his story—whether time is creative or destructive, objective or subjective, constant or fluid, important or only casual. And he must relate that understanding of time to the time of performance of the play.

The relation of historical patterns and meanings to dramatic art becomes even clearer when we remember that Christendom has spoken traditionally of history as a drama. It has sometimes referred to "the drama of history," sometimes to "the drama of salvation." I have not been able to discover when such terminology came into use, but as we know that at least as early as the fourth century certain Christians were either producing religious plays or were drawing analogies between the liturgy and drama, I suspect it was very early.[18] The Christian patterning of history suggests the idea of a drama for many reasons, the most important of which are, on the one hand, the sense of role-playing involved in the idea of the Incarnation, as suggested by the debates over the terms ὑπόστασις and *persona* in Christological discussion; and, on the other hand, the structuring of history around a center (Christ) which then becomes determinative for the beginning and end of history: "For Christian thought Christ is the

---

[18] See Allardyce Nicoll, *Masks, Mimes, and Miracles*, p. 210. The fact that the theatrical references of the fourth century are primarily connected with the Arians points to the temptation of Christian drama toward the heretical reduction of the Incarnation to the level of theatrical illusion, thus to lose the full humanity of Christ as well as the genuinely historical character of revelation. It is here, rather than in matters of exhibitionism or morals, that the fundamental tension between the Church and drama lies, although the latter have at times occupied the forefront of the discussion. However, I would also maintain that the tendency to move from the realm of historical tension into that of illusion is as dangerous a temptation for any type of drama as it is for the Christian.

center of history in which the beginning and end, meaning and purpose of history are constituted." [19] This Christian interpretation of history stands between the Greek tragedians and the drama of the Renaissance. It harmonizes more closely with the "Christian" drama of Shakespeare than it does with classical drama for the simple reason that the Shakespearean drama is to a large extent modeled upon it. Yet the Christian interpretation of history could hardly have been envisioned at all had it not been for the Hellenic perception of form and structure in all things, of which the Aristotelian discussion of beginning, middle, and end in tragedy is a good example. Here the cross-fertilization between dramatic and historical thinking is evident. The historical consciousness of Judaism (which, as I shall show in Chapter III, already contains drama-ritual elements) is refined and shaped into the Christian drama of history as it comes into contact with Greek dramatic patterns.[20] Later, that "drama of history" in turn exerts a powerful influence on the dramatic literature which, after many centuries, arises in an essentially Christian culture.

This summary is enough to indicate that parallels, affinities, and mutual influences do exist between dramatic and historical thinking. Basically the connections are located in two areas. On the one hand, both drama and history are concerned with events not only as objective phenomena, but also as part and parcel of human thought, feeling, and choice. On the other hand, both drama and history are concerned to discover meanings and patterns in the flux of events. The one concern points to human freedom in a physical world; the other, to significance adhering to a total temporal process. Together, they point to an understanding of both drama and history as a "compound of meaning and action." [21]

[19] Paul J. Tillich, *The Interpretation of History*, p. 251.

[20] I have two things in mind here: (1) the influence of Greek dramatic ceremonies, through the mystery cults, on Christian rituals; and (2) Hellenic patterns in symbolic thinking such as are discernible in the Fourth Gospel. The latter work has many quasi-dramatic elements, and they arise from the attempt to achieve patterns and meanings in the life of Jesus which are not nearly so much in evidence in the Synoptics. Hellenistic influence on the Fourth Gospel is usually acknowledged.

[21] This interesting phrase, which seems to embody both the dramatic and the historical idea, is found in Hartley B. Alexander, *God and Man's Destiny*, p. 51. It occurs in Chap. II, entitled "Drama as the Cosmic Truth," in which Alexander holds that the compound of meaning and action represents a philosophical principle apart from which the world is not intelligible. History, he says, is meaningful only as drama. He then rightly observes that such understanding is essentially religious: "It is the religious insight not that the world is artificially dual—so that here is phenomenon and there reality, here knowledge and there its object—but that it is inherently dual, the Action of itself lifting into being a meaning, and the World arising as the compound of meaning and action."

The connection between drama and history is further shown by the fact that time is a constituent element in dramatic structure. The drama is performed in a moment of time, in a social situation. It therefore exists in an historical moment quite as much as it reflects an historical view. It is related to time and historical occurrence not only as the latter are subject matter, but also—on a different plane—as they are concrete factors in its very existence.

As the term "history" will recur with great frequency in this study, the reader is entitled to a word concerning its usage. I take the concept of history to involve three elements, two of which form a unit and have been discussed already. Those two are (1) a concern with the free and deliberative, the human side of events occurring in time; and (2) an understanding of patterns and meanings in the flow of events. History involves an assertion of man's freedom without finding the sole locus of meaning in that freedom.

The third element I find in the concept of history may be described as the communal and cosmic setting of time. When one speaks of history one is assuming a time which is relevant to a certain community. There may, of course, exist a completely subjective "history" in which time is set in the context of purely individual psychological experience. So-called "stream of consciousness" writing suggests this. Or there may exist an ideational "history" where time is set in the context of the flow of ideas. Shaw's *Don Juan in Hell* sequence is a case in point; significantly, he has to remove the scene from earth in order to put time in such a setting, essentially to negate time. Such subjective and ideational "histories" I mean to eliminate by speaking of the "communal setting" of time. History thus points to what goes on, or is supposed as going on, in the objective world which the society shares together. To escape the world or society is to escape history. It was with such an idea in mind that Diderot spoke of historic art as the basis of dramatic art.

To this social setting of time I have added "the cosmic setting of time" in order to point not only to the fact that history has usually been thought to involve more-than-human factors, but also that history must always be supposed to take place in some arena. Time and space are coordinates.

For these reasons, I shall sometimes speak of an escape from history, meaning an escape from the world of social and cosmic events into a private, uncosmic, or timeless world. Such retreats are sometimes exciting for drama, but they are not natural to it. They are blind alley off-shoots rather than avenues to new growth. The theater by its very constitution reflects the arena of time and the social setting of time. It stands in the present history of its community. From there it turns its attention to the meanings which it sees in the actions of men.

II

HELLENIC HISTORICAL CONSCIOUSNESS: THE EQUILIBRIUM OF NATURE

The first thing to remember about the Greek historical consciousness is that it is, in essence, unhistorical. That is to say, the Greek mind in its search for orientation in the world was not concerned with history as a major component of the world picture. More than that, it had no conception of history at all in the sense that word has come to have in our culture, which owes so much to its religious roots in Hebraism.

Generalization of this kind needs preliminary defense at two points. First, is one entitled to make such all-inclusive statements about any people, involving abstractions like "the Greek mind"? Second, what is meant by history that its presence can be so emphatically denied in the Hellenic experience? To the first question I would reply that my statements will be seen as an attempt to show the drift, the tenor of Greek thinking. "Greek mind" there may not be, but Greek literature, philosophy, and art do show a remarkable consistency in their attitude to time; and my attempt is to delineate some of that consistency in order to show its effect upon the dramatists of Athens. This persistent quality of Greek thought will become even more clear and more homogeneous in appearance when it is contrasted with Hebraic modes of thought set out in the following chapter. Within itself, the Greek world shows some variety; but in contrast with a different view, it shows a distinctive solidarity.

As to the second question, regarding what is meant by history, the reader will recall that, in Chapter I, history was said to involve three elements: consideration of the deliberative side of events (what Collingwood calls the "inside"), discovery of patterns and meanings in the flow of events, and a picture of the communal and cosmic setting of time. History thus involves the actions of human agents not entirely determined in their responses, plus an over-arching meaning and significance, and a reference more inclusive than the purely individual and merely human. The Greek thought tends to slip through a net woven to catch this complex, not because any one element is lacking entirely, but because the components are not bound into a single entity, not held together in dialectical tension. Where the Greek was concerned with human freedom and choice, as in many of the Socratic dialogues for instance, he tended to forget patterns and meanings in temporal events. Likewise, where he was concerned with patterns and meanings in events he tended to lose the freedom of the individual. Moreover, the patterns and meanings he discovered were not so much *in* the flow of events as they were principles which *controlled* the flow of events, as by cause and effect. This outlook precluded his finding (or seeking) any *one* pattern or aim in the occurrences of time. Histories (illustrative stories) tended to replace history.[1] As for the communal and cosmic setting of time, it also was viewed in a different way. Time tended to be absorbed into the cosmos in such a way as to become a function of cosmic space, rather than a different order of reality.

Thus the mentality we may call historical was not coalesced in Greek thought. It was diffused, broken up into many parts, because another principle and way of approaching reality was, for Hellas, dominant and formative.

The tenuous relation which Greek thought bore to historical modes of thinking—nay, the antipathy it had for such thinking—has been expressed by R. G. Collingwood in *The Idea of History*. Following a discussion of Herodotus' achievements in the realm of historiography, he feels it necessary to add a paragraph on the "antihistorical tendency of Greek thought," in which he points out how strange it was that Herodotus should have turned the scientific spirit toward historical inquiry,

for he was an ancient Greek, and ancient Greek thought as a whole has a very definite prevailing tendency not only uncongenial to the growth of historical thought but actually based, one might say, on a rigorously anti-historical metaphysics. History is a science of human action: what the historian puts

---

[1] "in Greek thought there is no view of the world as history, even though there is no lack of historiography as a report of the confusion of human movements and as an example of politics." Tillich, *History*, p. 244. Cf. Collingwood, *Idea of History*, p. 27, who observes that Greek historical methodology prevented the construction of one all-embracing history, since it relied upon eye-witness accounts. The sources therefore perished with each generation, and each work stood alone, self-sustaining.

before himself is things that men have done in the past, and these belong to a world of change, a world where things come to be and cease to be. Such things, according to the prevalent Greek metaphysical view, ought not to be knowable and therefore history ought to be impossible.[2]

The difference between permanence and change, and the Greek passion for what is permanent, to which Collingwood here refers, lies at the base of the Greek attitude to history. Few people lived in a milieu more subject to change than did the Greeks, and few strove harder than they to find a reality beyond it which was not subject to its ceaseless coming to be and passing away.

The foremost changing element in the Greek environment was nature. The roots of Greek culture were agricultural. Her life was, in its earlier period, bound to the rhythm of the changing seasons, the planting and harvesting of crops; and even in the later periods, in the fifth century B.C., for instance, her festivals were still marked with the signs of an agricultural community. In this respect she was not different from most of the other peoples of the Eastern Mediterranean. Since the appearance of Sir James Frazer's *The Golden Bough*, there has emerged a continually growing body of literature devoted to exploring the roots of virtually all Near Eastern culture and mythology in the ritual observances of planting and harvesting, and the ceremonies of fertility.[3] The Hebrews appear to have been the one exception to the general pattern in that part of the world, adapting and changing the prevalent nature-orientation to an historical concern. The Greeks, however, fall into the majority group. Sustenance and the general well-being of the community depended upon the proper relation to the forces of nature, which were personified and deified as goddesses and gods.[4]

Where the primary attention is directed to the flux and change of things in nature, the desire of the community will be to understand and to control. Achievement of control is attempted through ritual, sympathetic magic, and the entire communal structure of required observances and taboos. This, as the Cambridge school of anthropologists has insisted, has important consequences in the rise and

[2] *Idea of History*, p. 20.

[3] See, for instance, works by T. H. Gaster, Jane Harrison, S. H. Hooke, E. O. James, A. W. Pickard-Cambridge, and George Thomson, cited in the Bibliography.

[4] For an excellent description of the type of relation thus established between man, the community, the crops, and nature, the reader may be referred to the first chapter of Theodor H. Gaster's *Thespis: Ritual, Myth and Drama in the Ancient Near East*.

formation of drama.[5] The attempt to understand the consistencies behind the variations in nature, however, is made through mythology, which led, among the Greeks, to a continued process of refinement eventuating in the rise of philosophy.[6] This type of understanding, I believe, is rooted in the desire to perceive the underlying forces and structures which make the changes in nature intelligible, an approach which is characteristic not only of the Greek philosophers, but also of the entire culture out of which they emerged. It is a culture which is at first myth-making; later the myths are subjected to critical analysis and revision, replaced by more sophisticated myths, until the structured outlines of philosophical thought begin to appear. This abstracting and universalizing type of thought does not appear in Hebraism, where nature, although an ever-present reality, is not a primary problem. The Old Testament is full of references to nature; but the understanding of natural processes, the laws of their operation, is never the object of concern. Rather, the focus is on the Creator of nature and the moral demands which seem consequent upon the fact of creation. In Greece, however, the desire to understand through the perception of eternal patterns is characteristic of the entire culture. It was finally given its most overt and intellectualized form in fourth-century philosophy, but it was operative long before in other forms.

Professor Werner Jaeger, in his study of the ideals of Greek culture (*Paideia*) puts the matter in these words, worth quoting at length:

In philosophy the force which produced the forms of Greek art and thought is most vividly displayed. It is the clear perception of the permanent rules which underlie all events and changes in human nature and in human life. . . . The *theoria* of Greek philosophy was deeply and inherently connected with Greek art and Greek poetry; for it embodied not only rational thought, the element which we think of first, but also (as the name implies) vision, which apprehends every object as a whole, which sees the *idea* in everything— namely, the visible pattern. Even when we know the dangers of generalizing, and of interpreting the earlier stage by the later, we cannot help realizing that the Platonic idea—a unique and specifically Hellenic intellectual product— is the clue to understanding the mentality of the Greeks in many other respects. In particular, the tendency to formalize which appears throughout Greek sculpture and painting sprang from the same source as the Platonic

---

[5] See the works of Jane Harrison, A. W. Pickard-Cambridge, and F. M. Cornford cited in the Bibliography.

[6] See, for instance, Henri Frankfort, *Before Philosophy*, especially pp. 248–62.

idea. . . . It was this tendency, too, to construct universal patterns, which distinguished Greek music and mathematics from those of earlier nations, so far as they are known today.[7]

It is significant that Professor Jaeger describes the Greek way of understanding as essentially visual. The eye perceives the form of objects. If the approach to reality is visual, we are led to expect a search for the *structures* of reality, the *forms* governing changing processes. This is just what the Greek quest was.

The Greek orientation in nature and the desire to see the structures in reality determined her attitude to time and history.

The world of nature embodies a process of change and return. Crops emerge from the ground, flourish, cast off their seeds, and return to the earth. The year passes from the cold of winter through budding spring, warm summer, ripened autumn, and returns to winter's barrenness. Man emerges at birth from an unknown existence and returns to another unknown at death.

In the manner of all agricultural peoples, the Greeks were, to repeat, intimately joined to the cycles thus observable in nature—so much so that it has been said that the Greek understanding of time itself is cyclical. Greek "cyclical" understanding has been contrasted with a Hebraic "linear" conception. For instance, Oscar Cullmann, in his study of *Christ and Time*, has set up the antithesis in these words: ". . . we must start from this fundamental perception that the symbol of time for Primitive Christianity as well as for Biblical Judaism and the Iranian religion is the *upward sloping line*, while in Hellenism it is the *circle*" (p. 51).

Erich Frank has described the Greek view in a similar way: "The Greeks thought that time was the time of this world since it was objectively determined by the revolution of the firmament. Time itself, in their opinion, was a circle—a periodical resuming of the same, a cycle in which even the life of the human soul was involved." [8]

In an extended note to the passage just cited, Professor Frank amasses evidence which shows how deeply rooted and how persistently held was the Greek tendency to regard time as cyclical.[9] He begins with the oft-cited quotation from Aristotle: ". . . and so time is regarded as the rotation of the sphere . . . and this is the reason of our habitual way of speaking; for we say that human affairs and those of all

[7] I, xxi–xxii.
[8] *Philosophical Understanding and Religious Truth*, p. 67.   [9] *Ibid.*, p. 82, n. 41.

other things . . . seem to be in a way circular, because all these things come to pass in time and have their beginning and end as it were 'periodically.'" (*Physics* IV. 14. 223b21.) Professor Frank then shows that although the best-known forms of the cyclical idea are the Stoic doctrine of world periods and the Pythagorean-Platonic notion of the migration of souls, nevertheless the concept "occurs with most Greek philosophers, with Heraclitus and Empedocles no less than with Parmenides and even with Aristotle, as is evident from the above quoted passage." [10]

Eudemus is quoted in these words: "But if one may believe the Pythagoreans . . . then some day I myself, with this staff in my hand, shall talk to you who will sit in front of me, just as you are sitting now, and the same will be true of everything else." (Eudemus, *fr.* 51, ed. by Spengel.)

A similar judgment on the prevailing tenor of classical thought is rendered by Reinhold Niebuhr, who recognizes that the cyclical view is the response of rational intelligibility to the world of nature: "For a classical culture the world of change and becoming was intelligible and real in so far as it participated in the changeless world through a cycle of changeless recurrence. For it, time is the cycle of 'coming-to-be and falling away,' of birth and death, of growth and decay."[11] A subordinate theme in classical culture, says Professor Niebuhr, is that the world of change gradually falls into non-being, a picture of decline rather than repetition. "But the dominant conception of the classical world is the cyclical interpretation of time." [12]

Paul Tillich also has remarked on the circular character of the Greek view of time in *The Interpretation of History*. His comments will suggest why I have called the Greek historical consciousness unhistorical and stated its ideal as "the equilibrium of nature": RESOLUTION

Where reality is viewed as Nature, it is governed by the symbol of a circle that returns in itself. This contains a double idea: first, of the inner dynamics, the tension of existence, which strives for development; then of the boundary of development, which by necessity is included in every factor of natural development: the urge to return into itself and to join the end to the beginning. Certainly by this symbol the being is not considered as simply resting. The circular motion can signify the deepest tension and unrest. But beyond all unrest and tension exists the state of rest, of ultimate equalization. The tension is

[10] *Philosophical Understanding and Religious Truth*, p. 82, n. 41.
[11] *Faith and History*, p. 43.　　　　[12] *Ibid.*, p. 44.

limited, the whole at last balanced. On this basis, true historical thinking is impossible. Thus throughout almost all Greek philosophy every deviation from the circular line is an expression of powerless being. Mundane things show their inferior character as contrasted with the heavenly in the very fact that they are not circular but move in centrifugal and intersecting lines. The deviation from the circular line involves a loss not an increase of power. . . . Even where the infinity of time threatens the picture of the circle, as illustrated in the idea of world-eras, the symbol of the circle is victorious in the idea of the "eternal recurrence of the same." [13]

The reader will perceive that when the cyclical view is linked to a nature-orientation, it is not meant merely that the Greeks possessed a naïve image of time based on simple observation of the rotating seasons, the movement of the stars, and the like. All peoples see that. What the Greeks did was to seek passionately after a rational understanding of these phenomena which would at the same time be true to their early religious experience of the sanctity and mystery of nature— an experience not divorced of course from an economic dependence upon nature. The early economic and religious affinity with nature was expressed in the mythology and rituals of the *chthonic* (earth) deities and the various fertility deities associated with them, the most important being that patron-god of the theater, Dionysus. Likewise, the longing for understanding, for seeing the eternally true beyond the changing, is symbolized for us in the Olympian deities.

The conflict between these two sets of gods and goddesses is not an ultimate conflict like that in Palestine, for instance, between Yahweh and Baal. It is a conflict expressing the tension which exists within a circular view of time and reality, as Professor Tillich has spoken of it; and it is capable of being resolved into that kind of sturdy unity which Aeschylus has so brilliantly celebrated in the last part of the *Oresteia*.[14] For if it was the Olympians who spurred man to find rational intelligibility in a circle of ultimately changeless recurrence, it was the fertility *daimons* who had first taught man the perpetual cycles of birth, death, and rebirth. Therefore, whoever would understand the essential qualities of the Greek world view must recognize first the cycles of change in nature, year to year, and second the ability of the rational mind to adopt the circle as a tool of understanding. The circle becomes a principle of Being—a way of harmonizing the changing and the changeless.

[13] *History*, pp. 243–44.   [14] See Chap. VI in this book.

Within such a system of intelligibility, time is necessarily subordinated to nature and to Being. Its function is to bring all things around again to their original state. ". . . . and so time is regarded as the rotation of the sphere."

The judgment that the Greek view of time was cyclical thus has much to recommend it. In general terms it is correct. However, it needs to be modified and set in a larger context. Greek thought about time is not always cyclical. There are linear conceptions as well.

The strongest indication of the linear element comes from the language. The tense-structure in Greek syntax is exceedingly precise. The tenses of the past are the imperfect, perfect, and pluperfect, in addition to the aorist. Those of the future are the simple future, the future perfect, as well as constructions known as future more vivid and future less vivid. Of course there is the present. The conception in such a system is that of a straight line stretching backward and forward from the present. The perfect tenses make it possible to describe action as extending over any portion of the line and being completed at any point. The pluperfect excludes an action from the present, for instance, and confines it to some anterior portion of the line. The aorist serves to describe an action pin-pointed in a moment of time— past or present—as if captured in a snapshot. The tenses of the Greek enable one to move in thought easily backward or forward along an imaginary time line, to divide the line into portions, and to stop at any particular point.

Such a system, in the main, exists also in English. The Western world is used to that type of precision and to such a linear way of imagining time. It is in sharp contrast, however, to Hebrew, where the only distinction in tense possible is between an action completed and one incomplete.[15]

The fact that the Greek picture of time seems in philosophy and

---

[15] The author does not read Hebrew, but the point is made in a popular article by Edmund Wilson, "On First Reading Genesis." Unfortunately, Mr. Wilson draws what I believe to be erroneous conclusions from his comparison of the two languages. He believes that Hebraic thought is timeless, eternal; and he quotes Renan: "Instead of narrating, Israel predicts, that is to say, systematizes. That is why it has prophets, not historians." But anyone who thinks Israel does not have narrative should re-read the Old Testament. Moreover, it is surely a superficial view of a prophet to think him primarily a predictor. He is essentially an interpreter of historical events, which he regards as revelatory, and because of which he issues a call to repentance and righteousness. As for systematizing, that is the Greek characteristic. Greek syntax is the reflection of a mentality which approaches time not as a mode of experience but as material to be measured, cut, arranged, and classified. Prophetic Hebraism did not thus systematize time; it remembered it, acted in it, and hoped for its future.

ritual to be that of a circle and in linguistic syntax to be that of a straight line leads us to look for another principle which shall be common to both conceptions. Such a principle has been pointed out recently by Thorlief Boman in a work entitled *Das hebräische Denken im Vergleich mit dem griechischen.* It does not greatly matter, says Boman, whether time is conceived of as a circle or as a straight line. The important point is that either the circle or the straight line is a *line.* It is not important, or at any rate is secondary, which form the line has. Both are conceptions drawn from space, and the distinctive feature of Hellenism is its tendency to translate time into spatial terms.[16]

Boman is not the first to see that space is the characteristic mode of thought in Hellenism, as time is in Hebraism. He refers to an essay by E. v. Dobschütz, "Zeit und Raum im Denken des Urchristentums." [17] Dobschütz had said that the Greeks thought only of space, the Hebrews of time. That is, says Boman, an overstatement of the matter, since both Plato and Aristotle had pondered the problem of time very deeply (they had been led to ponder it because it presented such a problem to the spatially oriented consciousness). Hesiod is cited as a literary example of concern with time. His story of the five ages of man—gold, silver, copper, heroic, iron—suggests a picture of an original paradise and subsequent fall similar to that in Genesis, which would imply an explanation of man's lot in which time had played an important role. There is a profound difference, however, in that Hesiod's five ages are not connected by any continuous history. Each comes to an end, and the next is created anew by the gods. There is no historical development, and the changes come about not through the guilt of man but through the will of the gods. The five generations are thus five free standing pictures without inner connection.[18] Time is cut. Also, says Boman, typically Greek are those distant places where the blessedness of the golden age is found in the present: Elysium, Atlantis, and the garden of Alkinous. Therefore, while it is too much to say that the Greeks did not pay attention to time, as Dobschütz had held, it is correct to see that their understanding of time is always brought back to subservience to a world-view which is dominated by space.

The common denominator for the images of the circle and the

---

[16] Boman, *Das hebräische Denken,* p. 106.
[17] *Journal of Biblical Literature,* 1922, pp. 212 ff. [18] *Ibid.,* pp. 104–5.

straight line, it appears, is that both are geometric conceptions. Here we see again the importance of nature. The study of nature as objective phenomenon means the study of forms in space. The Greeks reduced even time to such forms. "One might say," in the words of Professor Tillich, "that in this sort of thinking space holds time enclosed within itself. To be sure, time is also there and removes from space the image of a rigid, dead simultaneity of all things. But space does not permit time to go beyond itself, just as physics, ontologically based on this conception of the world, was able to consider time a dimension of space." [19]

The spatial orientation of Greek thought is symbolized in Aristotle's description of time, not in terms of memory or purpose, as a historian would need to view it, but in terms of movement:

Time must either itself be movement, or if not, must pertain to movement and change. . . . Movement, then, is the objective seat of before- and after-ness.[20]

The Greek view of time, therefore, may be seen as a view which absorbs the category of time into that of space. To regard Greek time as cyclical is not erroneous; but it needs to be shown, as I have tried to show, that the Greeks also thought of time as a straight line, and that both line and circle are attempts to bring time into intelligibility by making it submit to a form.[21]

The result of the Greek view of nature and time which I have been describing is that time inevitably takes on a negative character. It was a problem to begin with, and the solution of the problem in terms of space left no positive role for time to play.

[19] Tillich, *History*, p. 244. Cf. Tillich, *Theology of Culture*, pp. 30–39.
[20] *Physics* iv. 11. 219a8. I am indebted for the quotation to Erich Frank, *Philosophical Understanding*, p. 80, who adds that Aristotle is afterwards a bit amazed to realize that some transcendent soul which can contemplate, count, and measure such time is a necessary consequence of the conception. If Aristotle had followed the consequences of that fact, which significantly he did not, he would have been led into that experiential understanding of time which actually was left to Augustine to expound.
[21] As all of these terms are metaphorical, it is useless to argue at length, as many have done, over whether Greek time is or is not cyclical, biblical time linear. The strength of Oscar Cullmann's book, for instance, is in the broad dichotomy he makes between Hebraism and Hellenism regarding time. Its weakness lies in the fact that he does not perceive the metaphorical element in the Bible's picture of time as linear. His literalism at this point betrays him into a rigid schematization which is, I feel, most unbiblical. (For discussion of the latter point, see John Marsh, *The Fullness of Time*, pp. 174–82.) No people thinks in purely cyclical or purely linear terms. In Chap. III we shall have to notice circular elements in Hebrew thought on the subject. It is simply the dominant tendency which is important, and that is very markedly different in Hellas and Israel.

For one thing, the Greek view of the future necessarily became closed. "The conception of time as a cycle of recurrence excludes the emergence of novelty in the world," as Professor Niebuhr has said, citing Epicurus: "Nothing new happens in the universe if you consider the infinite time past." [22]

When the future became closed, of course, the present lost its decisive character. That is, it lost any claim to uniqueness, because nothing done in the present could possibly contribute to anything new in the future.[23] Therefore, although the present is important in philosophical ideas of eternity,[24] and although it is glorified in the Homeric epics in those vivid moments of the heroes' ἀριστεία, it is not, and cannot be, in the final count, of any fundamental consequence. The result is that the past takes on a decisive and determinative character. "Man, accordingly, had no definite aim, no real future. Time, to him, was essentially past." [25] This dominance of the past is true even though the Greek memory of the past is very short, in sharpest contrast to Hebraism and the modern world, which share long memories and great future expectations. For the Greeks the past was not long remembered, but it dominated the present and the future. This is a fact which has the strongest implications for literature, especially the drama.

Time for the Greeks not only was essentially past, it was also destructive. It did not create; it tore down. Professor Niebuhr regards this as a subordinate theme in Greek thought,[26] but it is in some ways a necessary corollary of the cyclical idea—at least psychologically, for the cyclical view is ultimately pessimistic.

Thorlief Boman has summarized the Greek attitude to time and space in this fashion:

Die griechische Zeitauffassung kommt nicht am wenigsten darin zum Ausdruck, dass die Zeit sowohl von Platon als von Aristoteles als etwas viel Geringeres als der Raum gewertet wird, z.T. als ein Übel. Aristoteles erklärt sich mit dem Sprichwort einverstanden, dass die Zeit verzehrt (κατατήκει ὁ

[22] *Faith and History*, p. 45.
[23] Let the reader not misunderstand. In a limited, cautionary way, present action could influence the immediate future. The Greeks were not insane. We shall see that the historians' writings were advanced largely to induce prudent action. But their advice turned out to be mostly negative—how to avoid past mistakes, rather than how to help fulfill a creative potentiality of history.
[24] Eternity could be described as the "eternal now." See Frank, *Philosophical Understanding*, p. 60, especially his note 16.
[25] Frank, *Philosophical Understanding*, p. 68.   [26] *Faith and History*, pp. 45–46.

χρόνος); alles wird alt unter dem Zwang der Zeit und wird vergessen im Laufe der Zeit, aber nichts wird neu oder schön durch die Zeit; daher betrachten wir die Zeit an sich eher als zerstörend als aufbauend. Das, was ewig existiert, z.B. die geometrischen Satze, gehört deshalb nicht in die Zeit hinein (Phys. IV, 12,22030 ff.) Diese Geringschätzung der Zeit durch einen so klaren und nuchternen Geist wie Aristoteles erzählt uns mehr von dem Unterschied zwischen griechischer und hebräischer Zeitaufffassung als alle Versuche, die griechische Zeitvorstellung philosophisch zu verstehen. Aus diesem Grunde wird auch alles, was nur dem Raume angehört, z.B. die Geometrie, so hoch geschätzt, und deshalb müssen sich die Griechen Gott und die göttliche Welt als aller Zeit, Vergänglichkeit und sogar Veränderung enthoben vorstellen, weil Zeit, Veränderung und Vergänglichkeit synonyme Wörter sind.[27]

Time is a curse.[28] It follows that the Greek idea of salvation must be that of an escape from the world of time into a world or place where time does not exist.

For the Greeks, the idea that redemption is to take place through divine action in the course of events in time is impossible. Redemption in Hellenism can consist only in the fact that we are transferred from existence in this world, an existence bound to the circular course of time, into that Beyond which is removed from time and is already and always available. The Greek conception of blessedness is thus spatial; it is determined by the contrast between this world and the timeless Beyond; it is not a time conception determined by the opposition between Now and Then.[29]

We may say that the Greek image of time as a repetitive circle, and the subordination of time to space, resulted in an attitude which found the future essentially closed, the present not unique, all time essentially past. If time brought any change it was destructive, and one looked for salvation in being delivered from its endless repetitions.

Since the picture I have described is certainly unhistorical, in the Judaic or the modern sense, the presence of two great historians, including the "father of history," among the Greeks might well give one pause. Herodotus and Thucydides certainly show that there was not lacking to the Greeks an interest in events in the historical realm. The two also show, however, that that interest was not allowed to develop into a genuinely historical outlook, but was held in tow by the desire to see the permanent structures in temporal events.

Herodotus' journeys over the greater part of the eastern Mediter-

[27] *Das hebräische Denken*, p. 109.   [28] Cullmann, *Christ and Time*, p. 52.   [29] *Ibid*.

ranean area are well known. The travels are not insignificant because they remind us of the investigative nature of much of Herodotus' work. His aim was to tell of the conflict between East and West, between Greeks and barbarians; [30] and his approach to that subject impelled him to travel in those regions and among those peoples concerned in order to investigate who they were, their customs and background. [31] Herodotus thus uses an empirical method of gathering material, and by virtue of that fact associates himself with the Ionian tradition of investigation into nature, and with the early meaning of the word ἱστορίη, which was, as we have said above, that of an inquiry or research. [32]

We have already noticed Collingwood's amazement that such inquiry should be directed toward human events and activities, because of the fact that these, being transient, would seem impossible objects of knowledge under the Greek doctrine that only the permanently real is knowable. [33] Collingwood believes it was a genuine *tour de force* on Herodotus' part, the work of a genius who could elevate the δόξα of his eye-witnesses to events into ἐπιστήμη—true knowledge. [34] Proof of the extraordinary character of that achievement lies in the fact that Herodotus had no successors. He founded no school and wrote the first chapter in no continuous history. Thucydides' kind of history is patently of a different order; the most you could say was that Thucydides set out to do what Herodotus had *not* done. It is equally remarkable that Thucydides himself had no successors. Greek historiography breaks off in the fourth century, while philosophy rises to its height—a philosophy, moreover, which takes no account of the work of the historians. [35] Fourth-century-b.c. philosophy did not, in relation to the fifth-century historians, attempt to take their conclusions or methods into its thought as has, for instance, twentieth-century-a.d. philosophy in relation to nineteenth-century historiography. The fact was, "the Greek mind tended to harden and narrow itself in its anti-historical tendency." [36]

Herodotus has very little of the mentality which I am in this work calling historical. The reason is that he is, or wishes to be, a *scientific*

---

[30] *Herodotus* i. 1.

[31] It may be that the history was written as a way of making use of the material collected in the travels, the theme of conflict between East and West being used as a principle of organization. At any rate, the method of first hand investigation is very important.

[32] See Chap. I, p. 6 of this book. Cf. Jaeger, I, 379.   [33] See pp. 20–21 of this book.

[34] Collingwood, *Idea of History*, p. 25.   [35] *Ibid.*, pp. 28–29.   [36] *Ibid.*, p. 29.

historian, with emphasis on the empirical, inquiring elements contained in that word. As a result, and also because of the intellectual climate in which as a classical Greek he moved, he was led further and further away from the freedom and creativity of events into the attempt to see what were the eternal forces at work in human life, the recurrent patterns. The overarching principle which Herodotus saw more clearly than anything else was the fall which followed *hybris*. Whether the destruction which came on the heels of too great power and prosperity was to be interpreted as the result of the gods' jealousy or as the consequence of man's stepping into a sphere in which he did not belong, it was, nevertheless, a recurrent pattern, and could be observed over and over again in the affairs of men.[37] An example is the defeat of Xerxes, which will be of interest to us because it is also handled by Aeschylus. A. W. Gomme points to the similarity of the interpretation put on this event by the poet and the historian. Both, he says, "have lifted it from the sphere of the local and the temporal, just the story of a Greek victory over barbarians, into that of the permanent, the record of the fate of a man and a people who have been guilty of just that kind of pride which is both wrong in itself and also leads to a fall." [38]

The drift is toward the permanent principle governing the phenomena, which is the scientific way of understanding reality. In such a view human freedom either is destroyed completely—all behavior subordinated to law—or it becomes narrowed to the very limited possibility of avoiding calamity by prudent moderation. This tendency to limit human freedom drives Werner Jaeger to say that Herodotus "subordinated all that he had seen and heard to his description of the power of destiny over individuals and nations." [39]

The full historical sense is therefore lacking in Herodotus—on the one hand because of his tendency to subordinate human behavior to destiny or to certain universal laws, and on the other hand because of his observing and describing the phenomena from the outside. The latter quality is partly due to a scientific type of concern; but also, as Werner Jaeger has pointed out, it is in line with the tradition of epic.[40]

---

[37] A. W. Gomme, *The Greek Attitude to Poetry and History*, pp. 81–82. Cf. S. H. Butcher, *Some Aspects of the Greek Genius*, p. 149.
[38] Gomme, *Greek Attitude*, pp. 82–83. Cf. F. M. Cornford, *Greek Religious Thought from Homer to the Age of Alexander*, p. xx.
[39] *Paideia*, I, 380.
[40] *Ibid*. "His work was, so to speak, a resurrection . . . of the epic tradition; . . . or rather it was a new growth from the old epic root."

Now, while the Greek epic is interested in the details of what happened, it is not interested in them as parts of any historical stream. Homer glorifies Achilles and Hector not because they represent a unique turning point in the history of mankind, but because they are especially noteworthy examples of the valor to which a man ideally may rise. One might argue that the Trojan War was remembered by the Greeks because of its historic significance in the life of their culture, but that element is not present in Homer. He sings their song because of what they embody of human *arete*, not because of what they accomplished. This is what Jaeger apparently sees also in Herodotus' possession of "the rhapsode's love of praising famous men." [41] The attitude is fundamentally unhistorical.

Thucydides, as we noted, had different aims and methods from Herodotus. Yet even more than Herodotus he seems to have been attempting to discover the universal and permanent in human affairs. [42] His point of departure was political rather than investigative as Herodotus' was, an approach which went hand in hand with the fact that his scope of reference was largely confined to Athens. Yet granted the political concern and the focus on Athens, within that area he searched for the laws to be deduced, and the lessons to be learned, from human events. It is this concern, in fact, which Werner Jaeger avers turned him into an historian, contrary to the more conventional theory that he was first a historian concerned about historical methodology and only later a student of Athenian politics. [43] Although Professor Jaeger says that in the days of the Peloponnesian War Athens' "serious political thinkers were compelled to develop a historical consciousness," [44] Thucydides being one of the most important of those thinkers, the main drift of his argument is that the historical mode of thought actually was foreign to them. They were forced into historical thinking by the circumstances—the need to understand the crisis to which Athens had come—but they went no further into it than necessary.

---

[41] *Paideia*, I, 380.
[42] See F. M. Cornford, *Thucydides Mythistoricus*, especially Chap. XIII, "The Tragic Passions." Cornford believed that Thucydides was much influenced by Aeschylus in the interpretation of historical events. He "inevitably borrowed much of the structure of Aeschylean tragedy," allowing its unhistoric principle of design to come in on top of his first, chronological plan (p. 250). Cornford believed that Thucydides' history of the wars is more tragedy than history.
[43] *Paideia*, I, 381–82.
[44] *Ibid.*, I, 381.

The test of that view, says Professor Jaeger, is in Thucydides' attitude to the past:

... his occasional digressions on problems of early history ... are either incidental or else written to explain the present by the past. ... He believes that the past history of the Greek people was unimportant ... because its life would not allow the creation of any political organization and the development of power on a large scale.[45]

Now the political and the historical are of course very closely allied, especially in that the political thinker is forced to regard the "inside" of events, the motivations and thought of those engaged in political struggle. Concern for the inside of the events may be seen, for instance, in Thucydides' speeches, imaginative reconstructions of the thoughts of historical agents. But the political is apt to miss the genuinely historical in failing to see a pattern of meaning and significance in the course of events. It is here that Thucydides reflects his Hellenic presuppositions. What he finds in history is not a significance inherent in historical development itself, or inseparable from it, but rather illustrations of permanently valid political wisdom. "It will perhaps be found," said Thucydides,

that the absence of mythology in my work makes it unattractive to listen to; but it will suffice if it is judged useful by all who wish to study the plain truth of the events which have happened, and which will according to human nature recur in much the same way.[46]

As Professor Jaeger has phrased it, "the true nature of history, he believed, was that it furnished political experience, not that it embodied any religious, ethical, or philosophical idea." [47]

It matters not greatly whether the reader wishes to agree with me that such an outlook is unhistorical or prefers to say that it is merely a different kind of historical consciousness from the modern, the Hebraic, and the Christian. At any rate, its tendency—one might say its very necessity—is to abstract *from* history rather than to pursue reality *in* history.

Though his work has the modern historical interest in separate events for their own sake, it tries to pass beyond them and to transcend what is strange and different so as to reach the universal and permanent law which they embody.[48]

---

[45] *Paideia*, I, 382.   [46] *Thucydides* i. 22. 4.   [47] *Paideia*, I, 387.
[18] *Ibid.*, I, 386. Collingwood, *Idea of History*, p. 30, thinks that Thucydides is the father of "psychological history," which is not history at all but a kind of natural science. Even a

The purpose in discussing Thucydides and Herodotus has been to show that while in some respects they provide exceptions to the picture of Greece as unhistorical, they do not contradict that view. Herodotus bears some of the signs of historical thought in his objective interest in events, Thucydides in his concern for the "inner" side of political warfare; but both attempt to overleap the temporal in search of permanent laws—Herodotus looking for moral or natural laws, and Thucydides for laws governing political behavior.

One further note regarding historiography may be made. Collingwood points out that the Greek historical methodology prevented the construction of any one, all-embracing history. As their history was based on eye-witness accounts, the evidence perished with each generation. Therefore each "history" stood alone, a self-sustaining work, hardly capable of substantiation or reinterpretation.[49] Whether such methodology is cause or effect I would not presume to know. We have noticed how the Greek attitude to time involved a short view, looking neither far ahead nor far back. The Greek saw what was immediately before him. He does not appear to have spent much time looking "before and after." Although the absence of an open, creative future tended to produce the belief that everything significant had already happened—still the Greek did not live in a historical memory. Perhaps just because the past, like that of Oedipus, was unknown, it was also feared. It was never turned to as the source of one's identity and function in life.

Although the next chapter will show how radically different from the Greek was the thought of Hebraism and Christianity, the reader of classical literature will already be familiar with the contrast between the historical and the unhistorical through the contrast between Vergil and Homer. It is possible to argue, I think, that apart from matters of literary sophistication and the difference between oral and written epic, the greatest difference between the two great classical epic poets is their contrasting assumptions regarding time. In Homer,

---

writer who disagrees with Collingwood here, such as A. W. Gomme, *Greek Attitude*, does not bring a very crushing argument to bear: "I cannot follow Collingwood . . . in his belief that Thucydides . . . was unhistorical. . . . In his *History* (which is all we have of him) Thucydides is more recorder than philosopher, even though we may feel certain that he was always thinking of general laws—but thinking about them rather than formulating them and giving them to the world" (p. 138). Even here, Thucydides' interest in general laws is acknowledged.

[49] *Idea of History*, p. 27.

time figures only as a literary device.[50] In the *Aeneid*, however, it becomes the very heart of the conception. The poem exists in the constant awareness of the difference between what was, what is, and what is yet to be.

This subject has been treated concisely by Professor C. S. Lewis in his *Preface to Paradise Lost*. Of the *Aeneid*, he writes:

> If I am not mistaken it is almost the first poem which carries a real sense of the "abysm of time." . . . I do not know a better example of imagination, in the highest sense, than when Charon wonders at the Golden Bough "so long unseen;" dark centuries of that un-historied lower world are conjured up in half a line (VI, 409).
>
> But Virgil uses something more subtle than mere *length* of time. Our life has bends as well as extension: moments at which we realize that we have just turned some great corner, and that everything, for better or worse, will always henceforth be different. In a sense, as we have already seen, the whole *Aeneid* is the story of just such a transition in the world-order, the shift of civilization from the East to the West, the transformation of the little remnant, the *reliquias*, of the old, into the germ of the new [pp. 34–35].

Nothing of that sort is to be found in Homer. In him, however grand and noble the event, it leads from no past to no future. "Nothing has a significance beyond the moment." [51] That accounts, in part, for Homer's remarkable clarity. The present image is not beclouded by any memory of a past moment, nor any dominant hope for the future. It stands absolutely free in itself, clear, distinct, immediate. Not that Homer never predicts the future: the *Iliad* is full of foreshadowings of the fate of Achilles, as well as others. But that fate is simply the black curtain of death, when timeless oblivion shall overtake the hero. It serves only the more to make vivid the fleeting but all-absorbing present, to remind us of its sun and color before the oncoming night. How different are the predictions of the future in the *Aeneid*—those of the first book, for instance, where the future of Aeneas himself is not only predicted but also surpassed in expectation of the golden age, the age of Imperial Rome, for the creation of which Aeneas has been led out of Troy, preserved through battle and storm, and repeatedly called to his mission.

---

[50] Time provides some element of romance in the *Iliad*, in that the great deeds occurred long ago when men were different from what they are now; and it adds some measure of suspense to the *Odyssey*, as Penelope weaves and reweaves the shroud; but that is all.

[51] Lewis, *Preface*, pp. 28–29. Cf. the similar views on Homer in *The Portable Greek Reader*, ed. by W. H. Auden, pp. 17–20.

In Homer, true to the Greek idea, and in anticipation of Aristotle's formulation, time is the measure of motion, of change from good fortune to bad and back to good again. In Vergil, according to a pervading historical consciousness, time is the measure of purpose.

In summary, four elements are found to make up the Greek historical consciousness, corollaries of the search for reality in the equilibrium of nature. To begin with that quality most recently mentioned, there is an absence in Greece of any controlling purpose in time, which is only another way of saying the absence of a continuous history. The Hellenic historical consciousness "was not a consciousness of agelong tradition; . . . it was a consciousness of violent περιπέτεια, catastrophic changes from one state of things to its opposite, from smallness to greatness, from pride to abasement, from happiness to misery." [52] Such alternation, seen in detachment, enables one to perceive an ultimate harmony in nature, a constant return to equilibrium. It is not an historical orientation, for, as Professor Tillich has said, "to see reality historically means to see it essentially out of balance." [53]

Second, the Greek world-view was characterized by an absence of belief in the possibility of novelty or new creation. The cyclical understanding of time prevented any such belief. Characteristically, this attitude concerning the future was thrown also into the past in conjecture about the beginnings of things. Greek thought has no place for a doctrine of *creatio ex nihilo*, which means no doctrine of true creation at all. "Nothing comes into being out of what is non-existent," said Aristotle; and the doctrine goes back to Parmenides. [54] Whatever exists, exists perpetually. The future is therefore closed.

That leads into the third aspect of the Greek world-view—its understanding of time as essentially past. Greek thought is pervaded by a melancholy which arises out of the awareness that if the future is to be only the past over again, all that really matters is already done. This accounts for much of the Greek love of physical beauty, of song, dance, and the evanescent pleasures of life. They are a bulwark in the present, erected against the haunting fear that the significance of life has already been lived long ago. [55]

The fourth, and most important, element in the Greek world-view

---

[52] Collingwood, *Idea of History*, p. 22.   [53] *History*, p. 245.

[54] *Physics* i. 4. 187a27. See Frank, *Philosophical Understanding*, p. 73.

[55] The reader is referred to S. H. Butcher's chapter, "The Melancholy of the Greeks" in *Some Aspects of the Greek Genius*, pp. 130–65.

is the concern with the permanent structures of reality. It was here that the Greek genius showed itself most clearly, here that the Greek legacy has been most valuable in philosophy and science, but also most at variance with the religious and historical genius of European culture, including the most significant dramatists. The Greek mind did not, in the end, know what to do with time. It therefore turned its attention in another direction, to the search for those forms and ideas which were beyond time, eternal, not subject to change. Whether those were the heroic virtues of Homer, the laws of *nemesis* seen by Herodotus, the laws of political behavior seen by Thucydides, the forms of geometry, or the eternal ideas of Plato, the quest was the same. The Greeks belonged to and loved nature. They found her full of change, growth, and decay, but also subject to recurring cycles, her life constantly returning to itself. Behind the immediate phenomena of flux and unrest they perceived a basic cycle of recurrence, a fundamental equilibrium. Wisdom consisted of knowing that equilibrium, and of coming into harmony with it. Although the moderation of Apollo and the ecstasy of Dionysus might seem to be contradictory principles, both shared the ideal of being at one with nature—either to seek for her fundamental rest, or to move in her periodic cycles. In either case, the locus of the real and the significant was not in history. The dimension of the historical was not a constituent part of the Greek situation. Its place was taken by nature, which led to the timeless.

Such was the Hellenic orientation in the cosmos. The following chapter will contrast it with the Hebraic and Christian, which had radically different presuppositions. Afterward, the way will be open to see how the anti-historical quality of Greek thought affected her drama—how, although the drama was sometimes in tension with the cultural presuppositions, it was fundamentally in harmony with them, searching deeply for an ultimate equilibrium of cosmic forces.

III

JUDAEO-CHRISTIAN HISTORICAL CON-
SCIOUSNESS: THE VOCATION OF ISRAEL

To pass from the Greek world to the Hebraic is to move from an orientation in which time is regarded negatively as an attribute of finite, imperfect existence into one in which time is taken for granted as the mode of existence proper to humanity responsible to a purposive God. The Greek genius was a particular outgrowth of a nature-orientation. Hers was a genius which flowered in philosophy, providing the Western world with its basic conceptual tools for rational understanding. The Hebrew genius, if one may call it that, was directed toward history. It emphasized the significance of action taken in the historical present.[1]

The concomitant of the Hebraic involvement in history was a sense of the religious, ethical, and personal importance of time. It is essential to distinguish that "sense" of time from a formal conceptualization. The Hebrews did not attempt to solve the problem of time (as Plato and Aristotle did) because, given their concern over purpose, right conduct, and the sovereignty of God, it was not a problem. The Old Testament has no abstract conception of time. Instead of reflecting on "time," the Old Testament simply sets it forth, a concrete datum of experience.[2]

The historical emphasis in Hebrew religion and culture has been so thoroughly expounded in recent theological literature that no new case need be made for it here. I intend simply to call attention to it under four headings: the importance of memory, the continued writing and rewriting of the religio-national history, the sense of temporal

---

[1] Mircea Eliade, *The Myth of the Eternal Return*, pp. 104 ff., has provided an excellent discussion of the way in which, in Israel, historical events for the first time gained a positive value.

[2] Werner Vollborn, *Studien zum Zeitverständnis des Altentestamentums*, p. 137.

perspective which informs virtually all Old Testament literature, and the Hebrew assumption of the potentiality of the new. Having done that, I shall point out some of the unique complexities in Israel's thought regarding past, present and future in a way in which, so far as I know, it has not been done before. That will prepare us for the even greater complexity of the historical consciousness in the New Israel.

When the ancient Israelite worshipper brought his basket of first fruits to the sanctuary, he recited a confession which was cast in terms of historical memory:

A wandering Aramean was my father; and he went down into Egypt and sojourned there, few in number; and there he became a nation, great, mighty, and populous. And the Egyptians treated us harshly, and afflicted us, and laid upon us hard bondage. Then we cried to the Lord the God of our fathers, and the Lord heard our voice, and saw our affliction, our toil, and our oppression; and the Lord brought us out of Egypt with a mighty hand and an outstretched arm, with great terror, with signs and wonders; and he brought us into this place and gave us this land, a land flowing with milk and honey. And behold, now I bring the first of the fruit of the ground, which thou, O Lord, hast given me.[3]

Remembrance of past events was vital to Israel because she owed her national identity to certain historical occurrences. Her religious life was given its particular character through interpretation of those events. Foremost among them was the Exodus from Egypt, in which Israel saw the preeminent example of the action of God in her past life. The deliverance from bondage was the first step in her coming to be a nation in her own land. It also led to the sojourn at Sinai where the covenant between Yahweh and his people was made. The covenant thereafter characterizes the faith of Israel and becomes the focal point of her past memory. "It is in the relation of the covenant God with a covenant history," says James Muilenburg, "that the Old Testament is to be understood."[4]

The covenant was a name which expressed Israel's belief that the meaning of the wilderness events was Yahweh's historic election of Israel to be his particular people—for his own purposes—and his requirement of certain conduct from her.[5] Here is the first among many

[3] Deut. 26 : 5–9. Cf. Deut. 6 : 20–24; Josh. 24 : 2–13.
[4] "The History of the Religion of Israel," in *The Interpreter's Bible*, ed. by G. A. Buttrick, I, 293.
[5] H. Wheeler Robinson points out that the earliest literature we have on the covenant is to be dated three centuries after Sinai. However, he says that the attitude was "virtually

examples we shall find, in this type of historical thinking, of the tension between the event and the interpretation of the event. The characteristic Hebrew reaction was to interpret these events, and others like them, not in terms of the manifestation of universal law, but in terms of the unique vocation of Israel.

That vocation had a double focus. On the one hand it referred to the ultimate purposes of God, who through Israel was bringing about his reign over the whole earth.[6] On the other hand, it referred to Israel's obedience and fulfillment of the commandments of the law. The personal and the historic met in the idea of vocation. In this connection it is significant that those who wished to exhort the Israelites to moral righteousness almost always did so by first reminding the people of their former history—the acts of God and the response of the people, never to be forgotten—which had brought them to their present situation.

The reformers responsible for the book of Deuteronomy, for instance, saw fit to preface the book—which is largely given over to exposition of the legal code—with a review of Israel's history from the sojourn at Sinai to the crossing of the River Jordan into Canaan.[7] The entire book is set in the framework of a summons to return to the original covenant at Sinai (and to later extensions of that covenant). Similarly, the book of Nehemiah recounts how at the return of the exiles from the Babylonian captivity—when the temple worship was reinstituted and the laws once more enjoined on the people—a new covenant was made in remembrance of the one at Sinai, and at the same time the history of the Israelites was told, from the deliverance from Egypt to the return from Babylonia.[8]

The memory of the covenant history in which God has watched over the fortunes of his elect people also lies at the base of the messages of the prophets. Indeed, one might say that the prophets are the very embodiment of the Hebrew sense of historical memory; for their message, from first to last, is a measurement of the present against the covenantal past. Out of that judgment arises the prophetic interest in the future, either in terms of warnings of doom (Amos, Hosea,

---

covenantal" from the very time of Sinai on, and that Israel's history is more intelligible if the national faith is regarded as then "formally ratified" and ceremonially established. *Religious Ideas of the Old Testament*, p. 189.

[6] Such a universal expression of Yahweh's purpose was, of course, a late development.

[7] Deut. 1–4.   [8] Neh. 9 : 6–38.

Jeremiah), or in terms of a new covenant (Jeremiah and Ezekiel), or in terms of the fulfillment of the true vocation of Israel by a holy righteousness (Second Isaiah). Thus Amos, who is shocked by the injustice of the cities of Israel, is animated by a dreadful awareness that a covenantal past has been violated:

> Hear this word that the Lord has spoken against you,
> O people of Israel, against the whole family which I
> brought up out of the land of Egypt:
> "You only have I known of all the families of the earth;
> therefore will I punish you for all your iniquities."   (3 : 1–2)

Hosea expresses the apostasy of Israel in terms of harlotry, the forsaking of the marriage vows, which is his vivid way of putting Israel's failure to remember her covenant with Yahweh. Hosea constantly uses images from the family. His specific mention of the deliverance from slavery is full of tenderness:

> When Israel was a child, I loved him,
> and out of Egypt I called my son.
> The more I called them
> the more they went from me . . .
> Yet it was I who taught Ephraim to walk. . . . (11 : 1–3)

The same covenantal setting for the prophetic message—Yahweh's deliverance and adoption of the people—is expressed in Jeremiah 2:1–7.

It was not only the reformers and the prophets who remembered certain definitive moments from Israel's past. Professor G. E. Wright, in *God Who Acts*, has pointed out how the entire religious life rested upon what he calls "recital" of the sacred history. The principal parts of that history are the election of the fathers in the Patriarchal period, the covenantal salvation at the Exodus, and the gift of a land in which to dwell.[9] "No Israelite was allowed to forget the simple history of God's acts," says Professor Wright. "The worshipper listens to the recital, and by means of historical memory and identification he participates, so to speak, in the original events. Then facing his own situation he confesses his faith and his sin; he seeks God's forgiveness and direction; and he renews the vows of his covenant."[10]

The pervasive importance of historical thinking for the national and religious life of Israel is strikingly evidenced in the way in which

[9] Wright, *God Who Acts*, p. 28.   [10] *Ibid.*

Israel transformed the festivals of the seasons into ceremonies commemorating historical events. The feast of Unleavened Bread, Pentecost, and the feast of Tabernacles were all originally festivals of the agricultural seasons, and as such connected with the prevalent Near Eastern nature religions which sought to insure fertility by means of proper seasonal observances. These festivals were of course attractive to the Israelites after they had settled in Canaan and adopted agriculture as a means of livelihood. Yet gradually the nature festivals were changed into celebrations of historical events from Israel's past.[11] The feast of Unleavened Bread became connected with the Exodus, Pentecost with the giving of the law at Sinai, and the feast of Tabernacles with the sojourn in the wilderness.[12] The same historical concern transformed the sprinkling of blood on the lintel from an ancient rite warding off evil demons into the Passover celebration of Israel's deliverance from Egypt through the slaying of the Egyptian firstborn.[13]

Such mutation of the meaning of the nature festivals found in the environment highlights the radical difference between the Hebrews and the other Near Eastern peoples (including the Greeks).[14]

[11] See Artur Weiser, *Glaube und Geschichte im alten Testament.*

[12] See Adam C. Welch, *Prophet and Priest in Old Israel*, p. 122. Cf. Henri M. Yaker, "Motifs of the Biblical View of Time," pp. 323–29. Mr. Yaker thinks it possible the postexilic historization of Exodus-Passover was a return to an original historical root.

[13] In Christianity the same historical orientation proved decisive in transforming the festival of the winter solstice into a celebration of the event of the birth of Christ. See Welch, *Prophet and Priest*, pp. 91–93.

[14] The subject of the importance of the vegetation rites in Hebraism has received much attention in recent years. The interested reader is invited to consult the works of S. H. Hooke, E. O. James, James Muilenburg, W. O. E. Oesterley and T. H. Robinson, J. Pedersen, and H. W. Robinson, cited in the bibliography. A recent literary study which has dealt with the subject is Herbert Weisinger, *Tragedy and the Paradox of the Fortunate Fall*; see especially Chap. V. Professor Weisinger's knowledge and handling of the sources is admirable. He sees clearly that "Hebrew thought in the very process of adopting the pattern [of birth, life, death, and rebirth] transformed it. . . ." (p. 189). He also sees that the major change which Hebrew thought made was that of breaking the cycle of nature's endless return to equilibrium: "the end of the cycle was not mere repetition but actual advance . . ." (p. 152). Given such a beginning, it is therefore the more unfortunate that Professor Weisinger's point of view has obscured his perception of the full difference which Hebraism made concerning the myth and ritual pattern. He sees the difference primarily in terms of the pattern's being "spiritualized" (p. 152). "The Hebrews," he says, "leaped out to a tremendous concept" (p. 152). They took a "dialectical leap from out of the endless circle on to a different and higher stage of understanding" (p. 189). This understanding was that by an act of will they could come into a relation of trust in "a God of universal compassion and justice;" one could attain to a new life in which "he is with his God eternally" (p. 189). Professor Weisinger departs radically from the Old Testament when he asserts that the Hebrews gave to the ritual pattern the one element it had lacked, "its permanent role as the means whereby man is enabled to live in an indifferent universe; they showed that man can, by himself, transcend that universe" (p. 189).

In this interpretation, God becomes entirely passive (the object, not the agent of the leap), and therefore the importance of history evaporates. Though he mentions Sinai several times, Professor Weisinger never mentions the covenant. For Hebrew religion, however, the Divine

In addition to the importance of the national religious memory—which we have seen manifest in the idea of the covenant, in the covenantal framework of the reformers' and prophets' messages, in the "recital" quality of various creedal confessions, and in the adapting of seasonal festivals to celebrations of past events—the historical orientation of the Hebrews is shown in their production of what may be called "epic history."

Modern critical study of the origin and composition of the Old Testament has revealed a people continually concerned with the writing and rewriting of history. Beginning with oral traditions arranged into a story of Yahweh's summoning of the patriarchs, his deliverance from Egypt, his covenant with the people, and his giving them a land over which, in David's time, they came to rule, they continually revised and adapted their historical narratives at each contemporary historical crisis and in line with developing religious beliefs. While the Hebrews had nothing of the modern scientific spirit of testing sources and looking for the original event *wie es eigentlich gewesen*,[15] they did have the typically Western concern to understand one's self in terms of one's past and to search continually for the most adequate interpretation of that past. That they did not possess scientific criteria with regard to evidence did not mean they felt free to change the stories at will, far less to abandon them. Their objective, rather, was to see the relationship of present to past, which means that their historical concern was not academic but existential. "Israel," says Professor Muilenburg, "sought in history an understanding of its existence and destiny."[16]

The early historical narratives represent the nearest Israel comes to epic literature.[17] Professor Erich Auerbach[18] has therefore illu-

---

initiative, covenant election, creation, and history form one indissoluble complex, and it is this which transformed the birth, death and rebirth pattern by adapting its festivals to acts of historical remembrance. For Professor Weisinger, the cycle was broken by a new insight, which represents an advance in the development of man. For Hebraism, however, the cycle was broken by the creative activity of Yahweh, which replaced the meaning found in patterned repetition by a meaning dependent upon Divine activity in the realm of human events. Professor Weisinger is afraid that Providence negates history by taking away man's freedom (p. 193). On the contrary, in Hebraism and Christianity history was made possible by the awareness of a Divine purpose which placed the greatest burden of decision upon man's capacity for choice.

[15] The phrase is from Leopold von Ranke's prefaces to his *Histories of the Latin and Teuton Nations*, quoted in Theodore H. Von Laue, *Leopold Ranke, the Formative Years*, p. 25.

[16] "The Faith of Ancient Israel," in *The Vitality of the Christian Tradition*, ed. by G. F. Thomas, p. 1.

[17] I refer here to the so-called *J* and *E* writings, found in parts of the historical books of

minated Hebraic and Hellenic differences by contrasting a passage from Homer with the story of the sacrifice of Isaac. If an epic is a poem "which makes you feel the way you feel after reading the *Iliad*," then the stories of Genesis are not epic. The main reason is that while they emphasize the stature of the patriarchs and the leaders like Moses and Joshua, they are devoid of the kind of ἀριστεῖα in which Homer abounds and which, indeed, are the characteristic feature of most epics. Standing above the human virtues of every hero in Israelite literature are both the purposive sovereignty of God and the historic destiny of the people of Israel. It is unity of purpose, implying the historic continuity of Israel, which separates Yahweh most clearly from Homer's Zeus.[19]

Professor Auerbach's analysis of the two selections shows clearly that their primary difference lies in the matter of historical time, which makes itself felt in every aspect of the literary intent, syntax, and style. His chapter [20] is so perceptive, from both a religious and a literary standpoint, that I cannot forbear devoting it some attention—the more so as it will serve to make clear the historical preoccupation of the Hebraic consciousness.

Choosing from the *Odyssey* the passage in which Euryclea recognizes the returned Odysseus by the scar on his leg,[21] a passage interrupted by a long digression of seventy-five lines relating how Odysseus in his youth had received the scar, Professor Auerbach shows how the Homeric style consistently portrays all objects and scenes in a distinct, fully illuminated manner. It has a need, he says, "to leave nothing which it mentions half in darkness and unexternalized" (p. 5). That means that Homer's focus is always directly on the subject immediately before him, without reference to perspective and without concern for past or future. Even when a "flashback" is used, as in the incident with the scar, the scene from the past quickly assumes the total interest of the reader, so that whatever Homer "narrates is for the time being the only present" (p. 4). Such exclusive focus on the immediate creates a

---

the Old Testament. Discussion of them and critical problems connected with their identification may be found in any good contemporary introduction to the Old Testament, for instance, R. H. Pfeiffer, *Introduction to the Old Testament*; or *The Interpreter's Bible*, Vol. I.

[18] *Mimesis: The Representation of Reality in Western Literature*, trans. by Willard R. Trask.

[19] It also gives him some resemblance to Vergil's Jupiter, except that the debt must be the other way around. For the suggestion that Vergil may have been influenced by the writings of the Hebrew prophets in translation, see Joseph Klausner, *The Messianic Idea in Israel*, trans. by W. F. Stinespring, p. 14.

[20] *Mimesis*, Chap. I, pp. 3–23.   [21] Book XIX. 386–473.

high degree of clarity, expressed in Homer's never failing to use all
necessary particles, adverbs, adjectives, and subordinating clauses to
express the distinct relations existing between the various objects of
his interest in a given scene. That interest extends to the most minute
details—clothing, physical appearances, sounds, smells, and the like.
All phenomena are "completely fixed in their spatial and temporal
relations" (p. 6). At the same time, "any impression of perspective is
avoided" (p. 7) because the past and present are not felt simultaneously,
nor are foreground and background; but rather, first one and then the
other is brought forward for immediate observation. Everything in its
turn becomes foreground. "Like the separate phenomena themselves,
their relationships," he says, "are brought to light in perfect fullness;
so that a continuous rhythmic procession of phenomena passes by, and
never is there a form left fragmentary or half-illuminated, never a
lacuna, never a gap, never a glimpse of unplumbed depths" (pp. 6–7).

The story of the sacrifice of Isaac stands in the utmost contrast to
the Homeric style. It is, says Professor Auerbach, "from a different
world of forms" (p. 7). Here we have "the externalization of only so
much of the phenomena as is necessary for the purpose of the narrative" (p. 11). When God speaks with the single word, "Abraham!"
and the latter replies, "Behold, here I am," we have no idea where the
two speakers are. What had they been doing just before? The God,
called Elohim, is not described by any physical attributes, nor indeed is
Abraham.

Such meager physical descriptions as do find their way into this
narrative are there because they serve to characterize the nature of
the act which Abraham is called upon to perform. The journey is begun "early in the morning," a detail mentioned not for the sake of
temporal precision but because it expresses Abraham's resolution,
promptness, and punctual obedience. The destination of the journey
is "Jeruel in the land of Moriah," [22] significant for no other reason
than that it has been selected for this journey by God. Isaac is described
as "thine only son, whom thou lovest," which again is not a description
of the person himself, but of his importance to Abraham and therefore
the severity of the sacrifice required.

The scene is formed not by any description of its setting in which we
might take delight, but instead by the imperative which comes to

[22] So in Auerbach, *Mimesis*, p. 10, although neither the A.V. nor the R.S.V. has the word
Jeruel, only "the land of Moriah."

Abraham and the nature of his response. The "purpose of the narrative" therefore entirely obliterates every conceivable intent to enjoy the natural world for itself. We are confronted with a literary form based upon almost complete preoccupation with actions taking place in historical time. "The human beings in the Biblical stories," says Professor Auerbach,

have greater depths of time, fate and consciousness than do the human beings in Homer; although they are nearly always caught up in an event engaging all their faculties, they are not so entirely immersed in its present that they do not remain continually conscious of what has happened to them earlier and elsewhere; their thoughts and feelings have more layers, are more entangled. Abraham's actions are explained not only by what is happening to him at the moment, nor yet only by his character . . . but by his previous history; he remembers, he is constantly conscious of, what God has promised him and what God has already accomplished for him—his soul is torn between desperate rebellion and hopeful expectation; his silent obedience is multilayered, has background [p. 12].

Such "multilayeredness," he continues,

is hardly to be met with in Homer [in whom] the complexity of the psychological life is shown only in the succession and alternation of emotions; whereas the Jewish writers are able to express the simultaneous existence of various layers of consciousness and the conflict between them [p. 13].

The latter point is extremely important, and will recur in my examination of Shakespeare.

The result of the complexity, perspective, and unilluminated depths of the biblical stories is that they constantly push at the limits of finite experience. They overleap the bounds of the literary situation and make claims upon the self in its historical existence.[23] "The Homeric poems," Professor Auerbach says, "present a definite complex of events whose boundaries in time and space are clearly delimited. . . . The Old Testament, on the other hand, presents universal history: it begins with the beginning of time, with the creation of the world, and will end with the Last Days, the fulfilling of the Covenant, with which the world will come to an end" (p. 16). The Hebrews took the

---

[23] "Their religious intent," says Professor Auerbach, "involves an absolute claim to historical truth." Even the modern critical approach to these Scriptures has not been able to free itself from the problem of historicity which the narratives involve. Nor has it sought to do so wherever its primary attention was centered on the significance of the narratives themselves.

48 INTRODUCTION

significance of historical action so seriously that they were driven toward an absolute, all-embracing historical view of man and the world.[24]

The Old Testament defines man in terms of history. The great figures of the Old Testament, says Professor Auerbach, "are so much more fully developed, so much more fraught with their own biographical past, so much more distinct as individuals, than are the Homeric heroes" (p. 17). It is the history of what has become of them as they played their elected part in the still larger history of Israel and the Divine purpose that occupies the Old Testament writers. Time touches the Homeric figures "only outwardly," whereas God continues to work on the biblical characters, "bends them and kneads them, and without destroying them in essence, produces from them forms which their youth gave no grounds for anticipating" (p. 18).

It is greatly to Professor Auerbach's credit that he has been able to elucidate so much of the persistent characteristic of the Old Testament in his exposition of the one story of Abraham and Isaac. Prophets, psalmists, and apocalyptists never depart from the fundamental historical orientation. As vast reaches of time are implied in the very style of the Abraham and Isaac narrative, so also the later editors wove the story skillfully into a cosmic history whereby God's promise to his chosen was faithfully kept from generation to generation, even though the threatened death of Isaac, as also other precarious events of history, seemed to place it in jeopardy. It was a later editor who added to the original story the postscript which reminds us of the historical continuity guaranteed by God:

By myself I have sworn, saith the Lord, for because thou hast not withheld thy son, thine only *son*, that in blessing I will bless thee . . . and in thy seed shall all the nations of the earth be blessed; because thou hast obeyed my voice (Gen. 22 : 16–18).

Professor Auerbach states that the Old Testament figures become, under the hand of God, something "their youth gave no grounds for anticipating." The concomitant of an historical orientation is the

---

[24] The Jewish propensity for thinking in infinite, limitless terms is described by Thorlief Boman in *Das hebräische Denken*, pp. 139–40: "ein religiöser Mensch nicht innerhalb seiner von ihm selbst oder anderen Menschen gesteckten Grenzen zur Ruhe kommen wird. Der geborene religiöse Mensch lebt in der unendlichen und ewigen Welt wie in seiner wahren Heimat (Fil. 3, 20). Es ist deshalb keine Zufälligkeit, dass die Semiten, die ohne Grenzen auskommen können, Schöpfer von drei Weltreligionen geworden sind. Für sie ist Unendlichkeit oder Grenzenlosigkeit kein Problem."

possibility of the new. This fact is expressed in the Bible under the idea of creation.

In Chapter II it was noted that Hellenic thought had no room for a doctrine of *creatio ex nihilo*. Wherever nature is the starting point in religion or philosophy, the doctrine will be absent, for creation demands acknowledgment of a completely sovereign, self-sufficient power supreme over nature. In fact, the doctrine of creation is but the corollary of belief in such a power. The Old Testament does not contain any specific enunciation of the principle of *creatio ex nihilo*.[25] Nevertheless, the doctrine is true to the spirit of Hebraic thought about the transcendence and power of Yahweh. It is implicit in almost every page of the Old Testament, and later theology was correct in elaborating it.[26]

In Hellas, the absence of a radical notion of creation went hand in hand with an understanding of time as essentially closed. The possibility of the new was excluded, for the reduction of time to the measure of change in a finite world meant that eventually all situations would recreate themselves.

In Israel, the conception of Yahweh's creativity meant an understanding of time as potentially open.[27] As Yahweh in the beginning had created man, earth, heaven, and all the natural beings, so he had created the people Israel in their covenant relation with him, had created their law, made them a nation, and preserved them in adversity. All this implied a purpose which, obviously not fulfilled now, would be made perfect in the future.[28] Thus the covenant was not simply made once, it is from time to time relived, and at each time the promises of Yahweh are renewed. Israel's history, as written and rewritten through successive historical crises, emerges with a long list of covenants made between Yahweh and the leaders of Israel. There is the covenant with Noah (Gen. 9 : 8–19), with Abraham (15 : 1–21), the covenant at

[25] The creation story in Genesis 1, having been in some measure derived from the Babylonian myth *Emuna eliš*, shows traces of the conception of primitive matter existing before the creative activity of God. See Cuthbert A. Simpson in *Interpreter's Bible*, I, 450, 465–68.

[26] See Frank, *Philosophical Understanding*, pp. 74–75.

[27] It is important to stress "potentially." Israel did not have the nineteenth-century view of necessary or inevitable progress. The new was not built into nature, from which it emerged developmentally. On the contrary, it depended entirely on the inscrutable, although faithful, creative power of Yahweh.

[28] Cf. Yaker, "Biblical View of Time," p. 162. See also Mircea Eliade, *Eternal Return*, pp. 106 ff., for a discussion of how the Israelites "saved" time by putting the primary reference to the future, changing the annual regeneration of nature by the king into an expectation of "a future and Messianic *illud tempus*."

Sinai (Exodus 24 : 1–8, renewed in 34 : 1–10). In Deuteronomy 29 there is a ceremony for the renewal of the covenant, another, as we have seen, in Nehemiah 9 and 10, at the return from Exile. Most important are the prophetic visions of a new covenant which God shall make with his people, one in which inner righteousness shall prevail over mere outward observance of the law, a covenant of perfect fulfillment:

"Behold, the days are coming," says the Lord, "when I will make a new covenant with the house of Israel and the house of Judah, not like the covenant which I made with their fathers when I took them by the hand to bring them out of the land of Egypt, my covenant which they broke, though I was their husband," says the Lord. "But this is the covenant which I will make with the house of Israel after those days," says the Lord: "I will put my law within them, and I will write it upon their hearts; and I will be their God, and they shall be my people. And no longer shall each man teach his neighbor and each his brother, saying, 'Know the Lord,' for they shall all know me, from the least of them to the greatest," says the Lord; "for I will forgive their iniquity, and I will remember their sin no more." [29]

The theme of the new covenant is taken up by Second Isaiah (Isaiah 55 : 3–5), who extends its promise to all the nations of the earth. It passed into the New Testament through the words of Jesus, whom the gospels portray as identifying the new community centering in himself with the new covenant promised of old:

Drink it, all of you; for this is my blood of the new covenant, which is poured out for many for the forgiveness of sins (Matt. 26 : 27–28).[30]

That the making of the covenant and the new covenant is dependent upon the God of creation is strikingly exemplified in Jeremiah, who, after the passage quoted above on the new covenant written in the heart, begins a new section in this manner:

[29] Jer. 31 : 31–34. This vision is similar in content to that of Hos. (2 : 19–20) and Ezek. (36 : 22–38).
[30] Professor E. O. James, *Origins of Sacrifice*, says that in Judaism, "the reason for the *Kiddūsh* of every festival and Sabbath is its historical significance. On the Sabbath the remembrance of the creation and the Exodus both occur because of the differing reasons in the two recensions of the Fourth Commandment (Ex. 20 : 10; Deut. 5 : 15). Jewish chronology is thus divided into two parts: from the creation to the Exodus, and the Exodus onwards. By identifying the cup with the blood of the covenant, Jesus made the Eucharist a new *Kiddūsh* introducing a new division of time" (pp. 171–72).

> Thus says the Lord,
>   who gives the sun for light by day
>   and the fixed order of the moon and the stars
>   for light by night,
>   who stirs up the sea so that its waves roar—
>   the Lord of hosts is his name:
>   "If this fixed order departs from before me,
>   says the Lord,
>   then shall the descendants of Israel cease
>   from being a nation before me for ever."
>
>   (Jer. 31 : 35–36)

It is the God who creates who is able to bring his creation to fulfillment:

> For behold, I create new heavens and a new earth . . .
>   for behold, I create Jerusalem a rejoicing,
>   and her people a joy.[31]

Again, the theme is carried into the New Testament, this time in the
apocalypse of John, who saw

a new heaven and a new earth. . . . And he who sat upon the throne said,
"Behold, I make all things new." [32]

There is undoubtedly a tendency here to push beyond history. But
if so, the point of departure is a very serious historical concern, alike in
Hebraism, Judaism, and Christianity. That concern involves the
assumption that events taking place in the history of the elect community have a decisive, even cosmic, significance. The God who has
chosen that community in a moment of history is the same as he who
created the world, and who has given indestructible grounds for hope
by making a covenant promise of an eventual new and perfect creation.

It is no wonder that it occurs to one to represent the Hebraic view
of time and history as linear, since time appears to proceed from an
original creation through various historical events to final consumma-
tion. Professor Cullmann says the picture is that of an "upward sloping
line." [33] As each new stage is reached, the past appears to be left behind, "the former things have passed away,[34] and a straight line appears to be the inevitable symbol.

Were that actually the case, the particular complexity and power of

---

[31] Isa. 65 : 17, 18. Cf. Isa. 66 : 22; II Peter 3 : 13.   [32] Rev. 21 : 1, 5. Cf. Isa. 43 : 19.
[33] *Christ and Time*, p. 51. See Chap. II, p. 23.   [34] Rev. 21 : 5. Cf. Isa. 65 : 17.

the Hebraic historical consciousness would be lacking. Actually, the Hebraic view of time was not nearly so cut and dried. Besides seeing the possibilities of newness in history, it had also a persistent tendency to mingle present and past. Even its visions of the future make constant use of images drawn from the past. The new future is a new *creation*, after all, suggesting a return to the goodness of the first creation.[35] It is pictured as a new Jerusalem, which echoes the past glory of the Davidic reign when a righteous king sat upon the throne, reigning over a God-given land in spiritual and political unity.[36]

Investigation will show that two principles are at work in Israel's life: the one, a radical emphasis upon historical time, the uniqueness of each moment and its decisions, together with the radical judgments and mercies to be expected from God in the future; the other, an awareness of the contemporaneity of time and the repetitive character of much human behavior. The tension between these two principles is observable in both what may be called the psychological and the sociopolitical spheres.

On the psychological side (by which I mean experience and conceptualization combined) the principle of contemporaneity and repetition is seen in the Israelite lack of precise chronology and in what Werner Vollborn calls *Vergegenwartigung*—making present.[37] For all of Hebraism's interest in history, it did not possess that concern for accurate dating which we today regard as one of the fundamentals of historiography.[38] The Hebrews do not seem to have imagined a line extending through the past with definite dates pegged along it, separated by certain numbers of years. To imagine that kind of thing requires a schematization of time which was foreign to most Hebraism.[39] The Hebrew language does not possess a flexible tense-structure which would enable accurate pin-pointing of events along a time-line, as does Greek.[40]

---

[35] On the use of the creation myth in the eschatology of the early Church, see T. H. Robinson, "Hebrew Myths," in *Myth and Ritual*, ed. by S. H. Hooke, especially pp. 195–96.

[36] See Rev. 3 : 12; 21 : 2.

[37] *Zeitverständnis des Altentestamentums*, pp. 209–10.

[38] There are two kinds of Old Testament interest in chronology. One is that of the Priestly Code, which is extremely precise but entirely fictitious. See Robert H. Pfeiffer, *Introduction to the Old Testament*, pp. 200–2; he calls *P* a philosophy of history rather than a history (p. 191). The other is like that of Isaiah (6 : 1), who makes the date of his vision very explicit by saying it was "in the year that King Uzziah died." The latter is the product of a mind which thinks in terms of historical moments, but it is not concerned with absolute, or objective, chronology.

[39] It is significant that the schematic chronology of the Priestly Code is of late origin and comes from the circles interested in preserving the minutiae of ritual and legal observances.

[40] See Chap. II, p. 26.

To date an event precisely, or to assign it an accurate past tense relative to the speaker, is to separate it from other events as objects in space are separated one from another. The Hebrew tended to bring events out of the remoteness in the past and to adopt them into present existence. This tendency is the result of a strange phenomenon. In the very degree in which time and historical occurrence become positive, constituent factors in the Judaeo-Christian consciousness, in that degree they also become ambiguous. For they refuse then simply to take their place in a chronology of the past. The event which *was*, meaningfully enters the *now*.[41] Hebraism and Christianity both are beset with a historical past which—because history is not only fact but also a mode of experience—refuses to remain in the past.

Israel's memory was an indication of her history-centered mind and her desire to pull all significant action into contemporaneity. Says Werner Vollborn:

Das AT sieht die Ereignisse der Vergangenheit nicht im ihren chronologischen Ablauf in Sinne einer knotinuierlichen Linie. Das AT sieht nicht einen zeitlichen Abstand zwischen ihnen, sondern begreift die Ereignisse als Geschenisse, die auf derselben Ebene leigen, in der Gleichzeitigkeit mit der Generation, die auf sie schaut.[42]

The same, he says, applies to future events. They also can be described as present, or even past, because they are already held firm in the will of God.[43]

Drawing the past and future into the present was the Israelite way of making all three times significant. Only in that way could "time" and "history" be concrete modes of experience. For action must be taken in the present, and a historical action must be taken in a present which is defined by appropriating the significant past and anticipating the hoped-for future. By such *Vergegenwartigung* was the Hebrew consciousness of history both complicated and given unique power.

Corresponding to the psychological sphere, in which the complexity of Hebraic historical thought is seen, there is the socio-political sphere, in which the same complexity is visible more objectively. I refer to the conflict between Israel's prophets and priests.

Scholarship has long noticed the severity with which the prophets were impelled to denounce the priestly functions—rituals, feast days,

---

[41] "The Lord our God made a covenant with us in Horeb. Not with our fathers did the Lord make this covenant, but with us, who are all of us here alive this day" (Deut. 5 : 3).
[42] *Zeitverständnis des Altentestamentums*, pp. 209–10.   [43] *Ibid.*, pp. 246 ff.

sacrifices, and the like.[44] This was always done in the name of ethical righteousness and accompanied by a call to return to the historic vocation of Israel as child of God, dependent upon His providence rather than upon the safeguards of rituals and sacrifices. In any discussion of the uniqueness of Israel's history-centered religion, it must not be forgotten that the Hebrews actually practiced a religion of ritual observances supervised by an elaborate priesthood.[45]

The role of the priest everywhere is to aid in the celebration of the necessary rhythms of life. The average man in any society lives not often in terms of historical crises or moments of ethical decision, but usually in terms of work and play, planting and harvesting, and the like. Religion for most is a matter of regular, periodic worship. It thus fits into the established orders of life and therefore is aligned with the establishment of legal systems and with the kingly functions of providing for the popular welfare, justice, and stability. As Frazer first pointed out, there is a direct line from the crops to the king.[46] No matter how important was the element of history in Israel's thought, it was a matter of practical necessity that she maintain a priesthood to preside over the natural, repetitive occurrences in the life of the people. The historical had to make concessions to the cyclical.

The prophets knew that, of course, Therefore, their protest against the priests was not absolute in character. It did not call for the abolition of the priesthood, but rather for its subordination to the more fundamental reality of the will of Yahweh. Recent scholarship has begun to see that there was not merely tension between prophet and priest, but also alliance. If it was the prophets who denounced the meaninglessness and idolatry of much of the temple worship, it was the priests, connected with the temple, who preserved the writings of the very prophets who attacked them. The cult embraced the prophets. And the convictions of the prophets necessarily involved, as Professor

[44] See, for instance, Amos 5 : 21–24.

[45] How similar these particulars were to those in the neighboring communities has been shown, for instance, by Professor W. O. E. Oesterly ("Early Hebrew Festival Rituals" in *Myth and Ritual*, ed. by S. H. Hooke), who also reminds us that behind all the Near Eastern rites lay the concern of harmonious and propitious relations to nature (pp. 111–46). When Israel settled in Canaan and became an agricultural people, her religion no doubt borrowed much from the agricultural festivals of the original inhabitants.

[46] This relation is touchingly expressed in Homer's description of that scene on the shield of Achilles in which the king watches over the harvesting being done by the laborers (*Iliad* XVIII. 550–60).

Welch says, "some means for maintaining the relation between the people and their God." [47]

The inter-relatedness of prophet and priest (and of the "ceremonial" and "historical" principles for which they stood) is confirmed in one of the most important books of the Old Testament. The book of Deuteronomy is an interpretative commentary upon the Hebraic laws, at once urging their re-establishment in Judah, and also setting them forth in the prophetic understanding of Yahweh's righteousness, power, and historically-manifested love for the chosen people. The book, says R. H. Pfeiffer,[48] is a compromise between prophetic ideals and the practical necessity of religious cult.

Compromise of that sort was required for the stability of the religio-national life. Deuteronomy may be seen as an expression of the wisdom of Hebraic religion, for it combined the radically time-centered religion of the prophets (ethical righteousness and historical vocation) with the cultic laws of the priests (the eternal, recurrent relation to Yahweh).

It was not in the ministrations of the priests that Israel's uniqueness lay. It was in the demand of the prophets for obedience to the creator-God who called Israel to his purpose. The latter is an approach to life which takes time with radical seriousness. It understands the past in terms of God's creativity and promise. It understands the future in terms of God's ultimate victory over evil. His creation of a new, perfect covenant. It understands the present in terms of that past and future, demanding obedience, repentance from apostasy.

The cyclical, simultaneous elements in Israel's thought are subordinate to that historical orientation. They begin to appear where the present is emphasized, for in order to exist the present must draw past and future into itself. The principle of cyclical repetition inheres in the priestly functions, especially where these are associated with agriculture and other natural phenomena. It was Israel's vocation to adapt the age-old seasonal celebrations into a form in which they could serve the purpose of a God active in the unique crises of human history. The

---

[47] *Prophet and Priest*, p. 72, see also pp. 69–75. Welch speaks of a growing use of the term "cult prophets" in Old Testament studies. He also supposes that not all the prophets attacked the priesthood.

[48] *Introduction to the Old Testament*, pp. 179–80. G. E. Wright's recent introduction to Deuteronomy (*Interpreter's Bible*, II, 325–26) follows Gerhard von Rad in challenging the over emphasis upon the prophetic side of the book, to which students following S. R. Driver had been inclined. But Wright does acknowledge "a definite prophetic influence on the book." He also notes that its ideal figure is Moses, "in whom both political and prophetic functions were combined."

relation of this God of history to cultic ceremonies was made possible in the principle of contemporaneity, by means of which the Israelites were enabled to celebrate in the immediate present the remembered acts of God. The characteristic present of Israel was a "historical present," made up of memory, anticipation, and responsibility. The characteristic present of Greece was an "eternal present," directed toward perceiving the changeless, recurrent, and eternal in the fleeting, kaleidoscopic now. Israel was a people to whom time and history were the fundamental realities and who, for practical reasons, had to adopt some non-historical elements. The Hellenes were essentially a non-historical people who were sometimes driven by extraordinary crises into a certain amount of historical exploration and interpretation. The theology of Hellas reveals the gods of nature and their relationships, one to another. The theology of Israel reveals the God of history.[49]

In Christianity, the relation of the historical and the eternal becomes, needless to say, much more complex. The heart of the new religion, and of this complexity, lies in the doctrine of the Incarnation. Jesus Christ is asserted to be both a historical event and also the summation of history. He is the completion of history, the expected Messiah, who nevertheless must come again in order to bring final judgment and the end of history. He is also a manifestation of the Divine in nature (flesh).

Inasmuch as Christ is viewed as a historical event, becoming in fact the most crucial turning point in all history, Christianity reaffirms and amplifies the historical orientation of Judaism. As in Judaism, the historical is its primary emphasis. The Incarnation might be described as a break-through[50] of the Divine into history (thereby creating a new history), and subsequent periods of reformation and renewed vitality in the Church can then be seen also as break-throughs of the original Incarnation event in power at particular moments. The creeds of Christianity are recitations of events in the sacred history. Its sacraments of Baptism and the Lord's Supper are, whatever else they may be, enactments in which original historic events are remembered.

Where Christ is thought of as an event, there is an emphasis upon

---

[49] Reinhold Niebuhr, *The Self and the Dramas of History*, p. 77: "For the one history is made into another dimension of nature; for the other nature is subsumed under history."
[50] This terminology is Paul Tillich's.

the work of Christ: "who for us men and our salvation came down from heaven . . . was made man . . . suffered and was buried, and the third day he rose again . . ." (Nicene Creed); "For God so loved the world that he gave his only son" (John 3 : 16). The four gospels are narratives constructed so that the events of Christ's passion, death, and resurrection form their climax.

Where Christ is thought of as an event, there is also the necessary attempt to recast universal history into such a pattern as will put the event of the Christ at its center. "For Christian thought, Christ is the center of history," as Professor Tillich says; [51] and the gospels of Matthew and John, as well as Romans, Hebrews, and Revelation, all deal with the central position of Christ in the history of the world from the creation to the last days.

The Church did not interpret Christ only as event. It also considered his person, status, and nature. It was concerned not only with what he did, but also with what he was (and is). These are not two separate or contradictory concerns, of course. The person of Christ, in fact, can hardly be discussed apart from his work. It is their conjunction in Christian theology which makes the questions of time, history, and historical interpretation more complex than in Judaism.

Without going into the early Christological discussions, we may, for present purposes, simply note two factors in the Church's interpretation of Christ which tended to soften the "linear" element in the Hebraic ideas of time. One was the doctrine of Christ as the Son who coexists eternally with the Father. The other was the interpretation of Christ as priest and king.[52] Both these ways of picturing him tend to accentuate what I have called the "principle of contemporaneity." They mean that in the Incarnation there was not an event which was totally new, but rather the complete revelation and fulfillment of that which had existed always. This was "the lamb slain from the foundation of the world" (Rev. 13 : 8). At the same time, the Church was at pains to maintain the "once-for-all" character of the redemptive act in Christ. Two points of view are therefore in tension—inevitably so from the very nature of the claim made in the doctrine of the Incarnation that the eternal God had entered human history in human flesh. Out of this paradox arises the peculiarly Christian interpretation of history, one in which there is constant tension between the historical

---

[51] *History*, p. 251.
[52] On the latter, see W. A. Visser't Hooft, *The Kingship of Christ.*

uniqueness of each event and the transcendent interpretation of the event.

Christian history always struggles in an effort to pin down historical events in their particularity. Its Hebraic inheritance demands that it do so. At the same time, it has a tendency to elevate the particular into the realm of the eternal by viewing it as participating in an eternal reality and revealing a meaning beyond itself. The event is more than a link in the chain of events.

No doubt this latter tendency of Christian thought owes much to the Greek way of thinking. It reflects the fact that Christ, the Messiah of Israel, was received by a Hellenistic world.[53] But it must be remembered that the way had been prepared for it in Hebraism's emphasis upon memory and *Vergegenwartigung*. Far from blunting the historical mode of thinking, this type of thought actually gave rise to history in its modern sense.[54]

The early Church found in the Old Testament a sacred history which gave meaning to, and received meaning from, the event of the Christ. The Church consistently rejected those who, like the second century Marcion, wished to abandon the Old Testament as Scripture. At the same time the new elements in Christianity demanded new interpretations of many Old Testament stories and prophecies. The humiliation of the Messiah by crucifixion called for his identification with the Suffering Servant in Isaiah (52 : 13—15 : 12). The belief in Christ's death and resurrection as an act through which once-for-all God had delivered his people from the bondage of sin meant that the story of the Exodus from Egypt was no longer the primary historical act of God's deliverance. Rather, the Exodus became a forerunner, a "type" of that complete deliverance achieved on the Cross.

[53] "Christendom was a product of Jewish historical religious experience and Gentile speculation upon an organization of that experience" (Auden, *The Portable Greek Reader*, p. 15).

[54] As an example of the tension between event and interpretation, the Gospel of John is instructive. Professor C. H. Dodd divides the Gospel into seven episodes preceding the Last Supper and sees all seven so narrated that the entire gospel is pre-figured symbolically in each of the episodes. See *The Interpretation of the Fourth Gospel* (Cambridge: 1953), pp. 384–86. The evangelist expects the reader to believe that the events described actually occurred as narrated, but also to see their symbolic meaning and their prefiguration of the Cross. As Augustine told his congregation:

"When you hear a symbolic exposition given of a passage of Scripture which records events, you should first of all get it clear in your mind that the event recorded took place as it is recorded; otherwise, if you take away the basis of fact, you may find yourselves attempting to build on air." (*Sermo*, II 6, P.L. xxxviii. 30, quoted by R. L. P. Milburn, *Early Christian Interpretations of History*, p. 155.)

Christian interpretation of Scripture, especially of the Old Testament, has been fundamentally of two kinds, one more history-centered than the other. The less historical method is that of allegory.[55] By its means, morally objectionable or inscrutable passages from the Old Testament were given a spiritual interpretation. Although there is in the New Testament a certain amount of allegorizing, it is comparatively rare.[56] The Alexandrian scholars were given to allegorizing—from Philo, who found Stoicism in Moses, to Clement and Origen—but by and large the Church resisted the method of allegory, or at least tried to apply brakes to it by insisting that it be measured against the meaning of the Bible as a whole.[57] The method was Hellenistic in character and tended to escape the realm of history.

The more historical method of Old Testament interpretation was that of typology. Here the events described were understood as having been genuine historical acts, chapters, as it were, in the story of God and Israel. But the events were also seen to bear analogical relationship to later, more complete revelatory actions. The earlier event, analogous to the later and therefore a foreshadowing of it, was a "type" of the later. I have already mentioned the Exodus as such a "type" of the Cross and Resurrection. Similarly, the prophecies of Jerusalem's destruction in 586 B.C. and again in 70 A.D. were "types" of the yet-to-be-fulfilled destruction of the world in the Last Day. Very important for the study of drama (because it has some implications for tragedy) is the prophetic Saved and Saving Remnant of the Old Testament (see Isaiah 11) which became the "type" of the Christian Church, "which had been raised up in the midst of the judgment by the mercy of God, a light to lighten the Gentiles and to be the glory—the fulfillment—of Israel's true vocation and history." [58]

Alan Richardson notes that the liturgical use of Scripture in the Church is based on the typological, rather than the allegorical, interpretation. His summary words will clarify the meaning of typology

[55] I am referring here to two of the four standard levels of medieval exegesis, which were the literal, the tropological, the allegorical and the anagogical. The distinction I draw is between the allegorical and the anagogical.

[56] *The Epistle to the Hebrews* has tendencies toward allegorizing, and Paul uses the method occasionally for hortatory or didactic purposes: I. Cor. 9 : 9 f.; I Cor. 10 : 4; II Cor. 3 : 13–15. Gal. 4 : 21–31 (Sarah and Hagar represent the New and Old Testaments) is the one place in the New Testament where the word "allegory" occurs. See Alan Richardson, *Christian Apologetics*, p. 180.

[57] Richardson, *Apologetics*, pp. 180–81.

[58] *Ibid.*, p. 189.

and provide a definition to which I will later have to return in showing
the patterning of events in Shakespeare:

> Hence the typological interpretation of the Bible differs from allegorical
> interpretation in that it detects a real and necessary correspondence in the
> structure and meaning of the original or "typical" event or complex of events
> to the new application or fulfilment of it. Accordingly the idea of the fulfil-
> ment of the Scriptures will mean for us the fulfilment of history, the making
> explicit of what was implicit in the pattern of the earlier historical events by
> the *denouement* of the later events, the deepening of the meaning of history
> itself as this meaning is revealed to the prophetic insight. . . .[59]

Canon Richardson traces the typological interpretation in the New
Testament, Augustine, Luther, and its modern resurgence following
the application of historical criticism to Scripture. He shows that
biblical literalism and allegory go hand in hand, but that the more
fundamental stream in Christian thought has been centered on historical interpretation and its handmaiden typology.

By means of typological interpretation, the past was reaffirmed in
significance while the old was transcended in the new. Event and
interpretation were put in tension, yet the interpretation itself arose
out of a new historical event, not out of something perpetual and unhistorical. The Incarnation wove all threads of time and history together, but it also put the divine stamp of validity upon the historical
arena—for it was that arena to which God came, in the fullness of
time.[60]

It is significant that Augustine, in whom the confrontation of
Greek and biblical thought reaches its apex, should have turned his
attention to the philosophy of history and the understanding of time.
The problem of time is considered in the *Confessions*, Book XI. There
the biblical experience of time is explored through philosophical
analysis. Augustine rejects the typical Greek view that time is the
measure of motion.[61] He perceives that he would have an intuition of

---

[59] Richardson, *Apologetics*, p. 190.

[60] For the ways in which the Christian concern with history worked itself out in actual
historiography and in numerous philosophies of history, the reader must be referred to other
studies. An excellent one is that of R. L. P. Milburn, *Interpretations of History*. The important
point to note is that virtually all major histories through the late Roman period, the Middle
Ages, and into the Renaissance, set their work in the context of the Divine history which
began at the creation of the world and will close at the Day of Judgment. For the importance
of these assumptions in Shakespeare's day, see E. M. W. Tillyard, *Shakespeare's History
Plays*, pp. 3–20.

[61] *Confessions* XI. 23, 29.

time even if nothing moved, so long as he were conscious. His consciousness of time, moreover, is an experience of the present, which strangely is made up of a future which is not yet and a past which is no more.

Thus my childhood, which now is not, is in time past, which now is not; but now when I recall its image and tell of it, I behold it in the present because it is still in my memory. . . . This indeed I know, that we generally think before on our future actions, and that that fore-thinking is present, but the action whereof we fore-think is not yet, because it is to come (xi. 18).

The experience of time is made up of memory, sight, and expectation. Augustine thus shows that the living experience of time is possible only because the soul in some sense transcends time in being able to create a present out of memory and expectation. It is only the non-existent past and future that enable the present to exist at all. This is paradoxical philosophical thinking based on a biblical-historical orientation to the self and the world. In it is present the biblical emphasis upon history and what I have called the Bible's "principle of contemporaneity." Past and future are drawn into the present, animating it.

Such paradoxical interdependence of past and present, future and present, could not come to full expression before the Christian era. For it depends upon an Aristotelian starting point, upon the Old Testament experience of God in history (with its emphasis upon historical memory), and upon the Incarnation event of Christianity (in which the radical future expectations of Judaism are drawn into the present). In Christianity, past, present, and future combine in a manifestation of the Eternal enacted in a moment of time—in what the New Testament calls *kairos*.

In the Hebraic and Christian orientations, history predominates over nature.[62] The approach to the ultimate meanings being through history, it follows that the cosmos itself participates in the historical acts of men. Thus it is that the world is created as time is created.[63]

[62] See Paul Tillich, *Biblical Religion and the Search for Ultimate Reality*, p. 40: "the whole universe is seen in historical perspective. The covenant symbol is applied not only to the relation between God and the nation but also to the relation between God and nature." That is to say, history swallows up nature. Cf. James Muilenburg, "The Faith of Ancient Israel," in *The Vitality of the Christian Tradition*: "The progress of Hebrew thinking proceeds from the grace of God as seen in history to the activity of God in nature. In this respect it stands in an interesting contrast to the development of Greek thought from the natural to the spiritual" (pp. 6–7).

[63] See Augustine *Confessions* xi. 13.

The fall of man involves a fall of nature,[64] and the prophetic vision of man's redemption involves the restitution of perfect harmony in nature.[65] Professor Tillich shows how the cosmic beginning and cosmic ending are thus "drawn into the historical vision of reality." "The historical vision of biblical religion," he says, "makes even the universe historical." [66]

With the beginning of the Christian era, therefore, we begin to find literature in which the cosmic world vibrates in sympathy with the moral, historical acts of men. The foremost example is in the synoptic gospels' accounts of the Crucifixion. Mark and Luke both describe the darkness which came over all the land, and the rending of the veil in the temple.[67] Matthew adds the earthquake and the opening of the tombs:

Now from the sixth hour there was darkness over all the land until the ninth hour. . . . And behold, the curtain of the temple was torn in two, from top to bottom; and the earth shook, and the rocks were split; the tombs also were opened. . . . When the centurion and those who were with him, keeping watch over Jesus, saw the earthquake and what took place, they were filled with awe, and said, "Truly this was a son of God!" [68]

I am indebted to Professor Auerbach for pointing out the literary importance of that passage. He links it with the Shakespearean participation of nature in human crises. In Shakespeare, says Professor Auerbach,

the cosmos is everywhere interdependent, so that every chord of human destiny arouses a multitude of voices to parallel or contrary motion. The storm into which Regan drives her old father, the king, is not an accident; it is contrived by magic powers which are mobilized to bring the event to a crisis.[69]

---

[64] Genesis 3 : 17:

> cursed is the ground because of you
> in toil you shall eat of it all the days
> of your life;
> thorns and thistles it shall bring forth
> to you. . . .

[65] Isa. 11 : 6–9; 65 : 25.
[66] *Religion and Reality*, p. 40.
[67] Mark 15 : 33–38; Luke 23 : 44. John does not mention these phenomena.
[68] Matt. 27 : 45, 51–52, 54. See also Milburn, *Interpretations of History*, p. 158, where an even more striking example is cited from the apocryphal Gospel of James (18 : 2). Milburn notes also: "The somewhat confused narrative of the *Apocalypse of Moses* records that the sun, moon, and stars were darkened for seven days after Adam's death" (p. 213).
[69] *Mimesis*, p. 323.

Later he adds that

the participation of the elements in a great destiny has its best-known model
in the earthquake at the time of Christ's death (Matthew 27 : 51 ff.), and this
model has remained very influential during the Middle Ages (cf. *Chanson de
Roland*, 1423 ff. or *Vita Nova*, 23).[70]

In later chapters, I shall show other examples of the way in which
Shakespeare has followed the Christian tradition in making "even the
universe historical." [71]

When Christianity combined the Hebraic historical orientation in
the world—including its expectation of a future Messiah, new covenant, new creation, etc.—with its own revelation that those expectations
had been fulfilled in Christ, it turned history into a drama. Prophetic
Hebraism had had the material for drama in the encounter between
man and God. Its view of life was dramatic. But it was deficient at the
point where the material of life needed to be envisioned in a form.[72]
The future, especially, was open in Hebraism, and the moral earnest-
ness of the prophets tended to keep it so, since it emphasized responsibility and choice. In that sense, Israel's experience of history was too
subjective to assume the formal pattern of drama.[73]

Form was, however, as natural to the Hellenic world as it was
foreign to the Hebraic. Incarnation was not a scandal to the Greeks
except insofar as the Christian version of it emphasized its place in a
temporal, historical scheme. The Incarnation made possible for Christianity a viewing of all history in terms of a formal pattern which is
essentially visible in Christ. By identifying Christ as the new Adam,

---

[70] *Mimesis*, p. 323.

[71] The involvement of nature in human deeds is to be found also in Seneca, notably in
Thyestes 11. 695–703, earthquake; 776–78, 789–884, the sun, moon, and stars disrupted
from their courses in consequence of Atreus' crime, with unnatural darkness at midday.
Parallels between Roman and Judaeo-Christian historical consciousness are striking. In
Chap. II, I noted the historical orientation in Vergil. See p. 45 in this chapter for the suggestion that Vergil may have had influence from Hebraic literature. Could the gospel writers
have been borrowing from Roman literary models of the time ? Or is the influence from
Judaism to both Rome and Christianity ? Or is it that the founding of Rome and the Sacrifice
of Christ both provide their separate communities (the Empire and the Church) with a
"center of history," in Tillich's sense, and thus similar historical consciousnesses arise ? If
there are two streams, they become one as the Church centers itself in Rome. The vitality of
the Christian interpretation of history absorbs and supplants that of the crumbling Empire.

[72] On the "borderlessness" of Hebrew thought, see Thorlief Boman, *Das hebräische Denken*,
pp. 136–40.

[73] I believe that this factor has much more to do with Israel's lack of dramatic literature
than the legalistic prohibitions against depicting things in heaven or earth (Exod. 20 : 4).
Rather, such prohibitions also are the product of a people who find reality in historical action
rather than in perceptible forms. The iconoclasm of Mohammedanism is another case in point.

and by seeing him as the one who will return to judge the world at the Last Day, the beginning, middle, and end of a dramatic history were constituted.

The appearance in history of the Christ who completes history creates a unique kind of time in the period which follows the Incarnation. The early Church was faced with the problem of interpreting the meaning of the time which comes after Christ's appearance *in* time. At first the destruction of the world, the Messiah's return, was considered imminent. Paul had to admonish his converts to keep busy at their work, for they apparently were ready to sit it out until Jesus should come again.

The Church solved the problem in the only possible way—it regarded itself as the community which bore witness to him during the interim between his First and Second Coming. In the Sacraments, Paul said, "You proclaim the Lord's death until he comes" (I Cor. 11 : 26).

History in the Christian era therefore takes place in a peculiar time which exists between what may be called the "constituting act" and the "fulfilling act." This present history is judged (that is, known for what it is) both by that which has gone before it and that which will come after it—Christ the Revealer and Christ the Judge of the World on the Last Day. The present is therefore seen as an interim period. It participates in the already-given body of Christ and it awaits his ultimate rule in power. The Christian drama of history depends upon an awareness of history's completion, manifest in the event of Christ which establishes the center of history.

This dramatic understanding of history arose in the minds of men at the time when the classical drama was in decline. The Church rose to power in the first four centuries of our era while the theater withered. The cosmos, whose powers and conflicts that theater had portrayed, was gradually replaced by the historical world of Christianity. As early as the fourth century, in Byzantium,[74] we may begin to trace the effect of the "drama of history" upon the history of the drama.

The factors in the foregoing discussion which the succeeding chapters will demonstrate to be most significant in the study of dramatic form are these: The Christian ordering of history around a center, the Incarnation, is immediately an ordering of time, beginning at Creation

---

[74] Allardyce Nicoll, *Masks, Mimes, and Miracles*, p. 210.

and ending at the Last Judgment. The order involves awareness that the Christian era exists in an interval between a constituting act and a fulfilling act of historical meaning. The order also establishes a universal history, claiming validity for all human occurrences. Even nature enters the realm of history in that claim.

The ordering of history in the Judaeo-Christian sense involves also the relation of time and form as one of tension. By the same token, event and interpretation are in tension. Neither exists solely for the other. These tensions mean that even the most mundane elements of life participate in the sublime, and do so in their uniqueness.

The importance of time and the importance of the unique combine to place an importance upon human personality in its capacity for decision which the classical world did not show. Christianity allows for, even demands, a certain internalization of history.[75]

The presupposition behind all these factors is that of Providence, which becomes the Judaeo-Christian alternative to Fate. It is distinguished from the latter by purpose, creativity, and personal demand.[76]

It is not my purpose to trace the interplay of these many factors through the centuries which lie between early Christendom and Shakespeare. I have tried to set forth the main elements in the Christian consciousness of history, which occur over and over again in the development of Christian thought. As for Shakespeare's day, the words of E. M. W. Tillyard may suffice:

the part of Christianity that was paramount was . . . the orthodox scheme of the revolt of the bad angels, the creation, the temptation and fall of man, the

---

[75] Cf. Collingwood, *Idea of History*, p. 57: "Man, for the Renaissance historian, was not man as depicted by ancient philosophy, controlling his actions and creating his destiny by the work of his intellect, but man as depicted by Christian thought, a creature of passion and impulse. History thus became the history of human passions. . . ." We may also note the three-fold effect which Collingwood says Christianity has had upon the conception of history (pp. 48–49): (1) the historical process viewed as "the working out not of man's purposes but of God's"; (2) historical agents seen as "vehicles of God's purposes and therefore as historically important"; (3) the demand for a universal history.

[76] In the Christian understanding of history, said Croce, "Providence guides and disposes the course of events, directing them to an end, permitting evils as punishments and as instruments of education, determining the greatness and the catastrophes of empires, in order to prepare the Kingdom of God. This means that for the first time is really broken the circle of the perpetual return of human affairs to their starting-point; history for the first time is here understood as progress, a progress that the ancient historians did not succeed in discovering save in rare glimpses, thus falling into inconsolable pessimism, whereas Christian pessimism is irradiated by hope" (*On History* [trans. by Ainslie], quoted in Milburn, *Interpretations of History*, p. 148).

incarnation, the atonement, and regeneration through Christ. And this is as true of the Middle Ages as of the age of Elizabeth.[77]

In Shakespeare's time, these conceptions were not only much stronger than they are in ours, they also were free of coloration from the modern progressive views of history. In Shakespeare—even though the tide of humanistic skepticism had begun to rise, even though he reflected its growth—the dramatic tradition of the Christian culture reached its fullest expression.

[77] *Elizabethan World Picture*, p. 16.

PART II: A NECESSARY EXCURSUS

IV

THE PROBLEM OF DRAMATIC FORM

The primary connection between drama and history is not in the drama's use of historical material as subject matter. It is, rather, in the influence of historical modes of thought upon the patterning of dramatic action. Study of that type of influence necessitates some preliminary attention to the idea of dramatic form.[1]

The reader should not anticipate that any canon of set forms will be placed before him. The best drama is not achieved by adhering to strict patterns. The freedom of the artist renders vain the attempts to discover laws of the drama, let alone certain necessary forms. But this does not mean that the finished work is formless or that the attempt to see the form is not the proper work of criticism.

Discussion of form in the drama inevitably evokes a certain interest and a certain embarrassment. Interest is stimulated because of the natural understanding that, in order to grasp the dramatic work of art *as* a work of art, its inherent principle of unity and structure must be seen. Such perception is always difficult in the drama, and therefore any attempt to elucidate it arouses interest. Embarrassment, on the other hand, arises from the fact that "form" is not a term which by strict propriety should be applied to drama. It can be so applied only as metaphor. Form is a spatial term; the drama is a temporal art. In what sense may one properly speak of the form of that which has its primary existence in the passage of time rather than in the delimitation of space? Werenskiold is said to have asked Ibsen: "You are interested

---

[1] In addressing the problem of dramatic form, I am not considering those characteristics which distinguish drama from other artistic media. There is no need to ponder the difference between, say, the form of the drama and the form of the novel. Rather, I shall attempt to distinguish between the form assumed by certain plays and that assumed by others. The aim is to attend not to the inclusive form of the genre but to the variant forms to be found within it.

in architecture?" to which Ibsen replied: "Yes, it is, as you know, my own trade." [2]

The architectural, sculptural, and pictorial parallels to dramatic construction are attractive. Especially has it been tempting for critics to perceive the difference between classical and Elizabethan drama in terms of classical and Gothic architecture. Thus, William Hazlitt:

> Sophocles differs from Shakespeare as a Doric portico does from Westminster Abbey. The principle of the one is simplicity and harmony, of the other richness and power.[3]

A few years earlier, A. W. Schlegel, in the famous lectures at Vienna, had employed similar language:

> The Pantheon is not more different from Westminster Abbey or the church of St. Stephen at Vienna, than the structure of a tragedy of Sophocles from a drama of Shakespeare.[4]

Schlegel also uses the comparison with sculpture. The great breadth of the Greek theater in proportion to its slight depth, he says, "must have given to the grouping of the figures the simple and distinct order of the bas-relief." [5] Although Schlegel's statement is not an observation on dramatic form, referring as it does only to physical appearances in the theater, the imagery is readily transferable to the play itself, as for instance when Harley Granville-Barker speaks of Ibsen in words like this:

> If a Greek play could be said to have some of the attributes of sculpture, with few of these lost there is now added to dramatic art something of the quality of a picture, the least touches of light and shade can be made to tell.[6]

Examples of such descriptions could be multiplied many times. If they often lead to over-simplification or tend to obscure a clear perception of the works themselves, nevertheless they are inevitable once the essentially spatial idea of form is applied to a temporal art such as drama.

It is true, I believe, that more unrest is felt when the Elizabethan

---

[2] Recounted in Ormerod Greenwood, *The Playwright; A Study of Form, Method, and Tradition in the Theatre*, p. 23.

[3] *Lectures on the Literature of the Age of Elizabeth*, p. 243. The lectures were delivered in 1820. Hazlitt proceeds to quote an article from the *Edinburgh Review* using the same kind of comparisons.

[4] *Lectures on Dramatic Art and Literature*, p. 21.

[5] *Ibid.*, p. 63. Cf. Hazlitt, pp. 241–42.   [6] *On Dramatic Method*, p. 173.

drama is compared to architecture than when the classical Greek is so compared. The fluidity, the freedom, the very complexity of structure in the Elizabethan drama resists analogy with the formal stability of architectural construction. By comparison, the Greek is obviously more static. It seems to lend itself more readily to description in terms of balance, proportion, and symmetry. The primary reason for the difference, as I shall show, is that the Greek drama reflects a culture in which space predominates over time, whereas the Elizabethan expresses the preconceptions of a culture in which time is more significant than space. Therefore the idea of form, with its architectural, sculptural, and pictorial analogies, more readily attaches itself to classical than to Medieval and Renaissance drama.

The difficulty of connecting a notion of form with the plays of Shakespeare has been so great that most of his interpreters have actually insisted that his plays show few signs of formal construction. They have maintained that he wrote not by design but by "nature," that his plays, rather than being carefully composed, simply grew. Only recently has criticism begun to rescue the greatest poet of the language from the charge of formlessness.[7] It is easy to see how his early commentators originated the misconception. They contrasted him with the criticism of his contemporary, Ben Jonson, and found that by comparison Shakespeare had none of the kind of construction which Jonson esteemed so highly in the classics and labored so arduously to popularize in England. With Jonson one could see the wheels turning; Shakespeare dazzled one by the brilliance of the achievement and the absence of any comment. Moreover, his models (with the single exception of *A Comedy of Errors*) were clearly not classical. As regularity of construction was the hallmark of the classics and the shibboleth of Ben Jonson, it was irrelevant to Shakespeare.

Ben Jonson himself originated the saying that "Shakespeare wanted art." William Cartwright wrote in 1647, in verses prefixed to the first edition of Beaumont and Fletcher's *Works*:

> Such Artless beauty lies in Shakespeares wit,
> 'Twas well in spight of him whate'er he writ.[8]

---

[7] The history of Shakespearean criticism from this point of view has recently been sketched so well that I need not repeat it here. See H. T. Price, *Construction in Shakespeare*. See also Max J. Wolff, "Shakespeares Form," in *Germanisch-romanische Monatsschrift*, S. 382–90; and Erwin Hernried, "Weltanschauung und Kunstform von Shakespeares Drama," in *Zeitschrift fur ästhetik und allegemeine Kunstwissenschaft*, S. 502–34.

[8] Quoted in Price, *Shakespeare*, p. 2.

By comparison with Fletcher, to whom the lines were addressed, Shakespeare must indeed have seemed artless; for Fletcher is perhaps the prime example of that tendency of the Jacobean dramatists to concentrate more and more upon the external form of the play, at the expense of genuine thought and emotion. What fun there is in Fletcher comes from seeing him work the thing out the way he does, rather than from any full experience through which the spectator may be led.

It was Milton who, even before Cartwright, had spoken of hearing "sweetest *Shakespear*, fancies childe/Warble his native Wood-notes wilde." [9] Never was there a writer more devoted than Milton to the study and imitation of classical forms. Few men have been less able, by taste and conviction, to perceive the possibility of a totally different idea of form from the strict disciplines which he so much admired.

The picture of the artless Shakespeare thus established has persisted until only recently, with few exceptions. In Germany, however, Lessing and Schlegel both started from the assumption that Shakespeare was an artist, not a sport of nature; thus they looked for the principle of unity upon which he usually worked. Coleridge followed them.[10] In contemporary criticism, certain voices have been raised on behalf of Shakespeare's construction—Max Wolfe and Erwin Hernreid in Germany, H. T. Price in this country. E. E. Stoll, who is certain of Shakespeare's artifice, while less certain of his care and attention to detail, has forced others to consider the element of design and construction in the master.[11]

If these voices, and others, particularly those who have sought the principle of unity in the imagery, such as Cleanth Brooks, Derek Traversi, G. Wilson Knight, *et al.*, can stimulate consideration of the problem of form in the greatest of our dramatists, the effect will be salutary; for the task of criticism lies precisely in that field. The work of art is not unrelated to life; in the final analysis it is not self-explanatory. But it does have a provisional, semi-independent existence apart from life, which gives it self-identity and the right to be known as art. The primary task of criticism is to elucidate that self-identity, which is another way of saying that it must discover the form of the work which it studies. If that task is difficult in drama, especially in Shakespearean drama, which exists so imbedded in temporal, rather than in spatial modes of thought, it is nevertheless necessary unless the

[9] *L'Allegro* 133–34.   [10] I am indebted here to Price, *Shakespeare*.
[11] See *Art and Artifice in Shakespeare*, and *Shakespeare and Other Masters*.

name of artist is to be denied the dramatist. For that reason, the present analysis of the influence of cultural conceptions of time and history upon the drama is directed to dramatic form rather than content. I am not looking for influences upon the ideas of the dramatist but for influences upon the artistic character of the finished work. The critic is concerned not only with the relation of art to a larger life, but also with the preservation of the work of art as a valid entity in its own right.

Dramatic form "is a question of harmony mainly, of just proportions, significant emphasis, congruities and arresting contrasts, of an ultimate integrity." [12] In those words a critic and man of the theater has given us an excellent definition of dramatic form in broad terms. What is needed beyond that, however, is a more specific definition which will serve as a guide for interpreting particular works. Mr. Granville-Barker himself becomes aware of that need when he turns to Shakespeare, as he does on the page following that just cited, where he suggests that the form of *King Lear* can be seen in terms of contrast, tension, climax, changes of pace, "by every sort of variation between scene and scene." These elements, he suggests, could be plotted on a chart, lines representing characters, plot and sub-plot, rising and falling to show volume of emotion, with a separate line to show increase and decrease of pace. "We can rightly call this form, I think, for all that it is form in motion." [13]

The introduction of a chart with rising and falling lines to show variations in interest and emotion represents a popular means of understanding dramatic form.[14]

The *locus classicus* for linear plotting of a play's form is Gustav Freytag's *Technique of the Drama*, where the action of a play is divided into rising action and falling action, with a turning point labeled "climax." A play, according to Freytag, can thus be plotted in the shape of a pyramid, a line leading up to the climax representing the rising action, and one leading down from it representing the falling action. It should be noted that Freytag's ascending and descending line does not necessarily reflect the rise and fall of spectator interest. Instead, it is a

---

[12] Granville-Baker, *On Dramatic Method*, p. 158. For his observations on the necessity of form in drama without insistence on regularity of construction, see pp. 26 ff. He seems to think of form as the result of disciplining the "rebellious human medium," the "close packing of matter and emotion."

[13] *Ibid.*, pp. 159–60.

[14] For instance, Brander Matthews, *A Study of the Drama*, p. 217: "This translation into a diagram of our fluctuating interest in a play is a test, primarily, only of the skill of the playmaker. It is a test of the form of the piece. . . ."

reflection of action taking place within the play. The climax is the point where the weight of opposing forces shifts, so that the hero either begins to take action formerly impossible to him or begins to feel the result of action taken in the first part of the play. The diagram so achieved by Freytag is therefore more objective than those envisioned by some others, but it is also much more rigid. He imagines that all plays will suit his scheme.

There have been other conceptions of form. Brief mention has been made in Chapter I of the Hegelian sense of dramatic structure in terms of force, opposing force, and resolution (thesis, antithesis, synthesis). Like Freytag's scheme, the Hegelian pattern attempts to see the one distinctive form in all drama, rather than the variant forms. It is thus of limited value in helping describe the difference between plays of two or more periods. Since its formula answers the question *how* the forces are related, the only question left is *what* forces are involved. It is doubtful whether dramatic form is indeed so consistent.

Another approach is to identify form with plot. That is perhaps the popular view of the matter, and it is what Eric Bentley referred to when he said that analyses of plays tell us how things begin, how they end, and where the climax lies.[15] The charge of confusing form with plot is laid at the door of the "neo-Aristotelian" critics of Chicago by Professor S. F. Johnson, who thinks that in practice their method reduces form to mere plot-summary and paraphrase.[16]

We need not dwell on the tendency of neoclassic criticism to identify form with obedience to the supposed rule of the three unities from Aristotle. At the opposite pole was the ability of romanticism to perceive a type of form related not to rules and outward symmetry but to inner consistency. Schlegel was perhaps the first to state it clearly. Defending Shakespeare against the charges of formlessness mentioned earlier, he said:

That we may answer this objection of want of form, we must first come to an understanding respecting the meaning of form, which most critics, and more especially those who insist on a stiff regularity, understand merely in a mechanical, and not in an organical sense. Form is mechanical when, through external influence, it is communicated to any material merely as an accidental addition without reference to its quality. . . . Organical form, again, is innate;

15 See Chap. I, p. 5.
16 *"Critics and Criticism:* A Discussion of the Chicago Manifesto," in *Journal of Aesthetics,* pp. 248–57. The book under review is *Critics and Criticism: Ancient and Modern,* ed. by R. S. Crane.

it unfolds itself from within, and acquires its determination along with the complete development of the germ.[17]

One is not certain whether Schlegel means to say that all good dramatic form is organic. In a sense, one feels the term is more readily applicable to Shakespearean drama and other modern works touched by the romantic spirit than to Greek drama. And yet one wonders whether it is meant that classical drama has mechanical form. Surely form is not communicated to classical drama "merely as an accidental addition without any reference to its quality." The beauty of Greek drama is its harmony of form and content. Is its form, then, organic? If it is, then must not organic be the description of all genuine form—a name describing inner coherence and consistency? We are back to Granville-Barker: form is a question of "an ultimate integrity."

There may be no greater wisdom which can be brought to the matter; yet there may be some insights which are useful as tools in critical analysis. It is my purpose now to suggest an analytical approach to the question of dramatic form. Rather than attempting to find ways of plotting a play's form on a linear graph, or reducing it to some resolution of forces, or describing it vaguely in terms of organic development, we shall find it more profitable to distinguish and elucidate the various components of the play which contribute to its form—factors to which one consciously or unconsciously refers when speaking of form in a given play. We shall ask what are the elements from which most, if not all, plays are constructed, without in the least suggesting that all dramas make use of them in anything like the same ways.

For this analytic task, we shall begin, as always, with Aristotle.[18]

"A tragedy, then, is the imitation of an action. . . ." [19] The helpfulness of the concept of action is derived from two implications which I believe are contained in the word as Aristotle uses it. The first is emphasis upon occurrence, upon something taking place, involving, as Aristotle says, a change from one state of affairs to another. The second

[17] *Dramatic Art and Literature.*

[18] The day has passed when Aristotle could be invoked as final authority for any particular view of dramatic art. It is not only that the meaning of so many of his terms is in dispute—none more so than "imitation" and "action"—but also that the idea of authority itself is in decline. Even if it could be established beyond debate what Aristotle meant, it would not follow in our age that his meaning is determinative. However, discussion has to start somewhere, and as a starting place Aristotle's position is, and is likely to remain, secure. I propose that an analysis of dramatic form should begin with Aristotle's description of tragedy as the imitation of an action.

[19] *Poetics* VI. Quotations are from the translation of Ingram Bywater, *Aristotle on the Art of Poetry.*

is unity. Had he allowed the word to imply merely change or movement, its helpfulness in analysis of form would have been negligible;
but he has repeatedly employed it in contexts which make it clear that
tragedy is not simply the imitation of action in general, but rather of
an action in particular. The article, of course, has to be supplied in
English translation, but Aristotle has left little room for doubt that it
should be understood. Thus, the famous definition of tragedy reads:

> A tragedy, then, is the imitation of an action that is serious and also, as hav-
> ing magnitude, complete in itself.[20]

It becomes even clearer that *an* action is meant when Aristotle deals
specificially with the question of unity in epic and tragedy:

> The truth is that, just as in the other imitative arts one imitation is always of
> one thing, so in poetry the story, as an imitation of action, must represent one
> action.[21]

This passage is worth quoting at greater length because it is the one
place in the *Poetics* where Aristotle discusses unity specifically. Everyone knows that it was a mistaken classicism which ascribed to him the
rule of the three unities, those of time and place being unwarrantably
based on v (1449^b 13) and xxiv (1459^b 25). The one principle of unity
which Aristotle does set forth unambiguously is that derived from the
unified and complete nature of a story's one action, which must be

> a complete whole, with its several incidents so closely connected that the trans-
> posal or withdrawal of any one of them will disjoin and dislocate the whole.
> For that which makes no perceptible difference by its presence or absence is
> no real part of the whole.[22]

More light is thrown on the Aristotelian idea of action when it is remembered that in the *Poetics* the word is usually found in the phrase
"imitation of action" (πράξεως μίμησις). As he uses "action" in
such a way as to prevent its being taken as mere activity, so he uses
"imitation" in such a way as to prevent its being understood as mere
mimicry (or so I believe was his intention). That which imitates the
total, complete action could not be merely the copying of gesture,
movements, tones, or even situations. For that reason, Aristotle most
often describes the imitator of the action as the μῦθος, a term usually
translated as story, fable, or plot. Thus the action, which is not seen

---

[20] *Poetics*, vi.   [21] *Ibid.*, viii.   [22] *Ibid.*

directly by the spectator, is imitated, or bodied forth, by the arrangement of the incidents. Μῦθος should not be read merely as plot, especially if plot means narrative. Μῦθος also means design, plan, order. The poet imitates his one central action by means of the total plan which he puts upon the stage, the audible and visible arrangements and sequences.

Professor Bywater, commenting on the Aristotelian use of μιμήσεις, says the word originally meant "to play the μῖμος," to reproduce the language, tones, and gestures of another.[23] Its usage was broad enough later to include the counterfeiting done by dancer, singer, painter, sculptor, musician, and in speech and literature. But, he says, Aristotle is responsible for a variation in usage when he applies the concept of imitation to the work of literature itself. Thus the total complex of elements in the epic poem, the tragedy, or the comedy becomes the vehicle for imitation of the one action which gives the piece its unity. As W. J. Oates has put it:

In saying that the artist "imitates" his models, Aristotle does not use the word in the primary sense of "copying," but rather is seeking to give a secondary meaning to the term. By the word he seems to mean the process which takes place when an artist creates his work of art. It is through *mimesis* that form comes to be imposed upon the artist's material, broadly conceived. Aristotle insists that "poetry is something more philosophic and of graver import than history, since its statements are in the nature of universals, whereas those of history are singulars." Hence poetry "imitates" universals.[24]

Desirable as a succinct definition of what Aristotle means by action would be, it is probably not possible without distorting his perception. Freytag came close to it, but was thrown off by an overly rationalistic understanding.[25] More recently Professor Fergusson's discussion in *The Idea of a Theatre* has been more helpful, while at the same time

---

[23] *On the Art of Poetry*, p. 100.
[24] Introduction to *The Complete Greek Drama*, p. xxiii. The quotation from the *Poetics* IX, is in Bywater's translation.
[25] "By *action* is meant, an event or occurrence, arranged according to a controlling idea, and having its meaning made apparent by the characters. It is composed of many elements, and consists in a number of dramatic efficients (*momente*), which become effective one after the other, according to a regular arrangement" (*Technique of the Drama*, p. 27). That is close to Aristotle, but its effect is minimized by passages like this, where too much is made of cause and effect: "the action must move forward with uniform consistency. This internal consistency is produced by representing an event which follows another, as an effect of which that other is the evident cause. . . ." (p. 29). But Freytag does see that action is the principal element in unity and form: "It is the business of the action to represent to us the inner consistency of the event, as it corresponds to the demands of the intellect and the heart" (p. 46).

showing that no precise formulation is easily to be achieved.[26] He shows that plot, characters, and thought are related to the action, and reveal it, by analogy. A clear reading of Aristotle demands a definite distinction between plot and action; yet plot, character, and thought participate in the action and thus present it to the audience by analogical rather than direct means. He says:

Thus by "action" I do not mean the events of the story but the focus or aim of psychic life from which the events, in that situation, result.[27]

In saying "psychic," Professor Fergusson does not mean "psychological." Neither he nor Aristotle is so subjective. I take it that both of them mean to include in "action" what Collingwood calls the inside and the outside of the event. The very difficulty in the concept is that action is on the one hand very inclusive, not to be identified with plot only, or characters, or ideas, or happenings; yet on the other hand it is internal—an interpretive unity at the core, from which all the other elements spring. It might be said that action is (in the root meaning) the "intension" of the events—that quality within them which puts them, as it were, into tension, and gives them a "tendency" to a certain outcome.

To go further in a definition of action would be prematurely to limit the concept. All dramatic action is not of the same kind. Enough has been said, perhaps, to indicate that, following Aristotle's lead, action may be regarded as the primary point of unity within the play—the focus, as Professor Fergusson puts it—and the imitation of action as the source of form in the dramatic work.

From that premise, certain elements in analysis of dramatic form may follow. Taking the cue again from Aristotle, a distinction may be made between the object of imitation and the manner of imitation. Aristotle himself distinguished between object, manner, and means of imitation, doing so for the purpose of classifying the various artistic genres, such as painting, music, and poetry, which he conceived of as several kinds of imitation.[28] We shall find it helpful here to use the distinctions for the purpose only of comparing various kinds of dramatic form. It will not be necessary to separate means from manner by a nice distinction. It will be useful, however, to think of the kind of action which is the object of imitation, and of the manner in which the particular action is set forth in dramatic imitation.

[26] pp. 47–48, 242–44, 248–50.   [27] Fergusson, *Idea of a Theatre*, p. 48.   [28] *Poetics*. I.

The *object* of imitation in any given play will be an action of a certain kind, and the primary task in the analysis of the form of the play will be to understand the nature of the action involved.[29] Analysis of dramatic form through dramatic action is the approach taken by Professor Fergusson. The principal kinds of action which he discusses in *The Idea of a Theatre* are those of Sophocles, Shakespeare, Racine, Wagner, and certain modern playwrights. These are described as "the tragic rhythm of action," "the analogy of action," "the action of reason," "the action of passion," and the "partial perspectives" of modern theater. In every case, a different principle of unity, a different focus is discovered.

If the object of dramatic imitation is a certain kind of action, contributing the first component in the form of the piece, the second component will be supplied by the *manner* in which the action is imitated. Theoretically, the same action or type of action might be handled in separate fashions by diverse playwrights, although the better the play, the closer the correlation between object and manner of imitation.

For the sake of completeness, I would divide the manner of dramatic imitation into four principal parts: (a) arrangement and relation of the incidents, (b) linguistic elements, (c) presentational elements, and (d) the division of acts and scenes. It will be well to describe what is meant by each of these.

The foremost element in the manner of dramatic imitation is in the arrangement and relation of the incidents of which the piece is composed. Aristotle referred to this as the construction of the $\mu\tilde{\upsilon}\theta\sigma\varsigma$ and admonished the young playwright to master the skill of handling it. This skill is usually thought of as "making the plot," a term which, as noted above, is adequate only if understood in a very broad sense. What is involved is not so much the narrative, but the design by means of which the total piece is conveyed to the spectator. This concerns many interrelated decisions, such as the order in which the events are presented, and which are enacted and which narrated. Especially it concerns the relationship of scene to scene: does one follow another because of demands of logic? or chronology? or analogical relation? or poetic imagination? Is chronological realism always obeyed, or do

---

[29] The average reader is aware of this fact, which is why in most cases, if one asks about a play's form, he will be given a résumé of the plot. The story is perceived as a way of getting at the action; or, perhaps more often, the story is identified with the action. At any rate, it is felt that if the action is described the form is also described, and such a perception is surely correct in the main.

scenes jump backward and forward in time? Do scenes which occur in sequence refer to simultaneous events? Does the play begin near the beginning, middle, or end of the action? This type of analysis is often imagined as exhausting the analysis of form. I am suggesting that, although it is extremely important, it is but one of a number of elements in the complete idea of dramatic form. It is, of course, closely related to the action itself. Many of the questions mentioned will be determined for the dramatist by the kind of action he is setting out to imitate; others he will have to choose and to think out carefully. The arrangement and relation of the incidents in a play is, I believe, what is usually meant by "structure."

The linguistic elements are among those parts of the play which the spectator perceives directly. Structure may not be apparent to him at first; the action may be discernible only after careful analysis; but the language of the play is a part of that outward form of the work which is observed immediately. Here are encountered such things as the employment of prose or poetry. If the latter, the particular verse form or forms is of interest. Under this head comes the use of imagery in the language, and the type and quality of symbolism. It is not possible to know thoroughly the form of a drama until one knows something of the demands made upon the imagination through these linguistic elements. No description of *Othello*, for instance, which stops with a retelling of the story, or even a description of the nature of the action is adequate unless it also manages to convey something of the experience brought to the listener by the association of images throughout the play. Among the linguistic elements, I would also include what may be called the "language reference" of the play: whether the language tends to imitate the natural speech of everyday life, or whether it seeks to achieve an elevated tone, or adopts some other style.

Those qualities of dramatic form which are closely related to performance may be called "presentational elements." Since the drama is complete only in actual enactment, it reflects in its form the type of theater for which it is conceived, together with the conventions of acting and staging which the author may imagine as determining the way his play will be performed. If one thinks of the play as it is in performance, these elements are present as the audible and visible forms in which the script has come to be embodied. If one thinks of the play as a literary piece on the printed page, these elements are understood as influences upon the author and explanations for certain characteristics of the play as written.[30] If the play is what is called "closet drama," it will be characterized by the very absence of dependence upon the conditions of performance in the theater. Presentational elements include also the use of settings and properties—whether they are necessary to the play, and if so, whether their use is primarily naturalistic, realistic, symbolic, or a combination of these. The relation of drama to theater, acting, and staging is an element in its form.

The division of the play into acts and scenes has been left to the last because it is not in itself a very important matter. Sometimes such division is purely a matter of literary convention, having more to do with the printed appearance of a play than with its existence as a piece for performance. Such appears to be the case with the Shakespearean act divisions.[31] That type of division has little or nothing to do with dramatic form as such. Sometimes act and scene divisions follow the conventions of theater practice, in which cases they are closely related to the presentational elements noted. This is true of Shakespeare's scene divisions, the short, rapid scenes being not only possible but also highly desirable on the Elizabethan type of stage.[32] Sometimes, however, the division of acts and scenes is intimately connected with the structure of the play with the arrangement and relation of the incidents. If this is so, it becomes an important consideration in understanding the form, because it is closely connected with the action and with the most important element in the manner of imitation—namely, structure.

Basing our discussion on the premise that the business of drama is the imitation of action, we have thus broken the idea of dramatic form into two components: the kind of action which is the object of imitation and the manner of the imitation itself. The latter was divided into four parts: structure, linguistic elements, presentational elements, and act and scene division. It is not implied that any of these

[30] "Very obviously a particular sort of stagecraft must be rooted in the opportunities of its particular stage. But I suggest that the whole fabric of a play's artistry will ultimately rest here; and that not merely the more plastic beauties of Greek Tragedy as it lived and moved and can now be re-created only in imagination, but its more intrinsic qualities too, those architectural qualities of spacing, proportion, cumulative effect, of repose and ordered power, which are extant still in the literary record, fetch their origin from the physical conditions of the theatre they could best adorn." Granville-Barker, *On Dramatic Method*, pp. 15-16.

[31] For an early statement of that opinion, see Brander Matthews, *A Book About the Theatre*, the chapter entitled "Why 5 Acts?" However, for a contrasting opinion, see T. W. Baldwin, *Shakespeare's Five-Act Structure*.

[32] I refer to the scenes as acted, not as chopped up, numbered, and assigned specific locales by his editors.

elements can be separated absolutely from the others. Analysis of any one of them should lead to each of the others and eventually to the action which lies at the base of the dramatic work. The better the form, the more closely will all the parts be related, especially if dramatic form is indeed a question "of an ultimate integrity." Nevertheless, this analysis has been felt necessary because it is believed that when one speaks of dramatic form he is speaking not of one factor but of many. He means unity of action, the structure of various incidents, the use of language, the manner of presentation, and the division into acts and scenes.

Of the various elements in dramatic form, by far the most important are the kind of action and the arrangement and relation of the incidents (structure). From these, in the main, the form arises. Perhaps it is better to say, they *are* the form, modified by linguistic, presentational, and scene division elements.

Now upon reflection it can be seen that what is most important for analysis of both the action and the structure is the element of time. It would be parading the obvious to say that time is the *sine qua non* of any action. But perhaps it is not so immediately evident that that very fact makes the sense of time underlying the action the clue to the quality of the action itself. Not the play's content, but the form and quality of the action will be known by the sense of time which informs it. If one wishes to know the kind of action underlying the *Oedipus Tyrannus* or *Macbeth*, he must ask whether things move fast or slow, backward or forward. He must ask whose time it is which is represented in each play, what is the setting in which time has its existence, whether the principal agents and powers in the action are subject to time, whether the action is regarded as occurring uniquely in a moment of unrepeatable time, or whether it is an illustration of that which exists eternally.

By the same token, if one wishes to understand the ways in which Sophocles and Shakespeare have structured the two plays, he must see the use to which they have put the factor of time. He must see the attention which each has paid to the clock and the calendar, where free and where strict with chronology and to what purpose, where moving forward chronologically and where doubling back, where the past is remembered and where the future is anticipated. And always the question is *whose* past and *whose* future, and in what setting.

These reflections lead me to reassert that the medium of drama is time, and that to speak of form in drama is to speak metaphorically of its particular temporal existence. The form of a play is the expression of a temporal action set within a certain social reference and a certain (explicit or implicit) cosmic frame. And since the social and cosmic setting of time is a part of the historical consciousness, analysis of the problem of dramatic form leads us to look for a relation between assumptions regarding historical time and the form of dramatic action.

PART III: COMPARISONS

V

NEMESIS AND JUDGMENT:
THE PERSIANS AND *RICHARD III*

Richard III

An important clue to the principle of construction of *Richard III* lies in the opening speech:

> Now is the winter of our discontent
> Made glorious summer by this sun of York. (I.i.1–2)

The words point to the importance of times and seasons. They introduce us to a mode of action which, as the play will disclose, is fundamentally temporal and historical in its conception. That is to say, it is action which is necessarily and indissolubly linked to the passage of time. It is action which must be understood as possible only at certain special "times" when all factors are in readiness. It is action in which time is not merely personal but has a social and a cosmic setting. It is, however, action in which personal character is very important because men's purposes run in some cases *with* time, in others *against* it. It is action which is fully meaningful not in general terms, but only in the unique historical situations wherein it occurred.

Technically, Richard's opening speech is exposition. Therein it does not differ from the opening chorus of *The Persians*, which describes the situation in Persia since the men have departed for conquest in Greece. Yet there is a striking difference, for the Greek passage describes the country, as it were, in a general condition. The Chorus is not specific, it presents us with vague forebodings of ill. We are given the picture of an existing situation, but one unfocused, not pin-pointed. Such focusing could be achieved only by the direction of the general situation toward a particular desire or will. This Shakespeare achieves at the outset of *Richard III* by making Richard serve as his own chorus, informing us simultaneously of the situation in England and of his own ambition to seize the throne.

By the time the opening monologue is completed we know exactly what Richard intends and what methods he will use to achieve his goal. As these methods are so drastic, we know also that he will in large measure succeed and that drastic steps will be necessary before he can be stopped. If there is a primary fault in the construction of the play it is that the audience knows so much so soon. Later plays will exhibit greater skill, revealing more gradually the forces at work, inducing suspense in the process. Even here, however, Shakespeare has a reason for his suddenness. If he exposes Richard at the outset, he guarantees that Richard in himself cannot become the paramount concern of the play. By a sudden disclosure of the character, the natural interest in this "Machiavellian" figure will be robbed of the augmentation it would receive from suspense, and what suspense there is will be directed toward the question of how far he can go and what can stop him. By indirection, the audience is forced to regard the larger situation of which Richard is, after all, only a part.

The personal and the collective are intertwined in the first lines of the play. The "winter of our discontent," which is now "made glorious summer," was neither only individual, nor only social. It was a winter in which the clouds lour'd not only upon the house of York but also—and in this speech more importantly—upon the grasping plans of Richard. It is not only "our discontent" but also "my" discontent which has been turned into summer by the rising of a York to the throne. After thirteen lines the plural is dropped, and Richard speaks on his own behalf.

In the context of the ensuing action, however, the speech has further ambiguities. Its character is ironic because it describes as "glorious summer" what is actually to be one of the bleakest winters in the history of England. Through scene after scene, the play will picture the winter of England's discontent while Richard possesses a brief—very brief—summer.

Yet at a still deeper level the lines are not ironic but prophetic. For the last scenes of the play will indeed show the winter of England's discontent made into true summer by a son of Lancaster and a daughter of York. In this sense, Richard's speech is premature. The true summer is not now but later. On the other hand, taking the play as a whole and in the context of the tetralogy of which it is a part,[1] the play is the "now" which shows the final blast of winter before the summer of Tudor power and peace.

Not all these levels of meaning would be caught by the audience at first hearing, of course;[2] but that is no matter. Shakespeare's construction usually involves the presence of meanings and connotations in early lines which are completed and fulfilled only in later passages. It is one of the most telling ways in which time finds its way into the fibre of the plays. The movement is toward a more and more complete revelation. This revelation, however, is not like the labyrinthine unraveling of the enigmas of oracles and perplexing situations, such as classical tales delight in, and such as motivates the plot in *Oedipus the King*.[3] Neither is it like the gradual disclosure of a pre-existent truth and accomplished fact, as in *The Persians*. It is rather the progressive fulfillment of meanings and significances which were present in earlier happenings (or lines), the full depth of which is sounded only later in the course of the action.

Richard III contains a very large number of specific references to time and times. Some deal with matters of chronology; the dating of events, the hours of the day, and the like. Others are lines which mention speed, rapidity of movement, or slowness, giving an indirect impression of the passage of time. Others are references to the present, the past, or the future. In her study of the presentation of time in the Elizabethan drama, Mable Buland says there is nothing in Shakespeare's previous work "to parallel the play upon notes of time" which this work contains throughout.[4] It has, she says, a strong "effect of rapidity of movement and definiteness in time-projection."[5]

---

[1] I follow Professor E. M. W. Tillyard in this view, regarding *Richard III* as the fourth in a tetralogy of which the first three plays are those named for Henry VI. See his *Shakespeare's History Plays*, pp. 147–49.

[2] Presumably, however, the audience would have a knowledge of the three *Henry VI* plays and of the chronicles, which means it would catch more of the meaning than might at first be thought.

[3] Incidentally, there is such an oracle in the opening speech of Richard (I.i.38–40), but it has only casual importance for the play as a whole. See also the enigmatic prophecy in *Cymbeline* (V.iv.137–51), where Shakespeare is playing at classical imitation. On the other hand, *Richard III* has many prophecies and curses which are not of the enigma type. See M. C. Bradbrook, *Shakespeare and Elizabethan Poetry*, pp. 129–30. These and their fulfillment re-emphasize the point made in the text. The oracles in *Macbeth* are treated in Chap. VII of this book.

[4] *The Presentation of Time in the Elizabethan Drama*, p. 101.

[5] *Ibid.*, p. 98. There is some debate on the number of days portrayed in *Richard III*. The Charlotte Porter ed. of *The Tragedy of Richard the Third* reckons there are twelve days of action plus various intervals (pp. 171–75). Daniels (*Shakespeare Variorum*), it says, had

The precision, or lack of it, which Shakespeare evinces in chronology need not detain us except to note that he is very careful about it.
That is, Shakespeare is careful to be accurate and consistent in his
references to the day and hour *where it suits his dramatic purpose* to be
so, and he is equally careful to be vague or imprecise where there is a
dramatic reason for that. The technique is neither one of slavish
obedience to clock and calendar probability nor of fanciful disregard
for credibility. He strives for an effect—an effect in which time is an
important element.

Miss Buland has described what she calls the double time-scheme,
which she finds in classical as well as Elizabethan drama.[6] It involves
the coexistence in one play of both a short and a long time-scheme. In
Richard III the short scheme appears to bring the whole action "within
the compass of a few days." [7] Events move very rapidly from the imprisonment of Clarence to Richard's death on the battlefield. On the
other hand, "the coexistence of a longer period of time is equally apparent." [8] Two reigns pass during the course of the play; Edward's vices
and Richard's tyranny become familiar to their subjects (III.v–vi.
and V.iii); there are uprisings throughout the country; Buckingham
journeys to Wales and returns with an army; [9] Richmond lands with
an expeditionary force, and so on.[10] By means of the double time-
scheme, Shakespeare satisfies two requirements at once. He achieves
dramatic intensity and excitement through the impression of rapidity;
and he satisfies the demands of the historical imagination, which thinks
in terms of protracted developments over months and years. The latter
has to do with the realism of a sequence of events as it might actually
have occurred. The former is an aspect of the dramatist's interpretation of the events. When Shakespeare turns "the accomplishment of
many years/Into an hour-glass," [11] he is not only bowing to dramatic

---

reckoned eight days (p. 175). Miss Buland finds ten days (p. 98). Miss Porter (p. 173) points
out that discrepancies arise mainly from two lines (IV.ii.93, 113) which appear in the Quarto
but not in the Folio.

[6] *Time in the Elizabethan Drama*, pp. 1–25.

[7] *Ibid.*, p. 98.   [8] *Ibid.*, p. 99.

[9] Buckingham's journey occurs in the space of forty-seven lines and (if the Quarto lines in
IV.ii be retained) the time only from ten o'clock until around supper of the same day!

[10] There is another kind of "double time" not touched on here—namely, that resulting
from the difference between time represented on stage and the time required for performance,
of which the clock scene in Marlowe's *Dr. Faustus* is a good example. Miss Buland notes still
another kind, that arising from the dove-tailing of two plots in one play (*Time in the Elizabethan Drama*, p. 9).

[11] *Henry V*, Prologue, 30–31.

and theatrical necessity; he is also turning the affairs of those years into their significant form.

The particular importance of time in *Richard III* is not, however, primarily connected with the question of chronology or the compression of time. It lies in the idea of "special" times, the particular ripeness of certain moments for certain events, and the unique character of particular times because of their past and future.

The irony of the story of Richard, as dramatized by Shakespeare, lies in the fact that he operates on a different schedule of time from the ultimately victorious forces. That is, Richard's desires and ambitions are, in the course of the play, to be proved vain. As "minister of hell" (I.ii.46) he cannot win against the "captain" of God (V.iii.108). Shakespeare, true to the religio-national character of his theme, has expressed the conflict of good and evil wills in something like the biblical understanding of a conflict of times.

We begin very soon to get indications that the times are out of joint for Richard—or rather, he for them. He tells us himself that he is

> Deform'd, unfinish'd, sent before my time
> Into this breathing world scarce half made up.   (I.i.20–21)

This motif is resumed twice afterwards. In the scene between the Duchess of York, Queen Elizabeth, and the young Duke of York (II.iv), the lad speaks of Richard's having chid him for growing so fast, quoting the old saw, "Small herbs have grace, great weeds do grow apace" (13). The Duchess objects that Richard himself was

> when he was young,
> So long a-growing and so leisurely
> That if this rule were true, he should be gracious.   (18–20)

She judges he grew too slowly rather than too fast, but the young Duke is not to be put off. He cites the popular gossip about Richard:

> Marry, they say my uncle grew so fast
> That he could gnaw a crust at two hours old.   (27–28)

When the Duchess of York meets Richard on his way to battle, he tells her he is in haste, drawing from her the comment, "Art thou so hasty? I have stayed for thee,/God knows, in torment and in agony" (IV.iv.162–63). This is an allusion to the tradition that Richard

could not be born naturally but only after long labor.[12] Later she amplifies the theme by speaking of all the abnormal stages in his life:

> A grievous burden was thy birth to me;
> Tetchy and wayward was thy infancy;
> Thy school-days frightful, desp'rate, wild, and furious,
> Thy prime of manhood daring, bold, and venturous,
> Thy age confirm'd proud, subtle, sly, and bloody.   (167–71)

In Act I, scene ii, Lady Anne echoes the tales about Richard's birth
by praying that if he ever have a child it may be "abortive . . . prodi-
gious, and untimely brought to light" (21–22).

Richard's actions are as untimely as his birth and growth. Lady
Anne laments the "untimely fall of virtuous Lancaster" (I.ii.4),
killed at Richard's hand; and Richard, adopting her point of view
in the wooing scene, refers to the "timeless [i.e., untimely] deaths/Of
these Plantagenets, Henry and Edward" (117–18). The imprisonment of the innocent Clarence brings forth from Brakenbury the sad
observation that "Sorrow breaks seasons and reposing hours,/Makes
the night morning and the noon-tide night" (I.iv.76–77).

Like many of the heroes in Shakespearean tragedy, Richard moves
too quickly. He is intemperate and hasty in fixing the day of the
Prince's coronation. "Tomorrow, in my judgment, is too sudden,"
says Derby; "For I myself am not so well provided/As else I would be
were the day prolong'd" (III.iv.45–47). The short scene of fourteen
lines wherein the Scrivener marks "how well the sequence hangs together" in the intemperate execution of Hastings is inserted solely for
the purpose of showing how much ahead of any proper order Richard
and Buckingham are acting (III.vi).

In Act IV, scene iv (l. 16), Margaret reminds Elizabeth that
Richard's outrageous acts have unnaturally changed her "infant morn
to aged night." In fact, Richard's whole campaign has so upset the
natural order of time that when the climax is reached on the day of
battle the sun refuses to shine (V.iii.275–87). According to clock and
calendar, which Richard consults, the sun "should have brav'd the east
an hour ago," but as it is, it will be "a black day."

It is possible for Richard (or any man) to get so out of harmony with
time because time in this play is not merely a quantity to be measured

[12] Hall wrote: "It is reported, his mother the duches had muche a dooe in her trauaill, that she could not be deliuered of hym uncut. . . ." (Quoted in Porter ed., p. 154.)

by the movement of stars or the flowing of sand in the glass. Time is laden with purpose, and therefore it tends to gather itself together, as it were, into certain particular moments when long-prepared actions are completed and great issues are decided. This quality is to be seen in small affairs as well as in the most consequential.[13]

The action of *Richard III* gathers toward two predominant "times" —the coronation of Richard and the Battle of Bosworth Field. Shakespeare has accentuated these "times" by building the rhythm of the play about them. Before each of them the pace accelerates. Before the coronation, the haste expresses, as we have seen, Richard's intemperateness. It does the same before Bosworth, but there it is even more important that the sense of acceleration expresses also the culmination of a decisive, judgmental action which has long been in preparation.

Near the end of Act II, the pace begins to quicken. Only the two young princes stand between Richard and the throne, and they are virtually no obstacle at all. The excitement first appears among the citizens (II.iii). Shakespeare wishes to show that events are stirring which involve the whole society. Thus the citizens, moving about exceedingly fast, for what reason they scarcely know themselves (1–2), pause only long enough to remark on the news of the king's death and to lament a land governed by a child who has not yet come to "his full and ripened years" (14), or else one governed by the Duke of Gloucester. They remark on the "untimely storms" (35) of the day's news and then hie themselves away. The next scene opens with the Archbishop's announcement that the crown prince and his escort will arrive in

---

[13] When Richard meets Clarence on the way to prison (and death), he greets him with the conventional, "Brother, good day," which in the context bears an ironic flavor (I.i.42). The two converse upon the reason why Clarence is "now" committed (61), upon related events occurring "this day" (69), and part with Richard's guess that the "imprisonment shall not be long," and his admonition, "Meantime, have patience" (114, 116). Clarence' short drama is completed in I.iii.339 to I.iv, where the sense of fateful time is reinforced in many lines. Richard receives from the murderers an affirmative answer to the question, "Are you now going to dispatch this thing?" He bids them be "sudden in the execution" (I.iii.346) and to be "about your business straight/Go, go, dispatch" (355–56). In prison, Clarence looks "heavily today" (iv.1); he passed a "miserable night" (2) not worth a "world of happy days,/ So full of dismal terror was the time" (6–7). In his dream, he and Richard had "cited up a thousand heavy times" (14) before Richard sent him to his "time of death" (34). Waking, he remembers with remorse that he has been guilty of all those wrongs which "now give evidence" against his soul (67). When the two murderers enter, they fall into a colloquy on the coming judgment day and where conscience is "now" (106–30). The murder follows, the murderers flee, and the next scene begins with Edward's line, falling ironically upon our ears, "Why so; now have I done a good day's work."

In the Clarence incident we see in miniature, and with but slight elaboration, the form which the play as a whole evinces.

London "tomorrow, or next day." A messenger comes with news which sends the women and the young Duke into sanctuary.

References to speed and haste now appear more and more frequently, and, according to Shakespeare's usual technique when the action is accelerating, there are increasing references to the hour and the day.[14] Rivers, Grey, and Vaughan are dispatched in a short scene of twenty-five lines (III.iii), and Hastings falls out of favor and loses his life before dinner of the same day (III.iv.97). Meantime, the nobles have assembled to decide "when is the royal day?" Buckingham wants to know if all is "ready for the royal time," Ely suggests "tomorrow" as a "happy day" (iv.3–6), which Derby believes is too sudden (45).

A slight lull now ensues as Buckingham and Richard unsuccessfully try to prepare the citizens to agree to the coronation (III.v), but at the end of the scene things speed up again.[15] The scrivener scene follows, devoted to the importunity of Hastings' death. The citizens are won in the scene with Richard "between two Bishops," and Buckingham gets his "consent" to be crowned "tomorrow" (III.vii.242, 244). In the following scene (IV.i), in which Lady Anne with unwitting irony bids her friends "a happy and a joyful time of day," (6), Stanley brings news of the coronation "one hour hence" (29) and bids Dorset flee to Richmond with "all the swift advantage of the hours" (49).

The impetuous movement is now interrupted, although not halted. The appearance of the women and their speeches of lamentation (in this scene and especially two scenes later in IV.iv) serve to slow down the movement, to give it perspective. In this post coronation lull, the second "special time" of the play begins to receive its preparation. Richmond's name is mentioned for the first time (IV.i.43) at the summit of Richard's success—less than an hour before the coronation. From that point forward, all acceleration of the action will be, although Richard does not know it, toward the Earl of Richmond's victory.

The precarious—that is to say, the temporary—nature of Richard's reign is emphasized by Shakespeare upon the very moment when we

---

[14] The prince urges "speedy haste" in the bringing of his brother (III.i.60). Hastings is summoned "tomorrow to the Tower/To sit about the coronation" (171). In the next scene he is being roused "upon the stroke of four" complaining about "these tedious nights" (ii.5–6). Catesby arrives, "early stirring," and is asked, "What news, what news in this our tottering state?" (36–37) Stanley enters and, although it is near dawn, urges them to the Tower because "The day is spent" (91). When Buckingham enters, he says he is bound for the Tower but cannot stay there long (120).

[15] Buckingham promises news by "three or four o'clock" (101). Lovel is dispatched "with all speed." The friars are bidden to come "within this hour" (103, 106).

see the tyrant wearing the crown. The scene of his pomp (IV.ii) opens
in this manner:

K. RICH. Stand all apart. Cousin of Buckingham!
BUCK. My gracious sovereign?
K. RICH. Give me thy hand. (*Here he ascendeth the throne. Sound.*)
                Thus high, by thy advice
                And thy assistance, is King Richard seated;
                But shall we wear these glories for a day;
                Or shall they last, and we rejoice in them?   (1–6)

The movement in the next forty lines is from long range hope that
"these glories" may last forever to recognition that the future may be
secured only by immediate, drastic action. The contrast between
Richard's "Or shall they last, and we rejoice in them?" (6) and his
brutal "Speak suddenly; be brief" (19) could not be more telling.

The fundamental irony of Richard's position is that, having reached
the crown by a succession of "untimely" acts, he wishes to hold his
crown forever, and does not know that time is already preparing for
him to be quickly dispatched from the world he had thought himself
free "to bustle in" (I.i.152).

With Margaret's speech at the beginning of Act IV, scene iv, the
tide clearly turns. Her first two lines are calculated to put one in mind
of the first two lines of the play.

            So, now prosperity begins to mellow
            And drop into the rotten mouth of death.[16]

The temporal quality of the play's construction could hardly be made
clearer than by the presence, at the opening and at the pivotal point in
the play, of these two speeches and their emphatic "now." The first
speech was cast in the imagery of warmth, sun, and ripening. This one
twists that imagery into a picture of decay, a growth past its time and
therefore certain of destruction. The meaning of this present time is
that Richard's time is over. The "now" of providence replaces the
momentary "now" of the "usurping boar."

We shall have to return to Act IV, scene iv later. It is constructed
almost entirely upon a notion of specific, contrasting "times." At the
moment we are seeing how the rhythm of the play creates a pause in

---

[16] Cf. also *As You Like It* (II.vii.26–27), with its wordplay on time, whoring, ripening,
reaping, and rotting. Also *Richard II* (II.i.153–54), and *Macbeth* (IV.iii.237–39). For a
discussion of these passages in connection with Edgar's "ripeness" and Hamlet's "readiness,"
see J. V. Cunningham, *Woe or Wonder*, pp. 9–15. See also Chap. VI, pp. 119–21 in this book.

this scene and then rushes on to the climax on the battlefield. At line 136, Richard enters with his train, meets his mother, and demands, "Who intercepts me in my expedition?" When she would speak with him, he replies he has a "touch of [her] condition" of impatience (156–57) and declares he is "in haste" (161). She manages to reprove him, however, and a long exchange follows (see p. 92 in this book), on the aberrant periods of his growth. Next comes the scene between Richard and Queen Elizabeth; as soon as she has made her exit, Ratcliff and Catesby enter to Richard's question, "How now, what news?" (432). The news stirs Richard into a frenzy of activity. He hurls orders left and right, and repeatedly changes his mind. Every entrant to the stage brings news—first Stanley, followed by four messengers and the re-entrance of Catesby. These rapid developments are followed by a scene of twenty lines in which Derby, dispatching Sir Christopher Urswick to Richmond, bids him "hie thee to thy lord" (19.)

The next scene (V.i, only twenty-nine lines) is remarkable. Its sole purpose is to establish the fact that the crucial time of judgment is at hand. With artful restraint, Shakespeare articulates this theme most explicitly in the mouth of Buckingham, leaving the application to Richard to be inferred by the audience. "Holy King Henry," Edward, Vaughan, "and all that have miscarried" are thought to "behold this present hour" (4–8). The day is none other than All-Soul's day, which Buckingham perceives to be his "body's doomsday" (10–12). The following lines play repeatedly upon the theme of "this day":

> This is the day which, in King Edward's time,
> I wish'd might fall on me. . . .   (13–14)

> This is the day wherein I wished to fall . . .   (16)

> This, this All-Soul's day to my fearful soul
> Is the determin'd respite of my wrongs.   (18–19)

> Now Margaret's curse falls heavy on my neck:
> "When he," quoth she, "shall split thy heart with sorrow,
> Remember Margaret was a prophetess."   (25–27)

When time is as laden with fulfillment as this, we are in the same kind of temporal understanding as the Fourth Gospel's "The hour cometh and now is . . ." (John 4 : 23).

The ensuing scene (V.ii) brings Henry, Earl of Richmond, to the stage, arriving in England at the height of the power of the homicidal king, when "this foul swine/Is now even in the centre of this isle" (10–11). The episodic Act V, scene iii, alternating between the camps, is full of references to time, especially to the morrow. On Richard's side, these references sound heavy, for he has "no alacrity of spirit" (73); but on Richmond's side they are light and beneficent, since "True hope is swift and flies with swallow's wings" (V.ii.22–23). The action draws itself to a climactic close according to a time schedule with which Richmond is in essential harmony and Richard at cross-purposes. Shakespeare has expressed this time schedule by accelerating the events which lead to Bosworth Field and by dwelling repeatedly upon the readiness and rightness of "the day."

The Shakespearean characters are never allowed to forget that they stand between a remembered past and an anticipated future.

We have noted already the manifestations of this theme in Richard's opening soliloquy—his description of the present "now" which stands between a past made up of "bruised arms," "stern alarums," "dreadful marches," (6–8), and a future in which he is "determined to prove a villain" (30) and so to reach his "deep intent" (149).

Richard's "deep intent" constantly throws attention toward the future; but in addition, an intent other than his is revealed to be at work. Queen Margaret is the principal oracle, especially in Act I, scene iii. 196 ff., where her curses project the sorrowful end of all those present, culminating in Gloucester himself. This scene, in its turn, later becomes a "past" which another "present" must remember. Margaret's words to Buckingham,

> O but remember this another day. . . .
> And say poor Margaret was a prophetess! (299, 301)

are recalled by him, long afterward, in the words, "Now Margaret's curse falls heavy," of which I have already spoken.[17] In Act III, scene ii, lines 57–61, Hastings expresses the vain expectation of laughing at Richard's pretenses in a twelve-month's time (cf. 121–23). But a wiser Hastings, at scene iv, lines 105–9, prophesies for Richard and England "the fearfull'st time . . ./That ever wretched age hath looked upon." Shakespeare also includes the oracular prophecies of Richmond's ascent to the throne (IV.ii.98–101), which Richard thinks to

---

[17] See also her prophetic words in Act IV, scene iv, lines 181–95.

circumvent (103–4), and of Richard's death at the Earl of Richmonds' hand (106–10).[18]

The future is frequently brought into consciousness by means of expressions of hope. Richard's "But shall I live in hope?" and Lady Anne's reply, "All men, I hope, live so," (I.ii.200–1) is but an early use of the theme. It recurs in I.i.145; II.iii (entire); IV.ii.60; and V.ii.23. Against these are played off continual forebodings of the future: I.iii.41, 76; II.i.1–6, 32 ff.; II.iv.49–54; V.iii.7–8, 213–22.

Likewise, the past is brought in deliberately and explicitly in terms of memory. Recollection of the past is, of course, necessary in dramatic exposition. But in this play the purpose is not so much to inform the reader of past events necessary to his understanding as it is to create a present situation which by its very nature involves the memory of a former history. The appearance of the corpse of Henry VI on its way to reinterment in Act I, scene ii is quite unnecessary as exposition, but is effective in showing Richard's present diabolism against the background of his ancient treachery.

If the past is forgotten, the present is meaningless to these characters. "Let me put in your minds, if you forget," says Richard,

> What you have been ere this and what you are;
> Withal what I have been and what I am.[19]   (I.iii.131–33)

Margaret—old, and widow of a former king—is a queen from out of the past. It is her entrance in Act I, scene iii which sets off discussion of past history and occasions foreshadowings of the future. She is a kind of chorus to the play, and it is not a little significant that she represents not the collective anxieties and forebodings of the populace, as do most Greek choruses, but the principle of historical continuity within which the play achieves its meaning. She is the only character who appears in all three Henry VI plays as well as in *Richard III*.

The matter of past, present, and future reaches its clearest expression in two key passages: Act IV, scene iv and Act V, scenes iii–v.

Act IV, scene iv, begins with Margaret's speech (see p. 95 of this book) signaling the approach of the fulfillment of justice. There follows the scene of lamentation among Margaret, Queen Elizabeth, and the Duchess of York. The recitation of past evils, going back as far as "When holy Harry died," (25) and up to the deaths of Hastings, Rivers,

---

[18] Lines 101–20 are not in the Folio, however.
[19] Cf. Act I, scene iii, lines 19, 70–73, 83–84, 121–24.

Vaughan, and Grey (69), creates the impression of vast time, an interminable history of flowing blood. At the line, "Richard yet lives, hell's black intelligencer" (71), we pass into time present, together with Margaret's assurance, "at hand, at hand,/Ensues his piteous and unpitied end" (73–74). There follow lamentations for the present (80–115) in which Elizabeth is said to have "no more but thought of what thou wast/To torture thee the more, being what thou art" (107–8).

Richard enters and speaks with his mother on the times of his life. She exits praying for his defeat, and Richard begins to sue to Queen Elizabeth for her daughter's hand. At line 291, their colloquy turns to the subject of time. Richard speaks of the irrevocability of the past and the repentance which follows evil deeds in "after hours" (291–93). He promises that the children of his marriage to Elizabeth shall comfort the queen's age, her youth having been full of vexation (305–6), and so forth in a succession of promises regarding a future which shall make amends for the past. When she doubts the validity of his word, he begins to swear, first by St. George and then a succession of other sanctities (366 ff.), each of which Elizabeth scorns as having already been profaned by him. The list exhausted, she asks, "What canst thou swear by now?" and receives the answer, "The time to come" (386). To this she replies:

> That thou hast wronged in the time o'erpast;
> For I myself have many tears to wash
> Hereafter time, for time past wrong'd by thee.
> The children live whose fathers thou hast slaughter'd,
> Ungovern'd youth, to wail it with their age;
> The parents live whose children thou hast butcher'd,
> Old barren plants to wail it with their age.
> Swear not by time to come; for that thou hast
> Misus'd ere us'd by times ill-us'd o'erpast. (387–96)

In this speech Richard's condition is described, as later Macbeth's will be, in terms of a history in which past has sinned against future and thereby created a hopeless present. Simultaneously, this history of Richard is interwoven with the history of the land, generation laced to generation in historical interdependency.

While Richard's condition is hopeless, England's in fact is not. That is because England is to receive one who will redeem the time. The news of his approach arrives immediately after the queen withdraws. By the eve of the battle, which follows after only 182 lines, time has

begun to be viewed as promising a redeeming hour to separate a glorious future from a darkened past. Richmond has urged his soldiers "to
reap the harvest of perpetual peace/By this one bloody trial of sharp
war" (V.ii.15–16).

The past enters the night preceding the battle in the person of the
ghosts of the murdered, who "sit heavy" on Richard's soul, but who
bring Richmond encouragements and prophecies of victory. Much
has been made of these visions as characterization of Richard in his
troubled conscience. One should, however, beware of pressing the internalization too far. The scene puts Richard and Richmond side by
side on the stage and shows that the same past which destroys Richard
is the basis of his conqueror's victory, through the help of "God and
good angels" (175).

The battle is the shortest in Shakespeare. The overarching pattern
is now so clear that there is no point in delaying the outcome. Richard's
choices were made earlier. Here he has none.

The short scene which follows the battle (V.v.) is, however, extremely important, for it summarizes the temporal pattern upon which
the play has been based. The day has been won by God and the soldiers' arms—a providential act in which the exertion of men is necessary.
The "bloody dog is dead." [20] The past is remembered in its infamy.
The "royalties" have been "long-usurped" but now are restored to
proper brows (4–6). Heaven has "long-frown'd" upon the country's
factional strife. "England hath long been mad and scarr'd herself"
(23), brother against brother, father against son, house against house
(21–28).

---

[20] Line 2. In the last scenes, Richard becomes increasingly a symbol of unmitigated,
rapacious evil. Throughout, however, he had been associated with the villainies of Herod,
a biblical allusion later to be exchanged for that of the anti-Christ. The Herod associations
have been pointed out to me by Professor S. F. Johnson. They center upon the slaughter of
the innocents:

> I do not know that Englishman alive
> With whom my soul is any jot at odds
> More than the infant that is born tonight. (II.i.69–71)

> Are you drawn forth among a world of men
> To slay the innocent ? (I.iv.186–87)

> Incapable and shallow innocents. . . . (II.ii.18)

> "Thus, thus," quoth Forrest, "girdling one another
> Within their alabaster innocent arms." (IV.iii. 10–11)

> . . . England's lawful earth,
> Unlawfully made drunk with innocent blood! (IV.iv.29–30)

See also Palmer, *Political Characters of Shakespeare*, p. 101.

All that is past. For the present, Richmond looks after the immediate needs: whether George Stanley lives, proper burial for those slain in battle, pardon for the soldiers "That in submission will return to us" (17), and, most important, taking the sacrament.

The word sacrament has deep poetic meaning here because it is symbolic of all which Richmond accomplishes, raised to a divine plane. By partaking of the sacrament, he becomes the priestly representative of England atoning for the past sins of the realm. The sacramental act recalls the shedding of blood. Thus it stands in sharp relief against the crimes of

> The wretched, bloody, and usurping boar,
> That spoil'd your summer fields and fruitful vines,
> Swills your warm blood like wash. . . . (V.ii.7–9)

The sacrament also recalls deliverance—from bondage in Egypt, and from the power of sin and death at Calvary.

Most important, however, is the fact that the sacrament means union and peace, and this theme Richmond proceeds to elaborate. He will "unite the white rose and the red," asking heaven to smile "upon this fair conjunction" (19–20). Past strife has torn the land asunder, but now the marriage of Richmond and Elizabeth, conjoined together "by God's fair ordinance" (31), will

> Enrich the time to come with smooth-fac'd Peace,
> With smiling Plenty and fair prosperous days!
> Abate the edge of traitors, gracious Lord,
> That would reduce these bloody days again
> And make poor England weep in streams of blood!
> Let them not live to taste this land's increase
> That would with treason wound this fair land's peace!
> Now civil wounds are stopp'd, Peace lives again;
> That she may long live here, God say amen! (33–41)

The entire speech, which ends the play, falls thus into a schematic design of past woe, present amnesty, royal marriage, and future peace stretching to the end of time. This pattern is apocalyptic.[21] To find its

---

[21] In his discussion of *King Lear*, John F. Danby, *Shakespeare's Doctrine of Nature*, refers to that play's "apocalyptical judgment" (p. 50). Professor Danby refers to the "biblical-political theme" in *Richard III*, and points out that "Richard is the last, the most formidable, the wickedest, and the greatest of the unsatisfactory kings" (p. 59). Cf. G. W. Knight's use of the word "apocalyptic" in his analysis of *The Winter's Tale* (*The Crown of Life*, pp. 117–18).

roots one must go to the Book of Revelation, which in turn finds its antecedents in the ritual patterns of ancient Judaism.[22]

Whether Shakespeare had the Book of Revelation consciously in mind, I do not know. It is more likely that he merely echoes the most basic assumption of his culture regarding the nature of evil and the historical framework in which its eventual overthrow is seen.[23] At any rate, the parallel is clear. Richard is a beast, entrenched in power at the center of the realm (V.ii.7–11), who must be overthrown in decisive battle (14–16). Bosworth is Armageddon. From its "one bloody trial of sharp war" will be reaped "the harvest of perpetual peace" (15–16), reminiscent of the angel's command in Revelation 14:15: "Put in your sickle, and reap, for the hour to reap has come, for the harvest of the earth is fully ripe."

The battle won, the reign of peace and justice is established by a royal marriage—a theme as old as the ritual marriages of the ancient Near Eastern gods but transformed into apocalyptic vision by the early church:

> Hallelujah! For the Lord our God reigns.
> Let us rejoice and exult and give him the glory,
> for the marriage of the Lamb has come,
> and his Bride has made herself ready.[24]

To the ringing description of the "fair prosperous days" ahead—which reminds us of the apocalyptist's vision of the new Jerusalem where there shall be no more death, nor mourning, nor crying (Rev. 21:4)—are added the resounding tones of the great amen. "What traitor hears me," cries Richmond, "and says not amen?" (V.v.22),

---

[22] See Theodore H. Robinson, "Hebrew Myths," in *Myth and Ritual*, ed. by S. H. Hooke, pp. 172–96.

[23] The religious character of the play's theme has been well stated by Professor Tillyard, *Shakespeare's History Plays*, pp. 199, 203–9, who holds that "the play's main end is to show the working out of God's will in English history" (p. 208). The reader is referred to Professor Tillyard's sane and lucid discussion of the relation of Shakespeare's own beliefs to those expressed in the play. The kernel of his idea is expressed in these words: "When, therefore, I say that *Richard III* is a very religious play, I want to be understood as speaking of the play and not of Shakespeare. For the purposes of the tetralogy and most obviously for this play Shakespeare accepted the prevalent belief that God had guided England into her haven of Tudor prosperity. And he had accepted it with his whole heart. . . ." (p. 204.) Although Professor Tillyard sees clearly the religious element of the play, he does not seem to have noticed that there is not only a "very subtle transfer of reference from the epoch of Bosworth" to the contemporary Elizabethan situation (p. 202), but also to the climactic battles of history in Christian apocalypse.

[24] Rev. 19:6b–7. Cf. 21:2, 9.

ending his speech with the triumphant, "God say amen!" It is in the same spirit as Revelation 19:1–4:

> . . . I heard what seemed to be the mighty voice of a great multitude in heaven, crying,
> "Hallelujah . . .
> he has judged the great harlot who corrupted the earth with her fornication,
> and he has avenged on her the blood of his servants. . . ."
> And the twenty-four elders and the four living creatures fell down and worshipped God, who is seated on the throne, saying, "Amen. Hallelujah!"

It becomes clear that *Richard III* is cast according to the pattern of the traditional Christian conception of history in which, at the proper time, decisive and redemptive action is taken. This conception of the world is radically time-centered, and that is why the play, which is not unique in this respect among Elizabethan dramas, is so full of references to time, rhythm, and the idea of preparation.

The structure and the language of the play (elements which in Chapter IV were said to belong to the manner of imitation of the action) are in harmony with and calculated to express the redemptive-historical nature of the action.

In the main, the order in which scene follows scene is chronological. That is, the incidents of one scene are presumed to follow in time those of the preceding scene; there is no "doubling back" in time, no long description of an important event which took place before,[25] and only one scene (V.iii) in which occurrences in two separate places are shown to take place simultaneously. Shakespeare begins at the beginning, as everyone knows, and tells his tale straightforwardly to the end. The reason he does so has nothing to do with any lack of subtlety; he does so because he understands human action in terms of historical development.

Within this general frame of straightforward advance, Shakespeare has not hesitated to point and interpret the action by compressing or delaying time where necessary. He has also, as was noted, utilized a short and a long time-scheme. Likewise, not every scene follows its predecessor by the law of natural progression: irony and contrast

---

[25] Two narrative sections do occur: Clarence' description of his dream (I.iv.8–63) and Tyrrel's of the murder of the two princes (IV.iii.1–22). Both refer to events immediately past; neither presents any action upon which later events pivot, and the dream, as dreams did before Freud, looks forward more than backward.

sometimes determine the succession. The entrance of Richmond (V.ii) ringing with a vigorous, clear poetry unlike any heard in the play before, is carefully inserted to follow Buckingham's repentance as he goes to "the block of shame" (V.i.28). Beginning in Act IV, scene iv and continuing to the end of the play, the scenes, mostly short,[26] alternate between Richard's and Richmond's side, accentuating the contrast in morality, courage, and hope. Compression, delay, irony, contrast, and one scene of simultaneous events are all mere techniques, however, with which Shakespeare achieves variety and emphasis within the dominant framework of advance from incipient beginnings to what is essentially an eschatological fulfillment.

The language of *Richard III* is that of a youthful genius. There is much patterned speech, impressing one with its contrivance and formality.[27] There are many sentences built upon the device of balancing words and ideas one against another. "Thou bloodless remnant of that royal blood!" says Lady Anne, addressing the corpse of Henry VI:

> O cursed be the hand that made these holes!
> Cursed the heart that had the heart to do it!
> Cursed the blood that let this blood from hence!   (I.ii.7, 14–16)

Such sentences lead naturally into a second type of speech patterning, namely, passages of repetition and refrain. These occur particularly in the scenes of lamentation:

> Q. ELIZA.   Was never widow had so dear a loss!
> CHIL.   Were never orphans had so dear a loss!
> DUCH.   Was never mother had so dear a loss![28]

They also are found, for instance, in Richmond's oration to his soldiers (V.iii.255–62). In addition, there is at least one passage of stychomythia (IV.iv.343–66).

Although this type of speech is evidently the product of Shakespeare's youth and may owe something to the influence of Seneca,[29] it also serves a function in the task of imitating the action of the play. Its echoes of ritual augment the sense of cosmic significance for the

---

[26] Act V, scene iii is long, but it is actually a series of short passages moving from one camp to the other.

[27] Bradbrook, *Poetry*, p. 129, calls this "Shakespeare's most patterned play."

[28] Act II, scene ii, lines 77–79. Cf. ll. 71–88; also Act IV, scene ii, lines 88–104 and Act IV, scene iv, lines 9–125.

[29] See T. S. Eliot, "Seneca in Elizabethan Translation," *Selected Essays*, pp. 69, 73–75.

action and prepare us for the final scene in which time is "rounded off" in a great recapitulation of the order which guarantees the meaning of the historic process.

Miss Caroline Spurgeon [30] says that the imagery of the play is dominated by the idea of trees, flowers, and gardens. The examples she quotes, however, and the summary she offers show that what is important about these images is the sense of continuity and development in the face of threatened destruction. The royal house is a tree, she says, "and the idea of this tree being planted, shaken by storms, grafted, rooted up and withered is constantly present."[31] W. H. Clemen points out that all the images in this play are short, well assimilated (usually as metaphors) into their context, so that the rapidity of the play's movement is in no way impeded.[32]

Here, as elsewhere, Shakespeare shows no fear of a mixture of styles. The language ranges from the lofty and rhetorical, in Richmond's addresses, to the mundane and comic in the quaverings of the Second Murderer. The language reflects the social as well as the cosmic breadth of the action. Between these extremes lies the whimsical, artificial, self-directed speech of Richard.

In *Richard III*, language and structure unite to create a form which expresses an action essentially temporal and historical in conception. Shakespeare looks for the larger, universal-historical action within which the smaller, transient one may be understood.

The Persians

To turn from *Richard III* to *The Persians* is to turn to so different a dramatic form that one may well ask whether, in truth, the latter ought to be called a history play. Indeed, if we call the action of *Richard III* historical, we cannot give that name also to *The Persians*, for *The Persians* is a history play which is not concerned with the continuity of history. History is its point of departure, but not, as in Shakespeare, its focus.

If in *Richard III* the underlying formative principle is time in its cosmic and universal-historical setting, in *The Persians* the formative principle is a notion of quantity. In *Richard III* one moves in an atmosphere of memory, decision, and expectation. In *The Persians* one moves in an environment created by expressions of weight, measure,

---

[30] *Shakespeare's Imagery*, pp. 219–20.   [31] *Ibid.*, p. 219.
[32] *The Development of Shakespeare's Imagery*, pp. 47–52.

space, and force. To these spatial references is added the recurrent motif of the contrast between light and dark.[33]

The result is that time in *The Persians* appears to be frozen. It is as if time had leaped up in one ecstatic moment—a moment essentially unrelated to any past or future—and there it is held as in a snapshot for the duration of the play, or heard in isolation like a scream through silence.

Lest the reader feel that this interpretation is due to our twentieth-century remoteness from the complexities of Greek history, rather than to the inherent form of the play, we must examine the language in some detail.

The foremost element in the poetry which tends to arrest the movement of time is the way in which time itself is described. The experience of living through time is not communicated. Time is understood quantitatively, as mere duration—not the stuff of existence.

In the opening choric ode, for instance, there are frequent references to age. We hear of "the ancient Cissian fortress" (τὸ παλαιὸν κίσσιον ἕρκοσ—17), of the Persians having been destined "of old" (τὸ παλαιόν) to risk all in war, of the elders who hold their council seats in this "ancient house" (στέγοσ ἀρχαῖον). Atossa, at her entrance, is greeted as "aged mother" (μῆτερ . . . γεραιά), and so forth. These passages give a picture of strength, stability, and permanence. Time has not been able to change Persia.

Other references to time in the opening song do add a note of unrest, but it is significant that they do it by dwelling on how long things have been quiet, how long since the arrival of news. Wives and parents of the soldiers lament the men's absence, and, "counting the days, they tremble in the long-protracted time" (ἡμερολεγδὸν/τείνοντα χρόνον τρομέονται—63–64).

This sense of immobility, of anxious calm, is of course deliberately induced in order that the news, when it arrives, may appear the more shattering. But that very contrast is part of the general sense of contrast in the whole play—force against force, light against dark, high against low—serving to militate against any feeling of development through time, while it reinforces the sense of space and order. We are being prepared for a sudden reversal (Aristotle would call it a περι-

---

[33] On the importance of light contrasted with dark, see especially ll. 225, 228, 299–301, 363–64, 376, 384, 429–30, 516–18, 536, 624, 632, 643 ff., 710.

πέτεια) of Persia's ancient condition. Time, which so far has seen nothing, will soon, and in one instant, see everything.[34]

References to the past and future are few, and refer to a very short period. Aside from the vague, generalized references to Persia's glory of old, the only specific incidents recalled from the past are Atossa's mention of Marathon (472 ff.) and the Ghost's speech on the leaders who built Persia's greatness (759–86). References to the future are to what is immediately at hand. They are full of foreboding and almost entirely hopeless. Wives and families fear for the return of the warriors (59–64); Atossa dreams an ill omen (176–214): Darius predicts destruction in the battle of Plataea (800–20). The main thought about the future is that it brings things to an end. Hope is gone and cannot return (261). Xerxes' hope was groundless (804). The temporal horizon is limited.

The most characteristic temporal expressions in *The Persians* are generalizing terms—"never," "whenever," and the generalized present. Thus the Chorus (in lines 86–99) describes the perpetual dominance of Persia's forces. Atossa speaks of the sufferings which "it is necessary for mortals to bear" (ἀνάγκη . . . βροτοῖσ φέρειν—293–94); she describes the fear which always arises "whenever a flood of evils comes up" (ὅταν κλύδων κακῶν ἐπέλθῃ) and the unwarranted confidence "whenever Fortune flows well" (ὅταν δ' ὁ δαίμων εὐροῇ). The Ghost of Darius declares: "It is the lot of man to bear whatever sufferings occur to mortals" (ἀνθρώπεια δ' ἄν τοι πήματ' ἄν τόχοι βροτοῖσ), because of the afflictions which constantly arise from land and sea (706–8). He describes how the Divine joins in the action "whenever anyone moves speedily" (ὅταν σπεύδῃ τισ αὐτόσ—742; see also 821–31, 840–42). These "whenever" generalizations are the more remarkable in contrast to *Richard III*, where the same sins (pride, impetuosity) are present, together with many chorus-like passages which comment on them. But in *Richard III* the focus is always on Richard's particular sins and his particular fate. I have been able to discover only two sentences which generalize time in the entire play of *Richard III*.[35]

---

[34] For the suddenness of the event, see especially the Messenger's announcement that Persia has lost everything "in one stroke" (ἐν μιᾷ πληγῇ—251) and his narrative which repeatedly emphasizes action taking place instantly, or εὐθύς (396).

[35] "Thus doth He force the swords of wicked men
To turn their own points in their masters' bosoms."
BUCKINGHAM, V.i.23–24.

"True hope is swift and flies with swallow's wings,
Kings it makes gods and meaner creatures kings."
RICHMOND, V.ii.23–24.

The descriptions and figures of speech which dominate *The Persians* belong, as I said, to another order, to quantity, weight, and space, rather than time. We are made to see force pitted against force as the might of the Persians meets the resistance of the Greeks. Into that balance is thrown the power of the gods, weighing down on the side of Hellas. The wealth and power of man is contrasted with the impotence to which Fortune can reduce him—the height he attains with the depth to which he may fall. The resultant drama of weight and force is played in a very clear-cut world of space, where geography counts for much.

The Messenger (340 ff.) knows the exact number of troops and ships on each side of the battle. Fortune, however, shifted the balance "weighing down the scales with unequal chance" (τάλαντα βρίσας οὖκ ἰσορρόπῳ τύχῃ—345–46). The size of the Persian military forces is frequently mentioned (12, 25, 532–33, 717, 789–800), and the idea of a great mass of strength is carefully built up. At Salamis it meets the power of the Greeks.

The picture of military power pushing against military power is, however, soon transcended with another idea—namely, that the weight of ills which falls upon the proud man is greater than the mass of his glories. Fortune's foot crushes the Persian race with "heavy stroke" (ἄγαν βαρὺς—515). The evils that befell the Persians at Salamis are measured quantitatively. Ten days would be required to tell the "great number of evils" (κακῶν δὲ πλῆθος—429) which came upon them there. When the Messenger has finished telling of the rout, he assures his listeners these are "not yet half the ills" (μηδέπω μεσοῦν κακόν—435). Others came which "weighed twice as heavy" (δὶς ἀντισηκῶσαι ῥοπῇ—437). The Chorus inquires of Darius what is the reason for this "doubly great measure of twice-lamentable wrongs" (περισσὰ δίδυμα δὶς γοέδν' ἁμάρτία—676). Darius replies: "In truth, sufferings occur for mortal man. For many evils come from sea, and many from land, if life is stretched out unto a greater length." [36]

Darius is harsh in condemnation of Xerxes because "being a mortal, he imagined he could over-power the gods and Poseidon" (θνητὸς ὢν θεῶν τε πάντων ῷετ' . . . καὶ Ποσειδῶνος κρατήσειν—749–50); and Darius fears that his great mass of wealth will be lost (751–52).

[36] The Greek is:

ἀνθρώπεια δ' ἄν τοι πήματ' ἂν τύχοι βροτοῖς· πολλὰ μὲν γὰρ ἐκ θαλάσσης, πολλὰ δ' ἐκ χέρσου κακὰ γίγνεται θνητοῖς, ὁ μάσσων βίοτος ἢν ταθῇ πρόσω.—ll. 706–9.

Mortal power is weighed in the balance against Fortune's woes, the height of man's attainment measured against the depth of degradation to which he is reduced. Xerxes, once great in honor and power, has been "cut down" by Fortune (οὖσ νῦν δαίμων ἐπέκειρεν—921). He has been "thrown down upon his knees" (ἐπὶ γόνυ κέκλιται—930).

The quantitative imagery demands a setting of limited space and definite geography. The description of the battle—usually regarded as an eye-witness account—delights in the details of the location of the ships, the plan according to which each was assigned its place (ἕκαστος ἦν τεταγμένος—381). The Persians, indeed, are defeated by allowing themselves to be lured into too small a space where they have no room to maneuver (413 ff.) and where the Greeks can surround them.

The attention to geography is specific throughout. When Atossa would inquire what sort of people the Greeks are, she opens by asking where, in what part of the earth, Athens is located (230–31). She also wants to know later, for no apparent reason other than curiosity about specifics, where the ships have been left (478–79). The locations of every battle (Salamis, the incident on the isle of Psyttalea, the later battle of Plataea), and the disaster on the waters of "sacred Strymon" are all sharply pin-pointed. In addition to frequent references to the land of Persia, mention is made of Boeotia, Phocis, Magnesia, Macedonia, Thrace, and many other regions.

The passages cited are only a few of the many which occur throughout the play. In their totality, the images and descriptive passages in the work combine to purvey with extraordinary consistency an idea of weights and forces, measured out in deliberate quantity.

It is interesting to compare the use of the idea of heaviness in *The Persians* with its use in *Richard III*. In the latter, the word occurs pointedly in only one passage. On the eve of battle, the ghosts of Prince Edward, Clarence, and Rivers tell Richard they will "sit heavy" on his soul on the morrow (V.iii.118, 131, 139). The ghosts of the two young princes will be "lead within thy bosom . . ./And weigh thee down to ruin, shame, and death" (152–53). Here the conception is that of a burden which must be carried, something which inhibits movement.[37] In *The Persians*, on the other hand, the burden of ills and

[37] In Act V, scene i, line 25 Buckingham asserts that "Margaret's curse falls heavy" on his neck. Here the image is not that of inhibited movement. On the other hand, the passage is dominated by the temporal idea of fulfillment, and the image of falling is not so much a picture of height and depth as of a particular event falling due. Cf. line 14.

sorrows, dwelt upon over and over again, is like a dead weight pressing straight down, as if the mass of ills and the earth formed a giant vise, between the arms of which man is crushed. The picture is static, an image not of movement but of a condition.

If the structure of the Shakespearean play is such that one sees the development from start to finish, the Greek structure is usually such that one sees the result of action taken earlier and now reported. The order of events in *The Persians* is given so as to produce maximum concentration upon *one* moment in time. That moment is one through which other moments may be seen, as if they stood inside each other. That is to say, *The Persians* is concentrated upon the moment of revelation.

The sequence of scenes shows the intention clearly. An opening lyric describes with foreboding the general situation in Persia. The Queen appears and relates an ill-omened dream, then asks for and receives a description of the Greeks whom her countrymen fight. The Messenger arrives, and in a *commos* announces he has bad news. In the following *episode*, he delivers at length a description of the Persian defeat. A choral lament follows, then a short *episode* in which Atossa decides to invoke the all-knowing ghost of the former king; then comes the choric invocation to Darius' shade, and after that the ghost appears. In his *episode* he reveals the moral meaning of Xerxes' defeat, how it was foreordained by the gods, and what ills it means for a Persia which once was ruled more moderately and wisely; he foretells further defeat. Upon his disappearance, a *stasimon* of lament follows, and then occurs the final *commos* in which Xerxes himself appears. The picture of defeat and abasement which Xerxes manifests in his person and about which he sings with the Chorus closes the play. The movement of the scenes is in a straight line from vague foreboding, to an ominous dream, to terrible news, to omniscient interpretation of the meaning, and finally to direct vision of the results of the catastrophe.

The time of the play is therefore a moment of revelation moving toward increasing clarity. Aeschylus is not interested in time as it passes during the play. *We* may ponder how long it might be between the Messenger's arrival and that of Xerxes, or how long it would take to move from the Council Hall to Darius' tomb, but such matters are of no concern to Aeschylus. If the play gives evidence of the so-called Unity of Time, that is because time is actually of little concern. What matters is the picture of a conflict of power in an enclosed world of space. The play's time is only the time in which that moral geometry is revealed.[38]

The outstanding presentational elements in Greek drama were the Chorus, the limited number of actors, the theater, and masks. All of these contributed to the externalization of the action. They went hand in hand with the tendency of Greek drama to depict an eternal or generalized present rather than a historical present.

The presence of the chorus, for instance, tended to "spread" the impact of the tragic events from the particular to the general. The chorus is auditory, passive, and descriptive, rather than hortatory, active, or decisive. Occasionally, it is true, the chorus offers advice or admonition. The Chorus in *The Eumenides* is exceptional in the active role it plays. In *The Persians* (623–80) the Chorus invokes the Ghost of Darius, at the queen's behest. Usually, however, the Chorus is moved to rhapsodic description of a situation which other agents have brought into being. This fact accounts, more than any other single element, for the impression of poise and stability which the classical Greek play conveys.

Because it is essentially descriptive, because it absorbs the shock of violence and transmutes it into the generalized emotion of lyric, the Greek chorus is priestly in character. It is never prophetic. The contrast with *Richard III* is startling. There Shakespeare has introduced passages which mark his closest approximation of the Greek chorus: the lamentations of the women in Act II, scene ii, Act IV, scene ii, and Act IV, scene iv. However, Shakespeare never separates the active from the passive in the choric personages. From recitation of woe, they turn immediately to admonition and imprecation, and since there is no permanent chorus as such, they return to their individual roles in the developing action. The principal "choric" figure is Queen Margaret. Her function is not only to lead the lamentation, as she does in Act IV, scene iv, but, even more importantly, to be the principal voice in the play for the prophetic denunciation of Richard. This prophetic role is not primarily that of forecasting events, although anticipation is heightened through what she says. Rather, it is to confront Richard with a moral alternative. The Ghost of Darius also foretells events and speaks of the king's transgression; but his tone and function are

---

[38] "The Greek mind . . . thought of the world as resembling a geometrical figure, which contains already within itself all those properties which can be deduced from it. . . . The work of time is to bring them from the potential to the actual. . . ." F. H. C. Brock, "Oedipus, Macbeth, and the Christian Tradition," in *Contemporary Review*, p. 177.

descriptive, oracular; whereas Margaret faces Richard as the denunci-
atory prophet.

What is said here about the generalizing tendency of the chorus
may seem to contradict what was said above regarding the concentration of the play upon one moment. The contradiction is only apparent.
We see here the characteristic complexity in Greek drama, namely,
the *universal meaning* perceived in the particular situation. The Greek
actor embodies the same complexity. Only two actors are needed for
The Persians. Four characters plus the Chorus complete the *dramatis
personae*. Such economy pin points the action, reduces it to its simplest
dimensions. Yet this practice, far from focusing our attention solely on
the leading character and presenting him fully realized in the many facets
of his personality, actually results in his being seen from one angle only,
that is, the angle defined by the nature of the moral law which he
illustrates, and which destroys him. This sacrifice of the uniquely individual to the universal was manifest visually in the use of the mask.
I do not think the mask was purely a necessity resulting from the vast-
ness of the theater nor the need for one actor to play several parts.
Masks are older than doubling and older than auditoria. Theater,
chorus, mask, and the small cast were all part of one dramatic complex
which on the one hand used extreme economy of narrative and situation, while on the other hand it reached for the most exalted and universal statements of truth.[39]

How then shall the essential action of *The Persians* be characterized? It is, to begin with, a simple action, involving one event: the defeat of the Persian force in its assault upon Greece. The ramifications
of this event, its possible manifold effects upon various persons and in
various places, are not involved. Some mention is made of wives and
parents, much is said of the land of Persia, but these are for emotional
color. They are not part of the action. Even Atossa, the wife of Xerxes,
who throughout has eagerly awaited her husband, is not present in the
scene of his return. The play is not concerned with her reaction to the
defeat, except insofar as through her anxiety the emotion of defeat may
be communicated.

The simple action of *The Persians* is not basically an historical
action. The focus of Aeschylus' concern is not the historical as we

---

[39] This is most emphatically the case in Aeschylus. Sophocles and Euripides do not destroy
the case, but they show the tendency of drama to move toward the historically unique, making
character more complex, the social situation more concrete.

understand it. That is, he is in no sense concerned with the continuity of history. Upon reflection, this fact becomes little short of astonishing. The battle of Salamis was but eight years past when the play was first performed. It was one of those battles which are decisive turning points in history, to be described in words like these:

> But had Persia triumphed on sea and land, and held its conquest in the fifth century, Greece had been orientalized. Then Aeschylus' voice had been quelled. There had been no age of Pericles, no Euripides. The Parthenon had never been restored. Thucydides had written no possession to instruct all time. Plato had seen no vision of the Good that is one with God. . . . And the language of Greece had not been the language of the Evangel.[40]

This historical view, however, is ours, not Aeschylus'. Although he had no way of knowing how far-reaching the effects of the victory were to be, he could not but have been aware of the political issues involved. How remarkable, therefore, is it that he should not once mention any of them. He describes nothing which was at stake in the battle, nothing which the Greeks stood to lose or the Persians to gain— neither freedom, nor justice, nor wives, nor land, nor wealth. Far from seeing the battle as part of a historical continuity in which Marathon saved the day and Salamis destroyed the Persian ability to invade, he omits virtually all reference to Marathon and makes Darius, who led the Persian forces there, a peace loving, virtuous monarch! If, as some have thought, this play is a celebration of a glorious Greek victory, it is the more astonishing that not a single Greek soldier or captain is mentioned by name. Persian names abound—becoming a rhetorical device as they roll from the tongue—but the Greeks are anonymous. The gods, not the Greeks, defeat Xerxes. And they do it not because any issue of history hangs in the balance (no past to save, no future to guarantee) but only because Xerxes is guilty of transgressing his apportioned limits through *hybris*.[41]

The action of the play is designed to reveal that fact of *hybris* to us. The play does not reveal primarily what happened in the battle. Every child knew about that. Neither was it designed to discover a meaning or significance which was inherent in that battle and inseparable from it. Aeschylus does not ask what it means that Greece should have had

---

[40] Herbert Weir Smyth, *Aeschylean Tragedy*, p. 91.
[41] H. D. F. Kitto has pointed out that the play is not a celebration of Plataea and Salamis, but a drama on the theme of *hybris* and its inevitable punishment. *Greek Tragedy*, pp. 38, 40, 42.

to fight at Salamis. On the contrary, the historical event was but his point of departure, one example among many possible ones which demonstrated the unchangeable laws within which man must confine himself if he is not to face destruction.

The play exists in order to reveal to the audience the law of *nemesis* operative in a particular case. The particular case (aside from the fact that in 472 B.C. it was a recent and vivid occurrence) is not so important as the universal law. That is why the poetry reiterates the expressions of weight, force, balance, space, and abrupt contrast. That is also why expressions denoting time are few and almost all express the idea of contrast, a former condition changed *suddenly* into the present one. Xerxes, whose power and audacity grew too great, falls subject to the retribution of *nemesis*.

Richard III, on the other hand, comes under divine judgment. That is why Shakespeare's play moves from early beginnings through decisive, climactic action to that fullness of time in which evil is put down and righteousness enthroned. The Christian idea of judgment involves the notion of a particular day upon which judgment will be made. That idea Shakespeare has carefully planted in the conversation of Richard's hirelings early in the play (I.iv.106–15).[42] The Christian Day of Judgment comes at the end of history and is, in its symbolic way, inseparable from the course of history which precedes it and prepares for it. "Judgment" is therefore the outgrowth and the culmination of action taken in the historical arena, and it is pictured in itself as another historical event in which decisive action is taken. It is particular, purposeful, redemptive; and it puts the final stamp of meaning onto the preceding ages of historical struggle.

Judgment gives meaning *to* history. *Nemesis* abstracts a meaningful law *from* history.[43] *Richard III* is built upon a temporal scheme and raises the question of what it means that the tyrant Richard became

---

[42] See also Edward's reference to "the general all-ending day" (III.i.78).

[43] For this reason I cannot agree with Bradbrook (*Poetry*, p. 129), that the theme of *Richard III* is nemesis, nor with R. G. Moulton (*Shakespeare as a Dramatic Artist*) who expressed the same opinion. The plot, said Moulton, "presents to us a world of history transformed into an intricate design of which the recurrent pattern is Nemesis" (p. 108). His analysis of the play strains to show a strict pattern of sin and retribution operating in every detail. Had Professor Moulton paid sufficient attention to the relation between justice and time in *Richard III*, and to the imagery, I believe he would have concluded, as I have, that the classical word *nemesis* is less applicable to the play than the Christian word *Judgment*, implying not repetition but fulfillment. Lewis Campbell (*Tragic Drama in Aeschylus, Sophocles, and Shakespeare*, p. 41) called Margaret "a human Nemesis." This makes *nemesis* something it never was in classical Greece.

king and was then defeated at Bosworth Field. Shakespeare concludes that the fight between good and evil imparts unique significance to each of the twists and turns of history because each act moves toward its judgment. *The Persians* is built upon a quantitative, proportional conception, and raises the question of why Xerxes was reduced to ignominy. Aeschylus concludes that an unchanging law insures the destruction of all who go beyond their apportioned limits, which means that everywhere and at all times *hybris* is followed by humiliation, according to a natural and moral equilibrium.

VI

SYNTHESIS AND PROVIDENCE:
THE *ORESTEIA* AND *HAMLET*

Hamlet's problem is the problem of responding to a call. In being summoned to a tragic vocation he is not generically different from most other tragic heroes, whom destiny requires to perform a necessary function of suffering for the well-being (may one say the redemption?) of their world. The difference between Hamlet and Orestes, however, is that Hamlet attends directly to the problem of his response to the tragic demand, whereas Orestes does not.

In this fundamental distinction is reflected the difference between Shakespeare's history-minded culture and the nature-orientation of Aeschylus' society. Upon this difference also rests the divergence of the dramatic forms. In the dramatic form which he inherited and further developed, Aeschylus could not, even had he wished, express Hamlet's vocational dilemma. No more could Shakespeare have utilized Elizabethan forms of drama to express the Aeschylean problem of a resolution of forces. The one form grows out of a concern for time in its social and cosmic setting; the other out of regard for the ultimate equilibrium of nature.

The vocational question begins early in *Hamlet*. In the opening scene we are led to anticipate the meeting of the prince with the ghost, and the anticipation is fulfilled in the fourth scene where the shade of the father calls the son to embark upon a certain course of action.[1] Even before the ghost speaks, Hamlet seems to assume that it has come to require something of him:

> Say, why is this? Wherefore? What should we do?   (I.iv.57)

[1] "The Hamlet formula, so to speak, is not 'a man who has to avenge his father' but 'a man who has been given a task by a ghost.' " C. S. Lewis, "Hamlet, the Prince or the Poem," p. 147.

Horatio, also, when he saw the ghost, had assumed some action was demanded, asking,

> If there be any good thing to be done.   (I.i.130)

The ghost beckons Hamlet to follow it. "Following" now becomes a key theme for some thirty lines. Marcellus and Horatio warn him not to follow; but Hamlet, perceiving that he must, replies,

> It will not speak; then I will follow it.   (63)

Later:

> It waves me forth again. I'll follow it.   (68)
> Go on, I'll follow thee.   (78)
> Go on, I'll follow thee.   (86)
> Where wilt thou lead me?   (v.1)

Echoing Hamlet's lines, Marcellus adds, "Let's follow" (iv.87) and "Nay, let's follow him" (91). Hamlet feels that the ghost is already laying a claim upon him which he may not resist:

> My fate cries out,
> And makes each petty artery in this body
> As hardy as the Nemean lion's nerve.
> Still am I call'd.   (iv.81–84)

The ghost speaks in the imperative mood. Hamlet is bidden to mark, to pity not, to hear, to revenge, and to remember (v.2, 5, 8, 24, 91). To each of these imperatives he responds with immediate assent. He is "bound to hear" (6); he will sweep to his revenge with "wings as swift as . . . thoughts of love" (29–31); he will remember "while memory holds a seat/In this distracted globe" (96–97).[2]

The imperative thus laid upon Hamlet is accompanied by—indeed grows out of—the ghost's revelation of the manner of his death; but the scene between Hamlet and the ghost is not primarily a scene of revelation but rather one in which a charge is laid upon Hamlet and he responds. After the ghost withdraws, Hamlet swears his allegiance, bids his sinews bear him stiffly up, and promises faith to "thy commandment." As soon as Horatio and Marcellus approach, he begins to instruct *them* in the course *they* must follow, binding them by an oath. Hamlet knows what he must do,

> For every man has business and desire.   (v.130)

[2] Note the conjunction of notions of time and the world. This is an example of what I have called the "cosmic setting of time."

The scene ends with the couplet in which Hamlet's vocational consciousness is given clear expression. The time is out of joint; Hamlet knows, against all his wishes, that he "was born to set it right" (189– 90).

The action upon which Hamlet embarks, therefore, is not one of his own choosing. He has been "prompted to [his] revenge by heaven and hell" (II.ii.613). When from it he has "laps'd in time and passion" he must be recalled by a second visit of the ghost, that his "blunted purpose" may be whetted (III.iv.106–11). Again Hamlet is stirred, he is responsive, and he speaks of "what I have to do" (129), words similar to those he later tells us he constantly says to himself, "This thing's to do" (IV.iv.44).

The question of vocation is the subjective side of a larger concern of the play which must be described by the term "providence." [3] *Hamlet* is built upon the assumption that the world is under a unified, purposive control. In the *Oresteia* the problem was to find one's way into an understanding of cosmic unity; but in *Hamlet* unity is assumed, and the problem is the relation of man's will and action to the will and action of that unified power. [4] Dramatic tension is achieved through outright opposition to the Divine will (primarily in Claudius), and through Hamlet's doubt and lack of resolution. The play represents neither a clash of equally matched cosmic powers nor merely a conflict of personal wills. Every struggle is placed in relief against a background of destiny, a destiny in itself purposive and creative, but not indifferent to the will of man.

The ghost which brings the "commandment" to Hamlet is surrounded with cosmic associations. [5] At first one may not be certain whether the ghost brings "airs from heaven or blasts from hell" (I.iv.41). Much of Hamlet's deliberation rests upon this double possibility. Yet the assumption is that it brings one or the other; and in the mouse-trap scene the ambiguity is removed, so that the only remaining possibility is that the ghost brought a divine

---

[3] See Chap. III, p. 41, where I have shown that in Israel the idea of vocation combined both personal and providential elements. On the importance of providence in *Hamlet*, see Bertram Joseph, *Conscience and the King*, pp. 132–41.

[4] "It deserves all possible emphasis that Shakespeare does not make Hamlet struggle with the inconsistency between a barbaric tribal code and the Christian code of morals in the matter of revenge, as a Christian Aeschylus might have made him struggle." Willard Farnham, *The Medieval Heritage of Elizabethan Tragedy*, p. 441.

[5] See Hamlet's invocation of "angels and ministers of grace" (I.iv.39) and of heaven, earth, and hell (v.92–93).

commandment.[6] At the second visit of the ghost Hamlet again cries for divine assistance:

> Save me, and hover o'er me with your wings,
> You heavenly guards!   (III.iv.103-4)

This prayer is not born out of fear of an evil apparition, for Hamlet addresses the ghost as "gracious figure" (104). Rather, it is the sign of terror inspired by what Rudolf Otto has called "the numinous."[7] The ghost arouses the dread of the unknown; but it also bears, as here there can be no doubt, a message reflecting the will of heaven. Thus Hamlet, when the ghost leaves, begs his mother to confess herself to heaven (149).

The will of heaven is more than once referred to in the play. The first occurrence is in the mouth of Claudius, who is far from incapable of giving voice to orthodox religious sentiment. Hamlet's behavior, he holds, shows "a will most incorrect to heaven," it is "a fault to heaven" (I.ii.95,101). Later, when Hamlet follows the ghost upon the rampart and Horatio and Marcellus express anxiety over the outcome of this business, Horatio affirms, "Heaven will direct it" (I.iv.91). So Hamlet, having killed Polonius, perceives that "Heaven hath pleas'd it so" (III.iv.173), going on to the belief that he must become heaven's "scourge and minister" (175).

The references to the will of heaven prepare the way for the two speeches in Act V in which Hamlet speaks overtly of the workings of providence in human affairs:

> let us know
> Our indiscretion sometimes serves us well
> When our dear plots do pall; and that should teach us
> There's a divinity that shapes our ends,
> Rough-hew them how we will.   (V.ii.7-11)

> we defy augury. There's a special providence in the fall of a sparrow. If it be now, 'tis not to come; if it be not to come, it will be now; if it be not now, yet it will come; the readiness is all. (V.ii.230-34)

---

[6] This internal logic of the play seems to me to obviate the necessity of the spectator's knowing the Elizabethan attitude to revenge, however interesting that knowledge may be. In spite of the biblical declaration, "Vengeance is mine, I will repay, saith the Lord" (Rom. 12:19), there can be no doubt that Hamlet's revenge is to be regarded as an injunction bearing heavenly approval.

[7] *The Idea of the Holy*, trans. by John W. Harvey. See especially pp. 5-11; on ghosts expressing this quality, pp. 28-29.

The latter speech combines the ideas of providence and vocation (here expressed by the word "readiness").[8] It is difficult to agree with those who find this speech fatalistic, or who see in it Hamlet's abdication of personal involvement in the course of destiny.[9] Professor S. F. Johnson has given an excellent treatment of this passage, as of the theme of providence in the play.[10] He holds that the unexpected events at sea, which rescued Hamlet from execution and returned him to Denmark where he might fulfill his task of killing the king, have impressed Hamlet with the fact that a providential purpose is at work in human affairs. Hamlet thus experiences a "regeneration," which shows itself in his becoming ready to perform his task according to the appointed time and under the direction of heaven. It would be strange indeed if, in order to express a fatalistic view of life, Hamlet were to make such an explicit reference as he does to the Gospel of Matthew (10:29), where the spirit is not that of indifference but rather infinite care. If the context of that reference means anything, we are not to take the speech to mean, "Become indifferent to destiny," but rather, "Be not anxious." When we remember that in Hamlet's former state of great anxiety he accomplished almost nothing, this wisdom does not seem out of place.

[8] For a discussion of this speech and its companion-speech in *Lear*, "Ripeness is all" (IV.ii.11), see J. V. Cunningham, *Woe or Wonder*, pp. 9–15. He shows that the meaning is the same as in the Christian belief in an appointed time for death.

[9] Such a view has been expressed by Kenneth Tynan, *He That Plays the King*, p. 187. For a contrary view, see Maynard Mack, "The World of Hamlet," in *Yale Review*, 502–23: if it is fatalism, "we must at least acknowledge that it is a fatalism of a very distinctive kind—a kind that Shakespeare has been willing to touch with the associations of the saying in St. Matthew about the fall of a sparrow, and with Hamlet's recognition that a divinity shapes our ends" (p. 521). See also Roy Walker, *The Time Is Out of Joint*, pp. 143–44, who holds that Hamlet becomes "an instrument of Providence."

[10] In his essay "The Regeneration of Hamlet," some of Professor Johnson's views on the providential action in *Hamlet* are developed from A. C. Bradley and others, as he has carefully acknowledged. See especially, Bradley's *Shakespearean Tragedy*, pp. 171–74. "It appears probable," says Bradley, "that the 'accident' [Hamlet's return to Denmark because of the chance meeting with the pirate ship] is meant to impress the imagination as the very reverse of accidental, and with many readers it certainly does so. And that this was the intention is made the more likely by a second fact that in connection with the events of the voyage Shakespeare introduces that feeling, on Hamlet's part, of his being in the hands of Providence" (173).
Earlier Bradley had said: "For . . . in all that happens or is done we seem to apprehend some vaster power. We do not define it, or even name it, or perhaps even say to ourselves that it is there; but our imagination is haunted by the sense of it, as it works its way through the deeds or the delays of men to its inevitable end" (pp. 171–72).
I am not able to reconcile these statements with Bradley's previous assertion that Hamlet's fifth-act statements to Horatio "express that kind of religious resignation which, however beautiful in one aspect, really deserves the name of fatalism rather than that of faith in Providence, because it is not united to any determination to do what is believed to be the will of Providence" (p. 145).

The idea of providence is found not only in the speeches. It is to be discerned, as Hamlet saw it, in the patterning of events which brings about an apparently "intended" result. Professor Fergusson has suggested that the main action of the play may be expressed as "the attempt to find and destroy the hidden 'imposthume' which is poisoning the life of Claudius' Denmark." [11] It is clear that such an action is accomplished not by the single will of any one person, but by the combined results of many wills and incidents. Professor Fergusson's use of the concept of Jamesian "reflectors" has helped to convey the understanding of the play's action in this more than individual way. Neither Hamlet nor Claudius nor the ghost nor anyone else can claim to be the motivating center of the action. Instead, the various characters and "occasions" all reflect an action which transcends each of them.

I believe the many references to "the will of heaven," to heaven, earth, and hell, plus Hamlet's problem of vocation and his fifth-act references to "divinity" and "providence," all force us to regard the main action as providential. I do not mean that the theme is pushed to anything like the degree found in preaching or in Scripture. But I do mean that the conception of the action involves more than the terms "Destiny" and "Fate" express. In common with the Christian idea of providence, it emphasizes unity, purpose, personal demand, and redemption. In the final scene of the play the hidden "imposthume" is found and destroyed, although in a way different from what any of the characters would have wished. A good and strong king assumes the throne, the incestuous usurper is slain. Yet the cost in bloodshed is greater than one's rational expectation would have assumed, and he who comes to rule is not the one imagined. The cost of this redemption is high; its result is a new creation. No man of himself can plan such a result. The most he can contribute to it is "readiness," a compliance of the will. [12]

If it is impossible to discuss *Hamlet* except with reference to will and purpose, it is likewise impossible to discuss the *Oresteia* except in terms of law, sanction, power, and authority. For the *Oresteia* is built upon

---

[11] Fergusson, *Idea of a Theater*, p. 117.

[12] See *OED*, which lists as the first meaning of readiness, "prompt compliance, willingness, etc." For instance, Fisher, 1509: "consyderynge the redyness of mercy and pyte of our sauyour Ihesu." The compliance of the will required of Hamlet involves also the cooperation of passion (not its elimination) and the disciplining of man's reason. See in this book, p. 134, n. 36. The play suggests that there is a passion which rightly transcends reason. In this relation of reason, will, and passion, I find more of Augustine than of the Renaissance exaltation of the reason alone.

the problem of a "conflict of sanctions."[13] Its interest rests not upon the providential outcome of a distraught situation but upon the reconciliation of opposing principles of justice.[14] In its climax, which is among the greatest scenes ever composed for the stage, it achieves a synthesis of apparently contradictory cosmic powers.

The conflict, of course, is between the Olympic and the *chthonic* deities. Primarily, and true to the Greek concern for space, this is the contest between gods of earth and of sky. The spatial concept of power is stated clearly in the Chorus' accusation against Apollo, in *The Eumenides*:

He made man's way cross the place of the ways of God and blighted age-old distributions of power.[15]

The contest is also between two conceptions of justice: that sprung from reason (δίκη) and that conceived of as ancient, irrational custom (θέμις). In addition it is a contest between maternal and paternal rights, and there are echoes of the rights of kingship over against tribal rule.

Aeschylus knows, as probably strong elements in the society would not let him forget, that no society can exist with sky gods only. The Furies are associated with earth, blood, and the nether world.[16] On their side are ranged motherhood, family loyalty, ancient custom, the practice of agriculture. As these are basic elements in any society, Athena (who votes to exonerate Orestes) *must* win them to her side in order to guarantee the stability of her city. Pure reason, beauty, and impartial justice do not provide the mortar necessary to hold a society together, nor the elemental urges to bear, clothe, feed, and defend its citizens. That is why the final visions of Athens' peace and victory cannot come until the Furies are won over and take their proper place in the cave beneath the Areopagus.

It is correct to say, therefore, that the aim of the play is to reveal the ideal adjustment between opposing principles and forces. The form of the trilogy manifests the concern for balance and symmetry. In

---

[13] I am indebted to Professor Moses Hadas for this phrase.

[14] Cf. George Thomson, *Aeschylus and Athens*, pp. 278–79. When, however, Professor Thomson accentuates the social significance of the conflicts to the virtual exclusion of the moral (pp. 289–90), I believe he goes too far.

[15] παρὰ νόμον θεῶν βρότεα μὲν τίων,
παλαιγενεῖς δὲ μοίρας φθίσας.   *Eum.* 171–72.
The translation is by Richmond Lattimore, *Oresteia*.

[16] See especially *Eum.* 179–97.

Agamemnon those forces represented by the Eumenides [17] are victorious. In *The Libation-Bearers* the opposing side is successful in revenge. In *The Eumenides* the issue is brought to trial, each side arguing its case so cogently that the vote is tied and must be broken by Athena herself, who thereupon steps down from her position as judge to enter debate with the Eumenides. By this time the question of the curse on the house of Atreus has been transcended. Had Aeschylus stuck carefully to that theme, he would have produced a play in which the historic mode of thought predominated. He did not do so. Orestes' exit from the play upon his acquittal is a clear indication that the interest lies elsewhere. The fate of the house of Atreus gives way to the glory of Athens. When the harmony of powers is secured, the play ends, as it must, in celebration.

The celebration is not of a victory, but of a condition. That is, it is not focused upon an event, but upon a cosmic and social structure which Aeschylus believes to have universal validity. He is asking what the ingredients of Athens' greatness are. To be sure, he puts this in narrative terms, as if, once upon a time, a trial such as this took place. But that is primarily an aetiological motif. There is much aetiology in Greek drama, notably in Euripides. In *The Eumenides*, it occurs not only as a theme in the whole trial by jury scene, but also specifically in Orestes' parting speech (754–77) which refers to the league between Athens and Argos of 461 B.C. Aetiology, however, does not necessarily reflect the historical mode of thought as I have described it. For it uses some past incident merely to explain a present custom or institution. It does not imply that the present in any sense stands under the past, or that the unique moment of the present leads into any future. Aetiology is a way of explaining what *is* (rather than what *is happening*), and that is Aeschylus' concern in *The Eumenides*. "The final act," says Richmond Lattimore, "comes down into the present day and seals within itself the wisdom, neither reactionary nor revolutionary, of a great man." [18]

The purpose of the narrative in the *Oresteia* is to reveal such wisdom. The basic action of the play, giving the clue to its form, is a movement from deeds performed by the characters to knowledge or wisdom. This may be put in a formula: event leads to knowledge. It is diametrically opposed to *Hamlet*, where knowledge leads to event.[19]

---

[17] Who, of course, do not appear until later.   [18] The *Oresteia*, p. 31.
[19] Cf. Preston Roberts, *Theology and Imaginative Literature*, p. 353: "The essential movement in every Shakespearean play is not from ignorance to knowledge but from knowledge to

Another way of putting the matter is that whereas in *Hamlet* action is a positive good because it is demanded by the vocation of the hero, in the *Oresteia* action is negative because it represents a disturbance of universal order. The "knowledge" which the play seeks is a vision of order. This is true in spite of the fact that Orestes has a divine mandate to seek vengeance upon Clytemnestra and Aegisthus; for that mandate is, in the total picture, limited and partial. Hamlet's is absolute.

An example of the way in which knowledge or vision takes precedence over events in the *Oresteia*, is the slaying of Agamemnon. From the opening speech of the Watchman, who has waited long years for the signal of victory, to the moment when the returning lord is persuaded to enter his house upon the crimson carpet, the expectancy is great. The tension thus built up is fulfilled—not in the scene of slaying, but in the visions of Cassandra (1076–1330). The long passage between Cassandra and the Chorus is the emotional high-point of the play and the portion where the writing is the most brilliant. Her chants in this passage use repeatedly the terms "see" (ἰδού) and "behold" (ὁρᾶτε). We are given not the event, but a picture of the event. Because the climactic events are hidden from view, the emphasis falls upon knowing what happens.

After Cassandra enters the house and the death-cries come from Agamemnon, the Chorus debates whether or not to act. One proposes calling the citizens to rally, another calls for breaking into the house, and so forth; but their conclusion is to do nothing on the basis of mere guess-work, and to wait until they "know for a certainty" (σαφ᾽ εἰδέναι —1369) what has occurred inside. At this point the palace doors open to reveal the direct vision of the crime. The moment of action has passed, and the play moves on to Clytemnestra's attempt to justify what she has done.

Were it not for the strong discipline of form, parts of Cassandra's speech might suggest a "historic" orientation; for past, present, and future are combined very skillfully. Cassandra recalls "the story of ancient wrong in this house" (λόγῳ παλαιὰς τῶνδ᾽ ἁμαρτίας δόμων— 1197); she pictures the terrible deeds upon which Clytemnestra and

___

idolatry and from idolatry to sin and from sin to judgment and forgiveness." Professor Roberts shows that a primary structural difference between Shakespeare and the Greeks is in the position of the recognition scene, which in Shakespeare occurs *before* the tragic deed rather than after it.

Aegisthus are now set, and prophesies the coming of "another one in his turn, our avenger" (ἡμῶν ἄλλος αὖ τιμάορος—1280). However, the form of the work turns all this "history" into a vision. Cassandra not only sees the past and future, she also sees the present action, which she reveals to us almost as if she were a messenger. Her vision compresses past, present, and future so closely together that we see all as parts of one picture, and the present becomes not a time of decision but instead one phase of a cycle.[20]

This muting of the action itself in favor of a vision of the act as *fait accompli* is, in the *Agamemnon*, an anticipation of the grand climax of the trilogy in which the act that Orestes commits, indeed the whole episode of Atreus' house, yields to a vision of cosmic unity embracing opposing powers.

The formative principle of the *Oresteia* is the desire for vision, not action, a fact which accounts for its ending in ritual celebration. The play's greatness, however, lies in the fact that the principle of "historic" action pushes against, but does not break, the "visionary" form.

Orestes' deliberation over the action before him makes his similarity to Hamlet very striking. Yet it must not be forgotten that the object of Orestes' deliberation is entirely different from Hamlet's. Orestes asks whether a man has the *right* to kill his mother in these circumstances, a question of truth, or wisdom, reflecting the play's attempt to harmonize two conflicting moral sanctions. Hamlet, however, has two questions. The first is, "Did Claudius in fact kill my father?" This is a question of fact. His second, more fundamental, question is, "Shall I act as I am bidden?" This is a matter of vocation. The sequence of these two questions shows that, unlike the *Oresteia*, the basic movement in *Hamlet* is from knowledge to event.

The movement from knowledge to event in *Hamlet* can be illustrated by two passages, the first a matter of style, the second a pivotal point in the play.

---

[20] Cassandra, says H. D. F. Kitto, *Greek Tragedy*, spreads "before us a filmy screen on which we see, as in a phantasmagoria, all the horrors of this House, past, present, and future. *Time and action are suspended*; or rather past and future action are made to live on the present stage" (pp. 80–81). The words italicized (by me) give the truth of the matter, I believe. Elsewhere Professor Kitto says that in the *Oresteia* "past horror is waiting to be reincarnated as a present horror" (p. 75), and "The Aeschylean concept demands that the past shall not be forgotten for a moment" (p. 76). That is true, but not in any such way as to suggest that there is any reciprocity between past and present. The Aeschylean present is bound to the past, which has the effect of suspending time.

The following passage occurs in the first scene of Act I:

> HOR. Well, sit we down,
> And let us hear Bernardo speak of this.
>
> BER. Last night of all,
> When yond same star that's westward from the pale
> Had made his course t'illumine that part of heaven
> Where now it burns, Marcellus and myself,
> The bell then beating one,—
>
> *Enter the* Ghost
>
> MAR. Peace, break thee off! Look, where it comes again!   (33–40)

Bernardo has begun a description of something seen on the previous night, yet we are not permitted to hear him out because the events of *this* night interrupt his speech. The narrative he began, and which in any Greek play he would have been allowed to finish, would have imparted a static quality to the scene. Shakespeare sees to it that rhetorical description is broken off by a new event demanding a new reaction. By similar means throughout the play, Shakespeare communicates a world of surprise, where the newness of things precludes comprehensive, detached knowledge, which is another way of saying that the life of reflection is continually disrupted by the demands of historical existence.

The movement from knowledge to event is the basis also of the "mouse-trap" scene. In the scheme of the total play (as in Hamlet's mind) the "Murder of Gonzago" is to be the occasion of providing the knowledge Hamlet needs in order to act ("If he but blench,/I know my course."—II.ii.626–27). Moreover, the trap not only is to provide knowledge as the basis for action; it is also set upon the premise that knowledge does, in fact, lead to action. Hamlet's assumption, entirely correct, is that when the king is shown the "mirror" of his own crime and thus is given the knowledge that others are privy to his secret, he will be forced into some overt act:

> Give him heedful note;
> For I mine eyes will rivet to his face.   (III.ii.89–90)

The king's knowledge will betray him into a visible act, which in turn will provide Hamlet with the knowledge he requires as the basis of his action.[21]

---

[21] The players "shall not only reflect true history but help in the making of it." Walker, *The Time Is Out of Joint*, p. 69.

This relation of knowledge and action in *Hamlet* is the formative principle upon which the twin themes of providence and vocation are hung. The ghost brings to Hamlet no mere revelation of fact, but knowledge which is intended to make him enlist in a certain endeavor.[22]

The encounter between Hamlet and Gertrude is abortive because through it Hamlet tries to avoid his role of avenger and to become Gertrude's enlightener. This was no part of his mission. He had been expressly warned to leave her to heaven and to her own conscience. The appearance of the ghost is therefore necessary to remind him that he is not to play the interpreter of past actions, but is to fulfill an action which remains at hand. In the midst of Hamlet's accurate description of Claudius as "a murderer and a villain," the ghost enters for the second time to move the play from knowledge to action.

The contrasting relationships between knowledge and event in *Hamlet* and the *Oresteia* provide the means for distinguishing the two types of dramatic action they portray. In *Hamlet* the play "imitates" the fulfillment of knowledge in a unique, purposeful event transcending our expectations. The *Oresteia* "imitates" a movement from deeds of bloodshed to the recognition and celebration of a more comprehensive form of justice. The manner in which these dramatic actions are imitated may be shown in reference to the handling of time, the importance of characterization, and the circumscription of the area of action.

In general, the handling of time in *Hamlet* is similar to that in *Richard III*. There is the same technique of compression, the same use of two time schemes (one fast and one slow), the same heightening of the significance of the present by showing its memory of the past and anticipation of the future.[23] There is not the same dwelling upon the day of judgment,[24] but there is set up the same feeling that all the separate wills and agents are moving toward the time of their trial.

The vocational problem which Hamlet faces is stated and resolved in the language of time. He has been born to set right a "time" which

---

[22] "Shakespeare makes man's will a component part of man's knowledge. . . ." John F. Danby, *Shakespeare's Doctrine of Nature*, p. 185.

[23] On the two time schemes, see H. H. Furness, *Variorum Hamlet*, pp. xiv–xvii. Miss Mable Buland, *The Presentation of Time in the Elizabethan Drama*, pp. 119–21, seems to feel that Shakespeare is simply inconsistent in his use of time in *Hamlet*, but the examples she cites are similar to those elsewhere used to show the presence of double time-schemes. On memory, note particularly I.v.91–112; I.ii.2, 143; III.ii.137–45.

[24] However, see Act II, scene ii, line 242 and Act V, scene i, lines 67, 252.

"is out of joint" (I.v.189–90), and his ultimate acceptance of the heaven-sent vocation is an obedience which stands in "readiness" for death, which comes in its own providential time ("If it be now, 'tis not to come," etc.—V.ii.230–35). Using the idea of time in two such crucial points, Shakespeare has, as it were, committed the play to the conception of right times and wrong times, therefore to the fulfillment of the action in the proper, the appointed time. The ghost "usurp'st this time of night" (I.i.46), it appears "at this dead hour" (65), the hour near one o'clock is "the season/Wherein the spirit held his wont to walk" (I.iv.5–6). Ghosts do not walk abroad in the season of Advent, "So hallow'd and so gracious is the time" (I.ii.156–64). Denmark's war preparations are so unnaturally hasty they "make the night joint-labourer with the day" (70–79), a phrase of which we are reminded later when Polonius assures us he will not discuss "Why day is day, night night, and time is time," which "were nothing but to waste night, day, and time" (II. ii.88–89).[25]

As usual in the Shakespearean play, part of the evil rests in the fact that events have moved too fast, which is the theme of the soliloquy in Act I, scene ii, with its invective against "wicked speed, to post/With such dexterity to incestuous sheets" (156–57).[26] Not only is this hastiness not good, says Hamlet, but, striking the note of anticipation and fulfillment, "it cannot come to good" (157). In contrast to his mother's speed, Hamlet himself is "tardy," "laps'd in time and passion" (III.iv.106–7); but Claudius is alert to dispatch him "with fiery quickness" (IV.iii.45, and cf. 56–59), while Laertes moves with "impetuous haste" (IV.v.100).

It is Claudius, so often correct in perception if not in motive, who puts the temporal nature of man's moral situation most clearly:

[25] For the sense of special times, see also Act III, scene ii, lines 266–67:

> Thoughts black, hands apt, drugs fit, and time
> agreeing;
> Confederate season . . .

> 'Tis now the very witching time of night
> When churchyards yawn and hell itself breathes out
> Contagion to this world. Now could I drink hot blood,
> And do such bitter business as the day
> Would quake to look on.   (III.ii.406–10)

(The latter speech shows how far Hamlet is from the mark. His business might well be done in the day, since it is just. Sometimes Hamlet would prefer to be agent of hell rather than heaven's "scourge and minister.")
Polonius' death is described as "untimely"   (IV.i.40).
[26] And see the return to this theme (III.ii.132–45).

That we would do
We should do when we would; for this "would" changes,
And hath abatements and delays as many
As there are tongues, are hands, are accidents;
And then this "should" is like a spendthrift sigh,
That hurts by easing.[27]   (IV.vii.118–24)

In *Hamlet* every man's situation is a temporal, that is, historical one. The wildness of Laertes' followers comes from the fact that they act as if "the world were now but to begin,/Antiquity forgot, custom not known" (IV.v.103–4). One could say the same of Claudius and Gertrude—that they forget the past and begin to make their own rules. Only Hamlet seriously attempts to remember antiquity and custom. The grave-digger scene, cutting through custom and class to discover the primitive qualities of manhood, finds both high and low to be creatures of time. In this primitive world where "gardeners, ditchers, and grave-makers . . . hold up Adam's profession" (V.i.34–35),[28] time is a destroyer. Only the grave-maker's houses last till doomsday (67). In youth, according to the first grave-digger's song, love is sweet, "But age with his stealing steps/Hath caught me in his clutch" (79–80). Yorick is not what he was "in's time" (116); the grave is for one that *was* a woman but *now* is dead (146); a man will last in the earth "some eight or nine year," a tanner a bit longer (181–91). In his graveyard mood, Hamlet would turn the conversation into a parable of time's reduction of all things to nothing. But the context of the play will not let him. A simple question about the grave-digger's years in his occupation draws forth memory of Danish history, of victory over Fortinbras, of the birth of "young Hamlet" (153–63). Man may be mortal, but he is still a creature of history. Even as Hamlet generalizes on the futility of all achievement, Ophelia's funeral procession enters, and he is thrown into new activity.

The historical world in which the action of *Hamlet* takes place, standing between Adam and doomsday, implies promise and fulfillment.[29] As Hamlet says, the air is "promise-crammed" (III.ii.100),

---

[27] Note how this "reflective" passage changes immediately into action: "But, to the quick o' th' ulcer:—/Hamlet comes back" (124–25).

[28] And note Hamlet's reference to Cain, "that did the first murder" (85).

[29] It is the clowns who talk about doomsday, just as in *Richard III* it was the comic murderers of Clarence who introduced the talk of judgment day. Even at its most primitive, most unceremonius level, Shakespeare's world is subject to a history which moves toward judgment.

or as the Queen puts it when the tragic end is near, "Each toy seems prologue to some great amiss" (IV.v.18).[30]

The formal way in which the sense of promise and fulfillment is communicated is through the convergence of several lines of action. The method is typically Elizabethan, the concomitant of the multiple plot. By linking several chains of events so that their crucial moments either coincide or reinforce one another, an idea of purposive control is generated. In *Hamlet* there are not what may be called separate plots, but there are diverse lines of action set up by the intentions of several agents. The ghost of the elder Hamlet represents one will. This will, entering the situation at court, sets up in young Hamlet several conflicting desires. He wishes to obey his father's spirit; he wishes to know the truth; he wishes to kill Claudius; he intends to restore Denmark to health; and at times, at least, he desires to die. Ophelia loves Hamlet, and her father is at work to have her wed. Claudius' aim, continually growing, is to remove Hamlet from the scene. In the background, from first to last, is the projected military campaign of Fortinbras. As the play draws to its climax, these various intentions either fulfill themselves, become eliminated, or shift into alliances, so that in the dueling scene a concentration is achieved. Ophelia's love having found expression only in death, and Polonius having fallen victim to Hamlet's aim to kill Claudius, the Polonius family's interests give way to Laertes' demand for revenge. This in turn is made the tool of Claudius' will. Hamlet's acquiescence to the will of heaven permits his many desires to become focused on the slaying of Claudius. When Claudius and Hamlet eliminate each other in the last scene, the latent action of Fortinbras takes over.

The pattern is of numerous strands woven together. The complexity and the combination of fulfillment and surprise remind us of historical reality, even when we see the careful management which the poet has exercised. By comparison, the *Oresteia* is utterly simple. The lines of force total only three: the law represented by the Furies, the law represented by Apollo, and the wisdom represented by Athena, the latter being the synthesis of the former two. The relationships here are logical in form, although the realities behind them transcend logic by far, creating the tension between form and substance which is the locus of the play's greatness.

[30] Cf. Act I, scene i, line 123, "prologue to the omen coming on," and *Macb.* Act I, scene iii, line 128, "happy prologues to the swelling act. . . ."

Time in the *Oresteia* is much more important than in *The Persians*. The reason lies in the subject matter, the theme of blood-guilt and family curse. In the *Oresteia* Aeschylus does not ignore history; he seeks to resolve its complexities in wisdom.

The *Agamemnon* begins late, after much water has flowed under the bridge; it deals with a fresh event in the chain of evil, and it looks forward to a future resolution. There are many references to time, beginning in the Watchman's opening speech describing his "long year's watch" (φρουρᾶς ἐτείας μῆκος—2), and carrying through to Aegisthus' parting threats regarding "days to come" (ὑστέραισιν ἡμέραις—1666). Two notions of time persist throughout. One is that time is simply duration, wherein all things change, negative in character, to be escaped if possible. "You will know the future when it comes," says the Chorus; "until then let it be, it is like sorrowing too soon" (τὸ μέλλον δ'/ἐπεὶ γένοιτ' ἂν κλύοις· πρὸ χαιρέτω·/ἴσον δὲ τῷ προστένειν— 251–53).[31] This is the more pervasive attitude in the play. Its leading symbol is the net, a recurrent image. The other notion is that of time bringing action to fulfillment. The long waiting is climaxed in a particularly eventful time. Clytemnestra can announce that the Achaeans possess Troy "this day" (τῇδ' ἔχουσ' ἐν ἡμέρᾳ—320); Agamemnon can speak of "the grace of this time" (καιρὸν χάριτος—787, using the word for a special time, rather than Aeschylus' more usual χρόνος); and Aegisthus can hail the light of what he calls the "day of retribution" (ἡμέρας δικηφόρου—1577).[32] The two notions of time find close juxtaposition in the Chorus' agitation at Agamemnon's death. One speaker strikes the note of punctual action, saying, "This is not the moment to delay" (τὸ μὴ μέλλειν δ' ἀκμή—1353), while another speaks of time quantitatively with the words, "We are wasting time" (χρονίζομεν γάρ—1356). Cassandra's prophecy of an avenger is very striking because it suggests that a future event will restore right to the

---

[31] Cf. the Herald's speech (551–82), especially 553–54: "Who except the gods escapes suffering through all his days?" (τίς δὲ πλὴν θεῶν / ἅπαντ' ἀπήμων τὸν δι' αἰῶνος). Also, for time as mere duration, see *Agam.* 8, 14, 67–68, 196–98, 521, 621, 629, 857, 915–16, 983, 1299, 1300, 1378.

[32] See also 1301, "The day has come" (ἥκει τόδ' ἦμαρ). However, one should beware reading into the Greek more of this type of expression than is there. Richmond Lattimore, in his usually excellent translation, has read the expression τὸ μόρσιμον as "the day of destiny" (*L.B.* 103, for example). Surely this is a case of attributing to the Greek a concept borrowed from Judaism and Christianity. See also his rendering of αἴλινον αἴλινον εἰπέ, τὸ δ' εὖ νικάτω (121, 139, 159) as "Sing sorrow, sing sorrow, but good win out *in the end*" (italics mine). Aeschylus stops with the idea of victory, not that of final culmination. Note further l. 674, where γένοιτο δ' ὡς ἄριστα becomes "may it all come well *in the end*."

tangled situation. "For there shall come another one in turn," she says, "our avenger" (ἥξει γὰρ ἡμῶν ἄλλος αὖ τιμάορος—1280), echoing the Watchman's prayer in the beginning for "release from labors" (ἀπαλλαγὴ πόνων—20). This shows that the historical (time-bound) story Aeschylus has chosen raises hopes for redemption in some temporal event, but the later parts of the trilogy abandon such hope in favor of new understanding. Orestes does come as avenger, but his act does not bring release.

We must take it, therefore, that the historical note does not come to predominate in the play. Just as in *Hamlet* the view of time as impartial destroyer is stated in the grave-diggers' scene but is not allowed to become paramount, so in the *Agamemnon*, time as purposive fulfillment is a stated theme but does not become paramount. Aeschylus cannot separate time from fatalism. Cassandra's "What is to come will come" (τὸ μέλλον ἥξει—1240) has no flexibility regarding either time or event, whereas Hamlet's "If it be now, 'tis not to come," hovers in time, ready for the moment which will be chosen.

In *The Libation-Bearers* Aeschylus comes closest to action in which time is important and in which history seems to be the arena of action. This is the part of the trilogy in which the deliverer returns, where "destiny is waiting" (τὸ μόρσιμον γὰρ . . . μένει—103). The words of the Chorus in 646–51 sound almost like the expectation of a Messiah:

The foundations of Justice are planted firm; Destiny, forging her sword, fashions her arms ahead of time; and famed, deep-brooding Vengeance is bringing the son into the house to requite at last the ancient pollution of blood.[33]

Even in this play, however, where Orestes' mission is paramount, the particular never becomes more important than the general. Destiny (Αἶσα) is not providence, and Vengeance ('Ερινύς) is not judgment. The language suggests the way in which firmly-planted Justice and armed Destiny *always* act. The image is that of a stain removed, throwing the focus into the past, so that we see not an incomplete act made

---

[33] Δίκας δ' ἐρείδεται πυθμήν.
προχαλκεύει δ' Αἶσα φασγανουργός
τέκνον δ' ἐπεισφέρει δόμοισιν
αἱμάτων παλαιτέρων τίνειν μῦσος
χρόνῳ κλυτὰ βυσσόφρων 'Ερινύς
Cf. ll. 929–30:
ἦ κάρτα μάντισ οὔξ ὀνειράτων φόβος
ἔκανεσ ὃν οὐ χρῆν, καὶ τὸ μὴ χρεὼν πάθε.

perfect, but a wrong righted. Insofar as *Hamlet* deals with the theme of revenge, it also focuses on the removal of a past wrong; but because the finding and destroying of the "hidden imposthume" in Denmark leads to a more comprehensive salvation than does Orestes' act of revenge, the emphasis is shifted to the historical fulfillment of a historical dilemma. This is entirely different from that which Athena achieves on the Areopagus, which is not, after all, the outcome of Orestes' actions. The "fulfillment" in *The Eumenides* is a synthesis achieved by Athena after the historical course of action has been completed. In this sense Athena is a *deus ex machina* who is necessary to resolve the ambiguities which history in the Greek understanding could not but perpetuate.

In the last analysis, therefore, time and history in the *Oresteia* are neutral. The choric ode which is sung when Orestes is slaying his victims refers to time as all-accomplishing ($\pi\alpha\nu\tau\epsilon\lambda\grave{\eta}s$ $\chi\rho\acute{o}\nu os$—965). And fortune is called a pair of dice which is about to fall out favorably ($\tau\acute{\upsilon}\chi\alpha\iota$ δ' $\epsilon\acute{\upsilon}\pi\rho o\sigma\omega\pi o\kappa o\hat{\iota}\tau\alpha\iota$—969). The image removes the idea of purpose, leaving that of time as mere change.

The use of such different expressions and descriptions of time in *Hamlet* and the *Oresteia* springs from the fact that Hamlet's problem of readiness is a temporal question, whereas Orestes' dilemma of the two moral sanctions is not.

In addition to their respective treatments of time, Aeschylus and Shakespeare have differed in the imitation of the action in *Hamlet* and the *Oresteia* by a quite dissimilar handling of character. By this statement it is not meant that Hamlet has one characterization and Orestes another, a matter of no interest in the study of dramatic form. The meaning is that characterization itself has one importance for Shakespeare and another for Aeschylus.

W. H. Auden has spoken of the difference between internal and external drama.[34] The external depicts the individual in a certain situation and taking a certain course of action, as seen from the outside with no introspection. This is the type of the Greek play. Internal drama deals with life as we experience it in ourselves, the individual's action toward his own states of being. This is the type of the allegorical morality play, such as *Everyman*. Shakespeare, says Mr. Auden, is "an attempt to synthesize both into a new, more complicated type" (p. xxviii.).

[34] *Poets of the English Language*, pp. xxv–xxviii.

The Shakespearean play, therefore, shows a high degree of internalization compared to the Greek, which means that the character of
its hero is much more germane to the fundamental intent of the play
than is that of the Greek hero. In the Renaissance, said Collingwood,
history "became the history of human passions." [35] This was one of
the results of the Christian view of history, according to Collingwood,
and its dramatic parallel is to be found in such a play as *Hamlet*, where
the "history" recounted is in such a large degree the history of Prince
Hamlet's passions. [36]

There is no need to devote space to the importance of Hamlet's
character. That is a subject so belabored that the task of recent scholarship has been to rescue the play from the domination of its hero; [37] for
after all, Hamlet's are not the only passions in the work, nor does any
one individual overshadow the role which social and historic forces
play. In *Hamlet* there is a wedding of individual, social, and providential forces which cannot be separated without upsetting the form. [38]

It is more necessary to show the externalization in the *Oresteia*. In

[35] See p. 65, n. 75.

[36] Although Hamlet says, "Give me that man/That is not passion's slave" (III.ii.76–77),
too much has been made of the play as an exaltation of reason over passion. Hamlet does not,
after all, ask for a man of no passion. On the other hand, he has several statements to the
effect that passion is proper to right action:

> Do you not come your tardy son to chide,
> That, laps'd in time and passion, lets go by
> Th' important acting of your dread command?   (III.iv.106–8)

>   What would he do
> Had he the motive and the cue for passion
> That I have?   (II.ii.586–88)

>   How stand I then
> That have a father kill'd, a mother stain'd,
> Excitements of my reason and my blood,
> And let all sleep . . . ?   (IV.iv.56–59)

Don Cameron Allen, "Shakespeare's Hamlet," in *Literary Masterpieces of the Western World*,
is nearer the mark when he locates Hamlet's plight as that of a man "who was so seduced by
the lure of reason that he wandered apart from the vertical road of faith" (p. 151).

[37] See Lewis, "Hamlet, the Prince or the Poem."

[38] For an example of Shakespeare's fusion of the social and the individual, see Act I, scene
iii, lines 19–24:

> He may not, as unvalued persons do,
> Carve for himself, for on his choice depends
> The sanity and health of the whole state;
> And therefore must his choice be circumscrib'd
> Unto the voice and yielding of that body
> Whereof he is the head.

The image of the king as head of the body is, of course, derived from St. Paul (Col. 1:18).
See also Claudius' opening speech (I.ii.1–25) which begins with private-royal matters and
changes abruptly (l. 17) to the subject of Fortinbras, as if personal-moral questions were
somehow connected with current history.

every case, character is defined by situation or dilemma, not by passion.[39] The individuals of the trilogy are not presented so that anything is to be learned from their individuality. Rather, they are illustrations of general types. Electra is a daughter before she is Electra, Orestes primarily a son, Aegisthus a lover and tyrant; even Clytemnestra, whose vivid characterization strains the form to the utmost, is pre-eminently mother, faithless wife, and lover. In Aeschylus, these are what may be called universal types, in contrast to the social types which they will become in Euripides and New Comedy. The matriarchal qualities of Clytemnestra in the *Oresteia* have an entirely different reference from those of the matron whom Euripides pictures in his *Electra*. Aeschylus is concerned with the individual only as he is defined by the conflict in which the play discovers him, and he is not concerned with the individual reaction to this conflict, but with what the tragic action can tell us about the nature of the conflict itself.[40] Character in Aeschylus is a product of situation and a means of imitating the dramatic action—the movement from deed to knowledge. In Shakespeare character is itself an inherent part—though not the whole —of the action.[41] Mr. Auden goes so far as to say that Hamlet's problem is that he would like to escape from the demands of his own individuality. Hamlet, he says,

defines his existence in terms of others: "I am the man whose mother married his uncle who murdered his father." He would like to become what the Greek hero is, a creature of situation.[42]

[39] See Kitto, *Form and Meaning in Drama*, p. 209. The Greek tragedians, he says, were always interested first in religious or philosophical conceptions, and they related story and character to that concern, whereas with the Elizabethans the balance was the opposite, "the balance between the constructive and the representational activities in the Greek and the Elizabethan respectively is considerable, and explains to a very great extent the differences in form and style." Aeschylus' interest in Orestes as a character, says Professor Kitto (p. 337), is exhausted when he has defined his dilemma, but in *Hamlet* we must see how the contagion spreads over the whole spirit and conduct.

[40] "The characters of the play are not merely blind puppets of higher powers; they have inward springs of motion, and yet these are agencies sent from God. Thus for a moment is the balance poised between the two sets of powers which shape human destiny." F. M. Cornford, *Thucydides Mythistoricus*, p. 236. Cf. Kitto, *Form and Meaning in Drama*, p. 36.

[41] Orestes' "character and his inner conflict are only a small part of the real drama," writes Kitto, *Form and Meaning in Drama*, p. 40. For a discussion of Orestes' lack of hesitation, inner conflict, and decision, see pp. 43–45. Professor Kitto believes that the silence of Pylades except for his one speech urging obedience to Apollo is a deliberate technique of Aeschylus' and is meant to give the impression that "the real protagonists are the gods" (p. 53). Pylades otherwise would remind us of Horatio, whose primary function is to show Hamlet more intensely as protagonist.

[42] *Poets of the English Language*, pp. xxiv—xxv.

The precedence of situation over character could not be more force-
fully demonstrated than in *The Eumenides* when Orestes is dismissed
from the stage. In *The Libation-Bearers* he had inherited the problem
of blood revenge from the villainous acts depicted in the *Agamemnon*.
He had acted upon this problem according to the behest of Apollo, and
this had led him in *The Eumenides* to the question of his own purification and exoneration from guilt. *The Eumenides* opens with his appeal
for divine aid, first at the shrine of Apollo, and then at the court of
Athena. However, since Aeschylus is not interested in the person of
Orestes in any unique sense—there being nothing in the action of the
play which cannot eventually be expressed abstractly rather than in-
carnate in an individual man—he must remove Orestes from the center
of attention. The trial is the perfect means for that accomplishment.
As Orestes has all along been the "creature of situation," he now becomes the object of debate, and then an illustration of a general issue.
His fate thus taken entirely out of his own hands, he ceases to interest
us as a character; and so, being given an acquitting vote by Athena, he
is allowed to depart. The protagonist absent, nothing is left on the stage
but the advocates and the issues they represent. The external character
of the action, which was indeed present from the very beginning of
the trilogy, is now manifest, and Aeschylus is free to conclude the play
with the establishment of the harmony of opposites which had been his
object throughout.

The entire relation of the audience to the Greek tragic hero is different from what it is to the Elizabethan. The Greek tragic hero is a
spectacle. The presentational elements of the Greek play—the design
and size of the theater, the elevation of the actors, the Chorus as
"screen" or "curtain" removing the actors a degree from the audience,
and the static quality, especially of the scenes of violence—reinforce the
conception of the hero as one seen externally, from a distance, as part
of an objective pattern. By contrast, the design of the Elizabethan
theater tends to promote a sense of identity between the hero and the
audience. Both are enclosed within the "wooden O." By numerous
devices, of which the soliloquy is primary, the audience is invited to
share the thoughts of the hero and thus participate in his experience.
For if the implication is that one should avoid the fate of the Greek
tragic hero (however cathartic it may be to watch), the implication is
also that to pass through what Hamlet or Lear pass through is somehow
ennobling. If this fundamental difference in the relation to the hero

is not an outgrowth of the religious rituals which lie behind the two theaters, it is at least parallel to them. For all the ecstasy of the Dionysian festivals, the efficacy of the sacrifice celebrated was entirely objective; whereas in Christianity the objectivity of the sacrificial Atonement was always mixed both with the willingness of The Lamb to become the sacrificial victim, and with the believer's obligation toward the imitation of Christ. So also, the spectator at a performance of *Hamlet* is intended to achieve a much higher degree of participation in the subjective state of the hero than at a performance of the *Oresteia*. He does not consider himself to be Orestes; he does consider himself to be Hamlet.

Aeschylus' imitation of a dramatic action which moves from deed or event to knowledge implies a certain conception of the limits of action which is quite unlike that implied for Shakespeare in the imitation of a dramatic action which moves in the reverse direction, from knowledge to event. Knowledge demands a circumscription of the area of study, an acknowledgment of boundaries within which the problem may be posed and a solution obtained. Events and historical occurrences transcend the limits of rational construction. Their limits, if they have any, are not apparent.[43]

The *Oresteia* takes place in a world with clear limits and deals with events which have a quite definite Beginning and End. Aeschylus has confined the story of the cursed House of Atreus to three definite episodes, two of which he enacts and one of which he mentions: Atreus served the children of Thyestes to him as a meal; Agamemnon was murdered; Orestes took revenge for his father upon Clytemnestra and Aegisthus.[44] Aeschylus does not, as he might, trace the curse upon the house further into the past, nor dwell upon the animosities between Atreus and Thyestes. No more is he interested in the future of Orestes or the house.[45]

---

[43] See Farnham *Elizabethan Tragedy*, p. 452: "Greek tragedy is willing to confine its scope to the action that immediately brings catastrophe and to let the audience feel all other motion indirectly. Gothic tragedy is normally not thus willing to limit its scope. It is keenly conscious of, and inclined to be directly concerned with, motion extended sweepingly through time and space in the theater of that active life which it first scorns and then tries more and more to understand."

[44] See *L.B.* ll. 1065–76.

[45] Aeschylus is not interested in the *particular* future of Orestes or his family. There *are* numerous references to a general future (especially the last speech of *L.B.*) and in *The Eum.* to the new era of justice in Athens which shall last "forever" ($\epsilon i\sigma\ \tau\grave{o}\ \lambda o\iota\pi\acute{o}\nu$—see *Eum.* 707–8, 851–54, 898, 907–9, 1031, 1044–45). Although this interest in the future illustrates one way in which Aeschylus' drama tends to move toward historical concern, it differs from the

As the limits of this "history" are carefully set, so is the cosmos clearly defined. Man's abode is on the earth, but there are gods and goddesses beneath the earth (*L.B.* 475; *Eum.* 115). The home of the Eumenides is beneath the ground (*Eum.* 71–73, 417, 395–96). Mortals, too, when they die, may go to the region beneath the earth, where Hades holds them in strict account (*Eum.* 273–4), and where they may be reached through supplication and the good offices of Hermes (*L.B.* 124–30). Worship rises for gods above (θεῶν . . . ὑπάτων) as well as those below, for the "gods of the heavens and of the market-place" (τῶν τ᾽ οὐρανίων τῶν τ᾽ ἀγοραίων—*Agam.* 88–90). Each divinity has its place, as the Eumenides remind Apollo (*Eum.* 574). Earth is the center and source of this cosmos. As Electra says, it is "Earth herself, that brings all things to birth, and after nurturing them, receives their increase into herself again" (καὶ Γαῖαν αὐτήν, ἣ τὰ πάντα τίκτεται,/ θρέψασά τ᾽ αὖθις τῶνδε κύμα λαμβάνει—*L.B.* 127–28).

By circumscribing the limits of the action (here he reflects the Greek tendency to think in spatial terms), Aeschylus is able to pose the problem of the two conflicting sanctions as one of a precarious balance. If space were infinite, or if time predominated in its capacity to bring forward new events, he could not do that; but where "history," and the cosmos, are limited, he can. Therefore the images in the *Oresteia*, as in *The Persians*, are primarily those of contrast: the contrast between high and low,[46] between light and dark,[47] and between new and old.[48] These images of contrast reinforce the passages where the struggle between the two moral sanctions and between right and wrong is made explicit.

The reiteration of height against depth, light against dark, new against old, suggests balance; and there are a number of important passages where this is the key idea. They occur in the middle section— *The Libation-Bearers*—where there is a balance between action and inaction, and where a deed is called for to redress a former wrong.

---

biblical and Shakespearean type in three respects: (1) it is primarily aetiological; (2) it describes a new state or condition, unchanging, with emphasis on a new resolution of forces; (3) it is not the fulfillment of prior history but a totally new state of affairs which could not have come about except for the intervention of Athena. Thus, while the *Oresteia* marks a change from one state of affairs to another, it does not do so in terms of historical continuity.

[46] See *Agam.* ll. 89, 456–74, 821–26; *L.B.* ll. 49–54, 347–48, 841–46, 963–64; *Eum.* 372–83, 1033–42.

[47] See *Agam.* ll. 20, 21, 100–1, 264–65, 281–316, 456–74, 657–58; *L.B.* ll. 535–37, 808–10, 816–18; *Eum.* ll. 692, 1021–24, 1033–42.

[48] See *Agam.* ll. 1376–80; *L.B.* 929–30, 956; *Eum.* ll. 150, 731–32, 778–79, 808–9.

ELECTRA: As judge or as avenger, meanest thou?
CHORUS: Say in plain speech "one who shall take life for life."
ELECTRA: And is this a righteous thing for me to ask of Heaven?
CHORUS: Righteous? How not? To requite an enemy evil for evil! [49]

(L.B. 118–23)

Electra prays at Agamemnon's tomb "that thy slayers may be slain" (καὶ τοὺς κτανόντας ἀντικατθανεῖν—*L.B.* 144) and the Chorus hears Justice cry,

For word of hate let word of hate be said . . . and for murderous stroke let murderous stroke be paid, while an aged precept runs, 'To him that doeth, it shall be done by!' [50]

Within the clear-cut cosmos, where the elements and moral forces balance one another, the limits of human life are equally clear. This is especially apparent wherever death is mentioned; for in spite of the fact that certain spirits of mortals may continue to live beneath the earth, death has a finality which it never possesses in the Christian world of Shakespeare. "When the dust has drained the blood of a man," says Apollo,

when he is dead, there is no standing up again. For this my Father has provided no remedies, although all other things he disposes, turning them to and fro. . . .[51]

When Agamemnon is slain, the Chorus prays that it, too, may die, may be brought its portion of "never-ending sleep" (ἀτέλευτον ὕπνον— *Agam.* 1451).

---

[49] The translation is H. W. Smyth's in the Loeb Classical Library ed. The Greek achieves the balance with the use of the words ἀνταποκτενεῖ and ἀνταμείβεσθαι.

[50] ἀντὶ μὲν ἐχθρᾶς γλώσσης ἐχθρά
γλῶσσα τελείσθω· τοὐφειλόμενον
πράσσουσα Δίκη μεγ᾽ αὐτεῖ
ἀντὶ δὲ πληγῆς φονίας φονίαν
πληγὴν τινέτω δράσαντι παθεῖν
τριγέρων μῦθος τάδε φωνεῖ. (*L.B.* 308–14)

The translation is by Smyth. Cf. *L.B.* ll. 461, 555–59.

[51] ἀνδρὸς δ᾽ ἐπειδὰν αἷμ᾽ ἀνασπάσῃ κόνις
ἅπαξ θανόντος οὔτις ἔστ᾽ ἀνάστασις.
τούτων ἐπῳδὰς οὐκ ἐποίησεν πατὴρ
οὑμός τὰ δ᾽ ἄλλα πάντ᾽ ἄνω τε καὶ κάτω
στρέφων τίθησιν . . . (*Eum.* 647–51)

One is put in mind of Hamlet's musings on the sleep of death:

> To sleep? Perchance to dream! Ay, there's the rub;
> For in that sleep of death what dreams may come,
> When we have shuffl'd off this mortal coil,
> Must give us pause.   (III.i.65–68)

Hamlet's thoughts upon this subject—as upon so many—run off into vague ends, where the limits of thought are met not by established boundaries, but by an area of mystery. For Hamlet, the region of souls after death is not a clearly defined place beneath the earth but "The undiscover'd country from whose bourn/No traveller returns" which "puzzles the will" (III.i.79–80). The very relationship to it, as to the earth also, is one of movement rather than habitation. The Queen reminded Hamlet that "all that lives must die,/Passing through nature to eternity" (I.ii.72–73). Hamlet's world is a prison "in which there are many confines, wards, and dungeons" (II.ii.251–53). Nevertheless, he says, "I could be bounded in a nutshell and count myself a king of infinite space, were it not that I have bad dreams" (260–63). In Hamlet's world, men have "thoughts beyond the reaches of [their] souls" (I.iv.56).

The difference here is not simply a matter of a Christian doctrine of immortality, a doctrine which Shakespeare's plays do not endorse distinctly. The difference lies in the fact that the movement from knowledge to event is an action which shatters the confines of rational thought and implies a world whose boundaries are indistinct. The relation, for instance, between human affairs and nature is not clear, although it is certain that they are in some way related. The references to nature are profuse throughout—the play contains more images drawn from nature than from any other single source.[52] Nature moves in sympathy with the action of the play.[53] At the same time, nature shades off into the cosmos, or the world beyond.

"The story has a cosmic background, a living frame of earth and heaven," says G. R. Elliott.[54] Some such adjective as "living" is necessary to describe the framework in which the action of *Hamlet* takes place, and this is what distinguishes it from the cosmic framework of

---

[52] See Caroline Spurgeon, *Shakespeare's Imagery*, p. 319.

[53] See especially Horatio's speech (I.ii.112–25). See Danby, *Nature*, pp. 37–38, for a discussion of Gloucester's belief in a connection between men and the occurrences of nature and Edmund's heterodox rejection of such belief (*Lear* I.ii).

[54] *Scourge and Minister*, p. 7.

the *Oresteia*. The nature imagery of *Hamlet* sets a quite different cosmic tone from the balancing and contrasting imagery of the *Oresteia*.[55] Professor Elliott, speaking of *Hamlet*, continues:

Again and again the author will make us feel the presence of the heaven above and the earth beneath, commenting with "secret influence" (Sonnet 15) upon the dramatic action: heaven with its night and day, stars and sun, gods and God, grace and Justice; earth with its stability and passion, evil and lovely growths, sickness and health, hells and purgations.[56]

This is language used to express a not-definitely-known relation between human actions and a sympathetic cosmos. The gods and goddesses of the *Oresteia* do not comment with "secret influence," they exercise their appointed powers; and while it is necessary that man should know what those powers are and how they operate, there is no intimation, as there is in *Hamlet*, that movements in nature are intertwined with human actions.

The result is that the dramatic form of *Hamlet* is as little definable in terms of the limits of action as is the situation of Hamlet himself. The strands of event which cross in it have too many interrelations and extend too far in every direction.[57] The folly in the question, "Where was Hamlet when his father died?" was not that it should have been asked, but that it should have been supposed that study of the play would reveal the answer. Questions of this nature are not irrelevant to the play, but the answers are. For *Hamlet* must be seen formally as a cluster of strands of event bound upon a center. This is because the underlying dramatic action which it imitates is one in which temporal events have precedence over rational understanding. Shakespeare has so interwoven the stories of Hamlet, Laertes, Claudius, Polonius, Ophelia, Gertrude, Fortinbras, Rosencrantz and Guildenstern, the First Player, and the state of Denmark, that all attempts at delineation of the scope of the action are humbled before the awareness of the events themselves. This is Shakespeare's fidelity to historical existence.

[55] These images predominate over the occasional *Oresteia's* images of growth, such as that, for instance, in the choric ode on Helen which compares her to a lion's whelp (*Agam.* 717–81).

[56] *Scourge and Minister*, p. 7.

[57] See Maynard Mack, "World of Hamlet," p. 504: " 'Hamlet' seems to lie closer to the illogical logic of life than Shakespeare's other tragedies. . . . If I may quote again from Mr. Tillyard, the play's very lack of a rigorous type of causal logic seems to be a part of its point." On the apparent irrelevancy of many details in *Hamlet*, such as Fortinbras and the Norwegian enterprise, see Walker, *The Time Is Out of Joint*, pp. 111–16. Cf. Kitto, *Form and Meaning in Drama*, pp. 336–37.

The reader will not suppose that one believes Shakespeare's characters to have a reality apart from the play. It is only necessary for the play to create that illusion. It is also immaterial if someone objects that much of the incident and unclear motivation in Hamlet came to Shakespeare from his inartistic sources. Surely no one is prepared to argue that Shakespeare could not have reduced the material to easily comprehensible form if he had wished.[58] Nor does it seem that anyone, apart from T. S. Eliot in the temper in which he wrote the now-famous essay on *Hamlet*, is ready to say that the play is lacking in artistic mastery. The truth is that to tie up all the loose ends and to make the motivation for all action perfectly clear would have destroyed the form in which Shakespeare was working. *Hamlet* is simply the greatest —but not the only—play of the period in which similar problems arise.

The form of *Hamlet* depends upon the tension between event and interpretation, a tension which could not be maintained if the audience felt itself possessed of a full delineation and comprehension of the events as they unfold. It was necessary to preserve the illusion of historical ambiguity in order to give the spectator a sense of participation in the tragedy of *Hamlet, Prince of Denmark.*

[58] William Empson, in an essay entitled *"Hamlet* When New," has argued that Shakespeare deliberately increased the quality of "mystery" surrounding Hamlet, a theatrical device to interest the audience in an old story. Mr. Empson does not enlighten the meaning of the play with this hypothesis.

VII

THE USES OF TIME:
THE *OEDIPUS TYRANNUS* AND *MACBETH*

Everyone agrees that Sophocles' *Oedipus Tyrannus* and Shakespeare's *Macbeth* are masterpieces of dramatic construction. It seems not to have been noticed, however, that one thing these two plays hold in common as a corollary to their admirable form is an acute awareness of the problem of dramatic time.

It would be possible in the present comparison of the two plays to deal with a number of the same problems which arose in the preceding chapter. They exhibit the same contrasting relationships between knowledge and event as do *Hamlet* and the *Oresteia*. There is the same difference between externalized action in the Greek and internalized action in Shakespeare. There is in Sophocles the same sense of the limits of action as was found in Aeschylus, and the same boundlessness in the Shakespearean world.[1] All of these topics in the *Oedipus Tyrannus* and *Macbeth*, however, are subordinate to the question of time, which is a matter of unique importance in these works. The procedure, therefore, will be to describe first the treatment and meaning of time in *Macbeth*, then in the *Oedipus Tyrannus*, and thereafter to compare the two.

Macbeth

In *Macbeth* there are three kinds of time: (1) time measured by clock, calendar, and the movement of sun, moon, and stars, which for the sake of convenience we may call "chronological time"; (2) an order of time which overarches the action of the entire play and which may

---

[1] I am indebted to Professor S. F. Johnson for pointing out the difference between size and scope, as applied to *Macbeth*. Although *Macbeth* is one of Shakespeare's shortest plays, it makes an impression of almost limitless scope.

be called "providential time"; and (3) a time scheme, or an understanding of time, belonging to Macbeth, which may be called "Macbeth's time."

Most of the techniques by means of which Shakespeare handles chronological time have been mentioned in Chapter V, but they may be noted here again because it is necessary to see the close relation in *Macbeth* between chronological time and the other levels of meaning which time achieves.

One such technique is that of compression, or foreshortening. Time in the original historical material is drastically reduced. For instance, whereas in Hollinshed the events depicted in the play spanned seventeen years, in Shakespeare they last about ten weeks.[2] This shortening not only assisted the imaginative unity, but it also involved eliminating some ten years of good rule by Macbeth between the murder of Duncan and that of Banquo,[3] a change which provided a dramatic value of its own.

Another form of compression of time appears in the difference between the time which actually elapses on stage during performance of a given scene and that which the audience is asked to suppose has elapsed. The technique has been described by Mable Buland as follows:

Shakespeare always felt at liberty to treat ten minutes of stage-action as representing a whole night. . . . A notable example of this presentation of time occurs in the great murder-scene in *Macbeth*. Banquo leaves Macbeth a little after midnight, Macbeth speaks a thirty-line soliloquy, the ringing of a bell summons him to his task, some twenty minutes full of horrors follow, when lo! a knocking is heard, and it is found to be already morning; Macduff enters, scolding the drowsy porter for having overslept, and apologizing for having almost slipped his hour.[4]

In *Macbeth*, Shakespeare also makes use of both a fast and a slow time scheme, woven together, much as he had done in *Richard III*. In Miss Buland's words:

The plot of Macbeth moves very rapidly; the banquet-scene is evidently part of the coronation-feast; Macbeth goes to the witches betimes the following morning, and sends at once to have Macduff's family killed; Macduff leaves England about the time of the banquet, before any subjects have suffered under Macbeth, and Ross brings him the first word of his wife's death.

---

[2] *Macbeth*, ed. by John Dover Wilson, p. xiii.
[3] *Macbeth*, ed. by Kenneth Muir, p. xliv.   [4] *Elizabethan Drama*, p. 16.

Yet the last part of the play is full of references to the lapse of a long period of time: Malcolm has to be informed of the misfortunes of his country, and Macduff talks as if Macbeth had misruled for years.[5]

As usual, the reason for the double time scheme is that the sense of historical reality demands the long one, while the dramatic construction, which is a part of the interpretation of the historical action, demands rapidity.

The play contains a very large number of references to chronological time; that is, to the day, the night, or the hour. There is no point in citing all of them, but one example may serve to show the deliberateness with which the hour is sometimes established. Act I, scene vii, in which the resolution to commit the murder of Duncan is made firm, takes place at supper time. The next scene (II.i) must establish that the hour has come for all to be retired, a matter accomplished in four lines:

> BAN. How goest the night, boy?
> FLE. The moon is down; I have not heard the clock.
> BAN. And she goes down at twelve.
> FLE.   I take 't, 'tis later, sir.
> BAN. Hold, take my sword. There's husbandry in heaven:
>   Their candles are all out.[6]   (II.i.1–4)

A similar exactness precedes the murder of Banquo, illustrated in the lines wherein Banquo takes leave of Macbeth before the banquet (the time words are italicized):

> MACB.   *Hie* you to horse; adieu,
>   *Till* you return at *night*. Goes Fleance with you?
> BAN. Ay, my good lord. Our *time* does call upon's.
> MACB. I wish your horses *swift* and sure of foot;
>   And so I do commend you to their backs.
>   Farewell.   (*Exit Banquo*)
>   Let every man be master of his *time*
>   *Till seven at night*. To make society
>   The sweeter welcome we will keep ourself
>   *Till supper-time* alone; *while then*, God be with you!
>   (III.i.34–44)

---

[5] *Ibid.*, p. 123. The passages to which Miss Buland refers which suggest a long time-scheme are Act IV, scene iii, lines 4–8, 170; Act V, scene iii, line 22; and Act III, scene iv.

[6] Note how the theme of time is woven into that of evil. These lines inform us that (1) it is past midnight; (2) that is the time when the stars usually shine; (3) the stars are not shining. This is an indirect use of the idea of the untimeliness of evil actions.

In addition to such specific references to time (of which there are many) the play contains a very great number of lines which give merely a sense of time, inducing in the spectator a kind of temporal anxiety. For instance, there is such a large number of speeches employing the words "when," "yet," and "until" that the effect is striking. As an example, the opening lines of the play:

> 1. WITCH.   When shall we three meet again
>   In thunder, lightning, or in rain?
> 2. WITCH.   When the hurlyburly's done,
>   When the battle's lost and won.

Throughout the play, adverbs of time are important because the weird sisters, at the beginning, put the future into our minds. In scene iv, Macbeth, having learned that two of the prophecies are true, talks with himself about the third:

>   Present fears
> Are less than horrible imaginings.
> My thought, whose murder yet is but fantastical,
> Shakes so my single state of man that function
> Is smother'd in surmise. . . .   (137–41)

At the end of the scene he invites Banquo to speak with him "at more time" regarding what has transpired, and arouses our expectations with the concluding phrase, "Till then, enough" (156).

In the scene in which Lady Macbeth induces her husband to "bend up/Each corporal agent to this terrible feat" (I.vii), she pin-points the action with reiterated "whens."

> When you durst do it, then you were a man.   (49)
>
> When Duncan is asleep . . .   (61)
>
>   When in swinish sleep
> Their drenched natures lie . . .   (67–68)
>
> When we have marked with blood these sleepy two . . .   (75)

In the next scene, which is immediately prior to the murder, the bloody "when" appears again. Macbeth tells the servant, "Go bid thy mistress, when my drink is ready/She strike upon the bell" (II.i.31–32). And in the following scene, the murder done, Shakespeare reaps in lines that crackle with excitement the harvest of expectation he has thus planted:

MACB.   I have done the deed. Didst thou not hear a noise?
LADY M.   I heard the owl scream and the crickets cry. Did not you
         speak?
MACB.   When?
LADY M.   Now.
MACB.   As I descended?
LADY M.   Ay.   (ii.15–18)

Before the murder of Banquo there are several speeches which
dwell upon the word "till" (see above), typical of which is Macbeth's
word to Lady Macbeth: "Be innocent of the knowledge, dearest
chuck,/Till thou applaud the deed" (III.ii.45–46). However, the
most outstanding use of this word comes in connection with the final
catastrophe of the play, which is first foreshadowed in the words of
the Third Apparition (IV.i.92–94):

> Macbeth shall never vanquish'd be until
> Great Birnam wood to high Dunsinane hill
> Shall come against him.

Macbeth is certain "That will never be," and repeats to himself the
"sweet bodements":

> Rebellion's head, rise never till the wood
> Of Birnam rise, and our high-plac'd Macbeth
> Shall live the lease of nature, pay his breath
> To time and mortal custom.   (97–100)

In the fifth act, "till" is reiterated very frequently, so that the spectator
absorbs the notion of time coming to its fulfillment:

> Till Birnam wood remove to Dunsinane
> I cannot taint with fear.   (V.iii.2–3)

MACB.   I'll fight till from my bones my flesh be hack'd.
         Give me my armour.
SEY.   'Tis not needed yet.   (32–33)

MACB.   I will not be afraid of death and bane,
         Till Birnam forest come to Dunsinane.   (59–60)

MACB.   Here let them lie
       Till famine and the ague eat them up.   (v.3–4)

When the Messenger brings word that he has seen a moving grove,
Macbeth threatens to hang him upon a tree "Till famine cling thee"

(vi.40). But of course the jig is up, and Macbeth knows it. The "till" and the "now" meet:

> Fear not, till Birnam wood
> Do come to Dunsinane; and now a wood
> Comes toward Dunsinane.   (44–46)

It is not only in the major events that this type of temporal speech appears. Malcolm, in the scene where he tries the virtue of Macduff, says of himself that he has

> All the particulars of vice so grafted
> That, when they shall be open'd, black Macbeth
> Will seem as pure as snow. . . .   (IV.iii.51–53)

Of Siward's son, it is said,

> He only liv'd but till he was a man;
> The which no sooner had his prowess confirm'd
> In the unshrinking station where he fought,
> But like a man he died.   (V.vii.40–43)

These lines have been quoted to show something of the technique by which Shakespeare plants in the spectator a feeling of time, quite apart from the many lines which mention time directly.

In *Macbeth*, Shakespeare, as usual, is careful in his "imitation" of chronological time. He is not slavish to detail,[7] but he strives for an effect in which the feeling of being in a real world of time is extremely important.[8] Shakespeare's adroit compression of time, his use of a fast and slow scheme of double-time, his concrete references to passing time, and the temporal note diffused throughout the speeches, all locate the audience in a temporal world and prepare it to accept time as a meaningful reality upon which rests much of the imaginative structure of the play.

Connected with chronological time in *Macbeth*, but not equated with it, is providential time, which is to say, time as an expression of social and universal righteousness. Many critics have spoken of the background of order in this play. "'Macbeth' is a play about a man

---

[7] See Buland's discussion (*Elizabethan Drama*, p. 124) of Act III, scene iv, in which "an exact report is given of events which have not then occurred."

[8] I am afraid Maurice Morgann "Essay on the Dramatic Character of Sir John Falstaff" was as misled by Macbeth as by Falstaff. He wrote, "we, the fools of amazement, are insensible to the shifting of place and the lapse of time, and till the curtain drops, never once wake to the truth of things, or recognize the laws of existence."

who violates the moral order, and is punished for it," Robert Pack has written; [9] Roy Walker has suggested that, "If *Hamlet* is a study of moral man in an immoral society, *Macbeth* is a study of immoral man in a moral universe." [10]

The moral order of *Macbeth* is expressed by Shakespeare in terms of a time against which Macbeth rebels. The conception is very similar to that already discussed in *Richard III* (Chapter V), a play which in more than one respect anticipated *Macbeth*.[11] In the later play, however, the idea of a providential time is made more explicit; it is related to the inner consciousness of Macbeth himself in a way which today might be called existential; it is plumbed to its poetic depth.

How does Shakespeare communicate the idea of a providential time? In the first place, he assumes an objective, temporal order, distinguished on the one hand from mere chronology and on the other hand from anyone's subjectivity. Early in the play, Duncan sets the order of historical succession:

> Sons, kinsmen, thanes,
> And you whose places are the nearest, know
> We will establish our estate upon
> Our eldest, Malcolm, whom we name hereafter
> The Prince of Cumberland; which honor must
> Not unaccompanied invest him only,
> But signs of nobleness, like stars, shall shine
> On all deservers.   (I.iv.35–42)

[9] "Macbeth: The Anatomy of Loss," (p. 536).

[10] *The Time is Free*, p. 218. A. C. Bradley, in his chapter, "The Substance of Tragedy," in *Shakespearean Tragedy*, speaks of the "evil that violently disturbs the order of the world" (34), which, I think, puts us first in mind of *Macbeth*. Later he speaks of the presence of an order similar to Providence in *Macbeth* as well as *Hamlet* (172–73).

[11] Similarities between *Richard III* and *Macbeth* have been noted by many. Thomas Whateley compared and contrasted the two royal villains in *Remarks on Some of the Characters of Shakespeare*, which drew in rebuttal a defense of Macbeth's courage from John Phillip Kemble: *Macbeth and King Richard the Third*. Bradley (*Shakespearean Tragedy*) has suggested a number of parallels, notably the use of irony, the influence of Seneca, and the similarity of Macduff's son to the young Duke of York (pp. 338, 390, 395). Tillyard (*Shakespeare's History Plays*, p. 316), has noted further the similarity of the murder of Macduff's children to the slaying of the princes in the tower, the resemblance between Malcolm and the Earl of Richmond, and the fact that in both plays "the body politic asserts itself against the monstrous individual." Professor S. F. Johnson has noted that Herod is an archetype for both Richard and Macbeth (see in this book, Chap. V, p. 100, and pp. 153–154, n.30). These similarities are interesting as showing how Shakespeare, late in his career ,was able to fuse history and tragedy. Says Professor Tillyard: "In *Macbeth*, Shakespeare settled the adjustment of the political man of action to the other parts of the tragic world" (p. 321).

Here is the proper relationship of past and future, the historical succession guaranteeing order a passage through the present into what comes "hereafter." To such historical order, Macbeth is immediately thrown into opposition:

> MACB. *(Aside)* The Prince of Cumberland! That is a step
> On which I must fall down, or else o'erleap,
> For in my way it lies.[12]   (48–50)

The prophecies of the weird sisters also contribute to an idea of objective time. They provide a sense of destiny, or an order in future events already set. The objectivity of the time they represent would, of course, evaporate if it were admitted that the weird sisters are primarily a symbol of Macbeth's imagination. That they are not.[13] They appear to the audience before they are seen by Macbeth, so that the spectator naturally takes them to have an existence apart from Macbeth.[14] The sisters therefore stand for a knowledge of the future, and the accuracy of their knowledge is confirmed in the unfolding events of the play.[15] After seeing them, the audience harbors a conception of what is *supposed* to happen, which it continually plays off against what it sees taking place.

The weird sisters' first speeches to Macbeth (I.iii) imply a fulfillment of time. "Glamis," "Cawdor," and "King" are not only names designating rank in the Scottish hierarchy, they are also, in this case, expressions of past, present, and future; Macbeth has been thane of Glamis, he this day becomes thane of Cawdor, and he shall "be

[12] Cf. "We'd jump the life to come" (I.vii.7) and "Vaulting ambition, which o'erleaps itself" (27).

[13] Coleridge seemed to imply the subjectivity of the witches, as apparitions, when he spoke of Macbeth's "superstition" and referred to the sisters as "the imaginative disconnected from the good" (*Lectures and Notes on Shakespere* pp. 369–71). Furness (*Variorum Macbeth*, p. 8) quotes Snider: "*It lies in the character of Banquo and Macbeth to see such specters.*" Macbeth, says Snider, is "controlled and victimized by the imagination, which sets up its shapes as actual." Cf. Pack ("Macbeth" p. 538): "they should be regarded as objectifications of Macbeth's imagination." N. Paul, *The Royal Play of Macbeth*, pp. 61–66, discusses the major views regarding the witches' reality. He thinks that Shakespeare thought of them as imaginary but left it open for others to believe they were women practicing black arts. For a contrary view, see Farnham, *Shakespeare's Tragic Frontier*, pp. 99–104.

[14] To reverse that assumption, to show the thing imagined before the one imagining it has appeared, would amount to a stunning theatrical *tour de force* in the first scene, of a kind which I believe no one has suggested.

[15] The weird sisters' relation to future time is unaffected by the question of demonology. It is enough that some figure a bit out of the ordinary describes future events. Unless later disabused of the notion, the audience will take the statement as oracular and test the succeeding events by it.

King hereafter" (I.iii.50). Banquo is amazed that the sisters seem able to

> Look into the seeds of time,
> And say which grain will grow and which will not.   (58–59)

But when Macbeth inquires after the source of their knowledge,

> . Say from whence
> You owe this strange intelligence, or why
> Upon this blasted heath you stop our way
> With such prophetic greeting,   (75–78)

they guard their secret by vanishing.

In Macbeth's second meeting with the weird sisters the temporal note is struck yet more distinctly. Macbeth is given assurance of victory until a certain event ("until/Great Birnam wood to high Dunsinane hill/Shall come against him"—IV.i.92–94). Although he does not know it, the moment of his defeat is set.[16] It is noteworthy that he is not given a certain number of days, but rather he is vouchsafed power until certain things shall come to pass. He is actually given a lease which will expire very shortly, while he confidently interprets it to be "the lease of nature" (99). In this scene also there is a return to the theme of historical continuity. The time which the weird sisters proclaim is partner to the time which Duncan had represented in establishing the historical succession upon his son.[17] The show of eight kings, which is set before Macbeth upon his own insistence to know the future of Banquo's line, implies a continuation of the historical succession through Banquo's descendants as far as the mind can reach:

> What, will the line stretch out to th' crack of doom?
> Another yet! A seventh! I'll see no more.
> And yet the eighth appears, who bears a glass
> Which shows me many more.   (117–20)

This vision of the ordering of the future, bringing the constituted authority in a straight line to Shakespeare's new monarch, James I,[18]

---

[16] "Time cowers like a wild beast which watches the movements of its prey and has only to stretch forth its claws at its own appointed hour." Henri Fluchère, *Shakespeare and the Elizabethans*, p. 104.

[17] J. Dover Wilson reminds us of the ancient connection between prophecy and historical succession: "all sound genealogical tales from the Book of Samuel downwards have opened with prophecy" (Intro. to *Macbeth*, p. xi). The connection between prophecy and historical succession was no whim of Shakespeare's, but came to him firmly rooted in the story.

[18] See H. N. Paul (*Royal Play of Macbeth*, pp. 3, 178–82). Mr. Paul has shown that the play was first performed before James I and Christian IV of Denmark on August 7, 1606, at Hampton Court.

and on to the rim of time, is a step which Macbeth cannot o'erleap. It is a "horrible sight" (122) and because of it Macbeth damns the time in which he stands: "Let this pernicious hour/Stand aye accursed in the calendar!" (133–34).

It is possible to see the full reality of providential time only when Macbeth's time is thrown into relief against it. More than one critic has noticed that a change takes place in Macbeth's understanding and experience of time. Murry sees the beginning of this change at the murder of Duncan.[19] The words of Macbeth to Lennox and Ross are ironically true:

> Had I but died an hour before this chance,
> I had liv'd a blessed time: for from this instant
> There's nothing serious in mortality.   (II.iii.95–97)

Says Murry, "His 'blessed time' is over: now the accursed time begins. There is a change in the nature of Time as he experiences it." Shakespeare now

clashes paradox against paradox to open the gulf between Macbeth's new condition of being and his former state. . . . He has murdered Sleep that is "the death of each day's life"—that daily death of Time which makes Time human. He has murdered that.[20]

Macbeth now tries

to shatter the frame of things . . . to wrench the pin of human time out of the nave of the universe; to annihilate the distinction between Has Been and Is: to make all Time like his own.[21]

Mr. Murry asserts that by artful reiteration of Macbeth's phrase "the time has been" (III.iv.78–79 and V.v.9–10), Shakespeare has enforced upon the imagination "Macbeth's dreadful experience of a change in the nature of time, a bottomless gulf dividing a blessed time from an accursed time, human time from inhuman time." [22]

Roy Walker has concurred with the Murry analysis, which indeed is remarkably sensitive, but he has added that what Murry calls "human time" is "essentially superhuman time." [23] In that, Mr. Walker is correct, for, as Mr. Murry himself has shown, the time which Macbeth is at odds with is one which is central to the universe, involved in "the frame of things," and by that token it transcends the

---

[19] *Shakespeare*, p. 332. The chapter on *Macbeth* is called, "The Time Has Been."
[20] *Ibid.*, pp. 332–33.   [21] *Ibid.*, pp. 333–34.
[22] *Ibid.*, p. 334.   [23] *The Time Is Free*, p. ix.

merely human. Mr. Walker also has noticed that at the end of the play, the time which stands over against Macbeth is resumed, expressed as he says, "by floods of daylight and summed in Macduff's words: 'The time is free.'" [24]

Stephen Spender has said that Macbeth knows three times: before Duncan's murder, during its enactment, and afterward.[25] Macbeth would like to keep these three times separate, but he cannot. This produces a chaos of time, symbolized by the fact that Macbeth cannot put an "Amen" to the prayer of Duncan's servants, nor indeed to anything.

There is no end within the control of Macbeth. In the fourth act, we even have a feeling that everything has stopped. The play seems to spread out, burning up and destroying a wider and wider area, without moving forward. "Tomorrow, and tomorrow, and tomorrow" is not merely the speech of a disillusioned tyrant destroyed by the horror which he has himself created; it has a profound irony, coming from Macbeth's mouth, because he of all people ought to have been able to make to-morrow different from to-day and yesterday. But all his violence has done is to create a deathly sameness.[26]

At the end of the play, "the emphasis of Malcolm is on time and measure and place, which he is restoring." [27]

There are, no doubt, many ways to describe the sense of time in the play; but the interesting thing is that each of the foregoing critics perceives a difference between what Macbeth does, or tries to do, with time and what he is ultimately allowed to do with it. "It was time," says Mr. Spender, "which, even more than in *Hamlet*, had got out of joint in *Macbeth*"; [28] and of course a time out of joint implies a prior state in which time is in joint.

However expressed, it is clear that Macbeth opposes a more ultimate time than his own. He would "let the frame of things disjoint" (III.ii.16); he would "jump the life to come" (I.vii.6); he murders sleep, that daily symbol of man's finitude in time; he destroys the meaning of tomorrow and tomorrow, the ironic consequence of his attempt to control the future.[29]

In his attempt to gain control over the future (like Richard III, he

[24] *The Time is Free*, p. ix.   [25] "Time, Violence, and Macbeth," p. 121.
[26] *Ibid.*, pp. 124–25.   [27] *Ibid.*, p. 125.   [28] *Ibid.*, p. 125.
[29] Cleanth Brooks (*The Well Wrought Urn*, pp. 41 ff.) has pointed out that Macbeth goes back to the weird sisters to force a control upon the future, which, because they already know it, cannot be forced. Professor Brooks has pointed out the significance of the children and images of babes as symbols of the future in this play.

wants to insure not only his own future but that of his heirs as well [30]—
cf. *Macbeth* IV.i.100–3 with *Richard III* IV.ii.5–20), Macbeth reveals that his experience of time is compounded of memory and anticipation. In order to gain control of the future, to o'erleap the steps
which lie in his way, he must create memories. Memories, the past
haunting the present as guilt, reduce Lady Macbeth to her pitiful end.
Her "What's done is done" of Act III (ii.12) later becomes, "What's
done cannot be undone" (V.i.76). It is as a bulwark against memories
that Macbeth erects his doctrine of the meaninglessness of life.

Much as he would like, Macbeth cannot separate the present from
the past and the future. By the act of murder he has made his own
history, and the rest of the play is the account of the fulfillment of that
history, ultimately self-defeating. His sin (skillfully portrayed by
Shakespeare as a combination of will and temptation) blinds him to the
meaning of providential time, while it does not remove him from subordination to it, nor does it remove him from his own inner historical
experience. He therefore continues, to the end, as R. M. Frye has
pointed out, to make use of biblical images of history and human finitude, although entirely without the biblical awareness of grace.[31] The
petty pace creeps in "To the last syllable of recorded time" (V.v.21),
a phrase which not only recalls Macbeth's earlier vision of the line
which stretches out "to the crack of doom," but which also reflects
biblical eschatology. This picture of the mortality of time is followed
by that of man's mortality, sketched in four images: the brief candle, the
walking shadow, the strutting and fretting upon the stage, and the tale
which is told, each of which has biblical parallels.[32] Even in his final
despair, therefore, Macbeth is made to speak of an order of time which
he has not been able to destroy, although that had been his hope when
he and his Lady stood in what proved to be a completely decisive
moment upon the "bank and shoal of time" (I.vii.7).

Oedipus Tyrannus

In *Macbeth* it is possible to speak of three kinds of time—chronological, providential, and that of Macbeth; in the *Oedipus Tyrannus*

---

[30] Macbeth is like Richard also in that, Herod-like, he resorts to the slaughter of children.
[31] See Roland M. Frye, " 'Out, out, brief candle' and the Jacobean Understanding," pp.
143–45. The same issue of *Notes and Queries*, pp. 142–43, includes an article by Paul N.
Siegel, "Echoes of the Bible Story in Macbeth," in which parallels are shown between
Macbeth and Adam, Judas, and Lucifer, between Lady Macbeth and Eve, and between
Duncan and the figure of Christ. A. C. Bradley noticed the strong religious tone in the play.
[32] See Frye, "Brief Candle."

there are only two, and perhaps even these two are one. There is, to begin with, chronological time, the time of the play's action: roughly, all the incidents from Laius' hearing of the oracle to Oedipus' exile from Thebes, including the narration of events which happened, as we say, before the play began. In addition, time also appears in the *Oedipus Tyrannus* as a deliberate, schematic arrangement of past and present. As far as the question of time goes, this is an advance over Aeschylus. It is yet a long way from the kind of historical consciousness which Shakespeare represents, but it is a more subtle mixing of action with time than seems to have been imagined before, and demonstrates the fact that as the drama becomes better able to depict character and situation, it also integrates time more closely into the heart of its conception.[33]

Sophocles' management of chronological time is extremely interesting. The Unity of Time is clear and believable. There can be no question but that Sophocles gave much thought to bringing his material within the compass of a short period which he could represent without a time lapse. Miss Buland notes two examples of what she calls "condensation of time": the herdsman, presumably summoned after l. 861, enters a few minutes later at l. 1119, although he must be imagined to have come from some distance away in the mountains; similarly, only a few minutes after Creon's return from an absence of several days, Oedipus says he has already twice sent for Teiresias at the suggestion of Creon.[34] Otherwise, the representation of time is quite realistic, and the action may be presumed to take place within a very few hours. For this reason, there is no double time scheme in the sense of a fast and a slow impression of time existing side by side, as in *Macbeth*.

The question of time in the *Oedipus Tyrannus* is directly related to that of structure. Sophocles actually is manipulating two segments of chronological time: the day of the action, and the events leading up to that day. The latter cover many years. The method of presentation he adopts is rather like putting a big box inside a little one. Within the narrative of one day's activity there is contained a complete story which begins before the hero's birth. Formally, therefore, the brief

---

[33] If something is gained in Sophocles over Aeschylus, something also is lost, namely, the awesome conceptions of justice which soar above the world of time. After Aeschylus, the drama has to wait for Shakespeare before the eternal again appears on stage so magnificently. But in Shakespeare the way to eternity lay through time.

[34] Buland, *Elizabethan Drama*, p. 189.

present is made to envelop the long past. This fact may be demonstrated from the following plot-outline of the play:

Incidents of the Plot	Structural Section
a. Introduction: we learn of the plague, the remedy prescribed by the oracle, and therefore the problem confronting Oedipus and Thebes.	Prologue
b. The *agon* with Teiresias, in which the play's ending is revealed.	Episode 1
c. Oedipus is thrown off the track by his suspicion of Creon.	Episode 2
d. Oedipus learns he probably slew Laius.	Episode 3
e. Jocasta tells of exposing her infant son.	Episode 3
f. Oedipus tells how and why he left Corinth, to avoid the prediction of the oracle.	Episode 3
g. The Corinthian Messenger brings the information that Oedipus is not Polybus' son.	Episode 4
h. The Herdsman brings the knowledge that Oedipus was the infant exposed by Jocasta.	Episode 5
i. Jocasta hangs herself.	Episode 6
j. Oedipus blinds himself.	Episode 6
k. Lament. Oedipus is visited by his children and asks for exile.	Ode 7 and Episode 7

Generally speaking, the story is told backward. The incidents are not exactly in the reverse of chronological order, being varied somewhat to avoid triteness, but on the whole that is the movement, beginning at the very end of Oedipus' career and rising to the climax when the facts of his infancy are disclosed.

In the outline given, items *d*, *e*, *f*, *g*, and *h* describe events of the past. They fall in the exact center of the list: three items precede them and three come after, while the lengthy expository section in the Prologue is balanced by the long lament and conclusion in the final Commos and Episode. Sophocles has imbedded the material of the past in the center of a series of events taking place in the present. Furthermore, the deeper the play probes into the past, the more violent the present becomes, as if to know the past were to shake the foundations of the present—a fact which Jocasta senses when she warns Oedipus not to persevere in his inquiries.

Thus the formal structure of the play leads into the more fundamental question of the schematic and problematic arrangement of past and present. On the one hand, past and present in the *Oedipus Tyran-*

nus seem two completely different things, quite insulated from each other. Oedipus arrived in Thebes and ascended its throne essentially as a man without a past. He became king by no right of succession but because he answered the riddle of the Sphinx. The play reads as if there has been no communication between Oedipus and Corinth since the day he left there. No more is Jocasta connected with the past, for there are no lines which emphasize the fact that she is older than Oedipus, nor is her role, at first, primarily that of the widow of Laius.

On the other hand, the completed play reveals that past and present are inextricably bound.[35] In fact, as the play moves forward we witness the past swallowing up the present, and finally achieving complete victory over it. In terms of formal structure, as we saw, the present contained the past; but in terms of meaning, the past contains the present. Here lies the basis of the play's irony. Professor Kitto has observed that "the continuous dramatic irony" in the *Oedipus Tyrannus* "seems overdone, if it is regarded as only a dramatic effect." [36] The very substance of the play is ironic: things as they appear on the surface are the exact opposite of what they are in truth, and nowhere is the opposition more striking than in the apparent and real relations between past and present time.

In either case, however, on either side of the time-irony, Sophocles is dealing with time as a quantitative matter or state. This is made evident through the very fact that he can treat past and present so schematically. For whether the past contains the present or the present contains the past there is, in this view, a hiatus between them. They are not related organically, but conceptually. It is not Oedipus as he develops who interests us, for indeed we are not shown his development. We are given his state of happiness in the beginning of the play, his past actions which were an affront to the moral law, and his final state of woe. The bridges, the points of decision, are conspicuously absent. Therefore it is clear that Sophocles has not given us anything which we could call Oedipus' history; [37] for the hallmark of history is

---

[35] "By starting the play at the end of the story, and showing on-stage only the last crucial episode in Oedipus' life, the past and present action of the protagonist are revealed together; and, in each other's light, are at last felt as one." (Francis Fergusson, *Idea of a Theater*, p. 29.)

[36] Kitto, *Greek Tragedy*, p. 144.

[37] Contrast Oedipus with this description of *Macbeth* which Wilson (*Macbeth*, p. xlvi) is able to give: *Macbeth* shows "the 'process' of the hero's 'change,' as Shakespeare first conceived it, which was no other than the history of a human soul on its way to Hell."

continuity and development, whereas the basis of the highly ironic *Oedipus Tyrannus* is precisely the discontinuity of time.

There is another way in which Sophocles' interest in time moves away from history rather than toward it. In Sophocles' mind there is a linkage between time and law. The moral law, which in principle is timeless,[38] works itself out in human affairs in the course of time. This means that Sophocles can represent time as an agent of law. Wilhelm Schmid, *Geschichte der griechischen Literatur*, has described the Sophoclean view of time in this manner:

Chronos erscheint bald wie Helios als πάνθ' ὁρῶν (vgl. O.R. 1213, O.C. 1454) καὶ πάντ' ἀκούων und darum auch alles (*fr.* 301), besonders das Recht (O.R. 614) aus Licht brigend (p. 462, n. 22).

Schmid says that Sophocles personifies time, a fact Professor Greene has amplified in his study of *Moira*, where he speaks of "the almost mystical way in which Sophocles regards *Chronos* and *Tyche*." He continues:

For Sophocles time (χρόνος) is not merely the duration of successive events; it is frequently conceived of as almighty (παγκρατής), alive and active and personal, with moral powers. Time "beholds all things" (O.C. 1453 f); it "soothes" (El. 179) or "confounds" and "destroys" (O.C. 609 συγχεῖ; Ai. 713 μαραίνει; El. 780 προστατῶν). The vicissitudes of nature's cycle and of man's life are alike both made and marred by time. So, too, the children of time, the months and the nights and the days preside over men's affairs, and mighty is the opportune moment (καιρός) (p. 142).

Later, commenting on the *Oedipus Tyrannus* l. 1212, he observes, "Time, like a judge, brings all things to trial and sentence." [39]

The important point here is the total supremacy and impartiality of time: all-seeing, all-hearing, all-powerful, making and marring. *Chronos* is one infallible, unbending aspect of the moral order which Sophocles posits behind the tragic experience of Oedipus.[40] Its power

---

[38] See the *Oedipus Tyrannus*, pp. 865 ff.

[39] Greene, *Moira*, p. 158.

[40] I cannot agree with Cedric Whitman (*Sophocles: A Study of Heroic Humanism*) that in the last plays of Sophocles "time enters into the fate of men as a mysterious and healing element; suffering is still intense, but time and the faithful act of living bring salvation" (p. 151). Professor Whitman applies this to the *Oedipus Colonus* and tries to show that Oedipus is saved through "endurance." Not at all. Oedipus is "saved," if one is to call it that (apotheosized would be better), through the mysterious connection between what is taboo and what is holy. His relation to law as "holy offender" is the key point, not his relation to time as duration.

and impartiality is a corollary of the power and impartiality of the laws to which man is subject. "Oedipus," says Professor Kitto,

is blasted as a man may be who inadvertently interferes with the natural flow of electricity. . . . Every detail in the *Tyrannus* is contrived in order to enforce Sophocles' faith in this underlying *logos*; that is the reason why it is true to say that the perfection of its form implies a world-order. Whether or not it is beneficent, Sophocles does not say.[41]

One must conclude, therefore, that the thought which Sophocles has given to the problem of time has not led him into anything that could be called historical understanding. Time is either a schematic, ironic compartmentalization of past and present, as manifest in the structure of the *Oedipus Tyrannus*; or, conceived of as duration, it is the moral eye which brings all things to light, to growth, to destruction. "For Sophocles," says David Grene,

the myth was the treatment of the generic aspect of human dilemmas. What he made of the myth in his plays was neither history nor the kind of dramatic creation represented by *Hamlet* or *Macbeth*. Not history, for in no sense is the uniqueness of the event or the uniqueness of the character important. . . .[42]

Sophocles' time is still the measure of change, although the change he is interested in is that which takes place according to law.

The Two Forms

The relation of time and form in *Macbeth* and the *Oedipus Tyrannus* will be clarified through a comparison of what has been said about each of the plays.

In both works, time appears as "fact" and as "meaning." In *Macbeth*, chronological time is simply time on the level of positive fact, but providential time and the time of Macbeth refer to time as it has taken on a meaning and therefore is capable of being used metaphorically. In the *Oedipus Tyrannus* there is also the presentation of chronological time, or time as "fact," but the structural arrangement of past and present is Sophocles' expression of the meaning of time.

The manner in which chronological time is imitated is very different in the two plays. The primary difference comes from the fact that, as we have seen, Sophocles begins his play at the end of the narrative, whereas Shakespeare begins at the beginning. In the *Oedipus Tyrannus*

[41] Kitto, *Greek Tragedy*, pp. 148–49.
[42] *Sophocles: Oedipus the King, Oedipus at Colonus, Antigone*, p. 7.

we are, for the most part, told what *did* happen. In using this method Sophocles has followed conventional Greek practice. The Chorus tells us about the plague which has come; Oedipus tells us about having sent Creon to consult the oracle; Jocasta tells about how Laius was killed and about exposing her infant son; Oedipus tells how he left Corinth; the Messenger tells how the infant Oedipus came to Corinth; the Herdsman tells about what he did with the infant who was given him and from whence he got it; the Second Messenger tells what Jocasta and Oedipus have done, etc. There is, of course, also present action, but it is never seen apart from an ironic relation to time past.

In *Macbeth*, on the other hand, we are presented directly with what *is* happening, the scene shifting from place to place and hour to hour as each new event occurs with the result that we are made to *feel* time as it unfolds. Shakespeare has the keenest sense of time as a mode of experience, and he is able to carry the audience along over a progression of time in such a way that when the spectator eventually stops to look back he is surprised at the varied terrain over which he has passed.

> I am in blood
> Stepp'd in so far, that, should I wade no more,
> Returning were as tedious as go o'er.   (III.iv.137)

This ability to present the *feel* of time passing is made possible by the "romantic" form in which Shakespeare wrote. The "classical" form of the Greek theater, which by and large strove to confine itself to one place and one time, could not present the sensation of passing time so well; and therefore it had to deal with time as concept if it was to do much with it at all. In a play such as *Macbeth*, where he is thinking consciously about time, Shakespeare presents us with a stream of metaphors:

> If you can look into the seeds of time   (I.iii.58)
>
> To beguile the time
> Look like the time.   (I.v.64–65)
>
> But here, upon this bank and shoal of time . . .   (I.vii.6)
>
> Away, and mock the time with fairest show.   (V.ii.81)
>
> The very stones grate of my whereabout
> And take the present horror from the time,
> Which now suits with it.   (II.i.58–60)

I will advise you where to plant yourselves,
Acquaint you with the perfect spy o' th' time,
The moment on't.   (III.i.129–31)

Only it spoils the pleasure of the time.   (III.iv.98)

> pay his breath
To time and mortal custom.   (IV.i.99–100)

Time, thou anticipat'st my dread exploits.   (IV.i.144)

She should have died hereafter;
There would have been a time for such a word. (V.v.17–18)

To the last syllable of recorded time.   (21)

And live to be the show and gaze o' th' time!   (V.viii.24)

> Behold where stands
Th' usurper's cursed head. The time is free.   (V.viii.25)

It is all the more interesting that these metaphors exist on so many different levels. "To beguile the time/Look like the time" is on the colloquial level, time meaning simply "present society." "The seeds of time" is Shakespeare's own poetic creation.

Sophocles has very few metaphors of time. On the contrary, he personifies time as the all-powerful, the all-seeing. The difference between metaphor and personification here is precisely the difference between a reality experienced in process and a reality conceptualized.

Shakespeare and Sophocles would not imitate time so differently, however, if the meanings which they saw in time were not also different, for in both cases form and content are exceedingly well paired. It has already been mentioned that the Sophoclean view of time is ironical. That is to say, it is intimately connected with the question of knowledge. When the past and the present, which at first are disconnected in the *Oedipus Tyrannus*, come together, Oedipus' "amnesia" (his ignorance of his own past and therefore of his own moral offense) is lifted, and the full irony of the situation is seen. Oedipus then understands that he has pronounced a curse upon his own head, and that there is no escape from a punishment already self-directed. It is time as the infinite discloser which thus brings together those two fragmented orders of time, the past and the present, and reveals the irony implicit in the situation of man, whose time, because of his limited knowledge, is broken and finite.

Shakespeare's view of time is not ironical. The irony in *Macbeth*, of which there is much, does not arise from an inherent discontinuity in the nature of time, but from the fact that Macbeth, as goaded by Lady Macbeth, vainly imagines that he can remake time into something which it cannot be. His struggle to establish a barrier between what is and what has been, his attempt to control the future, and his desire to put a stop to a time which cannot be controlled, all form part of the illusion which envelops him ever more completely as the play progresses. The equivocating irony [43] is that he who starts out to "mock the time with fairest show" comes in the end to face the prospect of living "to be the show and gaze o' th' time." This is not an irony in the understanding of time itself, but in Macbeth's opposition to the fundamental time scheme of the universe.

Shakespeare's view of time is inseparable from his view of freedom. It involves the possibility of the new, the possibility of decision. In *Macbeth* we witness two courses of action from their beginning. In the first act we see a Macbeth of noble character and high repute who has been rewarded by the king for his valour and loyalty, and who becomes tempted and falls. We watch him plot a course of action which will, as he thinks, put matters into his own hands. In the fourth act we see the planning of Macbeth's opposers. We watch them initiate the course of war which will dislodge him from his throne. In both cases, there is the situation, the individual's response to the situation, and the ensuing action taken as a result. In this sense, always in *Macbeth* "the time is free."

Not only do Sophocles and Shakespeare imitate chronological time differently, and not only do they see different meanings in time, but they also present differently the relation between time as "fact" and time as "meaning". Sophocles deals with "lumps" of time. We must imagine the time he presents to us spatially or quantitatively: time past, time present, time as infinite duration (all-seeing).[44] Shakespeare deals with several interconnected levels of meaning of time. He does not describe providential time as something apart from chronological time, or as something which is perceived when chronological time is divided up according to various tenses, rearranged, conceptualized. On the contrary, his meaning rises from the interplay of two understandings of the same kind of time. Chronological time is the basis

[43] See Muir, *Macbeth*, p. xxx, for a good discussion of the "equivocation" theme in *Macbeth*.
[44] See the discussion, Chap. II, p. 26 in this book, on the syntactical structure of the Greek language as contrasted with Hebrew, and its relation to quantitative conceptualization and measurement of time.

upon which providential time is raised—or, providential time depends upon chronological time for its expression.

The close correspondence between providential and chronological time may be observed best in that remarkable scene (I.vii) in which Macbeth and Lady Macbeth prepare themselves for the murder of Duncan. Here Macbeth's time, providential time, and chronological time are in the closest juxtaposition, the scene depending for its effect on the interplay between time in its most specific and literal sense and time as an avenue of human understanding. The stage directions set a definite time (supper) and place (outside the dining hall):

Hautboys and torches. Enter, and pass over the stage, a Sewer, and divers Servants with dishes and service. Then enter Macbeth.

When he enters, however, he begins to speak of time in a general and metaphorical way:

> If it were done when 'tis done, then 'twere well
> It were done quickly. If the assassination
> Could trammel up the consequence, and catch
> With his surcease success; that but this blow
> Might be the be-all and the end-all here,
> But here, upon this bank and shoal of time,
> We'd jump the life to come. (1-7)

The first sentence grows directly out of the immediate situation, communicating the swiftness and the finality of the act. But in the next line Macbeth is aware that no act is so final it does not have consequences (whatever Lady Macbeth may suppose), and this thought leads into the metaphorical idea of time as an island. On the one hand there is the "bank and shoal of time," "the be-all and the end-all here"; on the other hand there is "the life to come." The image, as Samuel Johnson said, is of a "narrow bank in the ocean of eternity." [45] Time is at once an image of finitude and of infinity.

---

[45] Johnson's edition of 1765 is quoted in *Macbeth*, ed. by Wilson, p. 113. This interpretation depends in large measure upon Theobald's reading of "schoole" (F¹) as "shoal," which most editors now accept. See Muir (*Macbeth*, pp. 38–39). However, even if the image were of a schoolroom and "the life to come" were only the future years of Macbeth's natural life (which some have held) the contrast between an insulated present and a larger time surrounding it would still be apparent. The image of an island or isthmus makes that clearer, however, and is therefore preferred. On "the life to come" see Muir (*Macbeth*) who sees echoes of the prayer book. See also S. L. Bethell, *The Winter's Tale: A Study*, pp. 125–28. He prefers the reading "schoole," but believes "the life to come," means life after death. The same meaning is attached to Autolycus' use of the phrase in *The Winter's Tale* (IV.iii.30).

Macbeth's thought now turns again to the specific instance, and he reviews the history of the situation in which he stands: the present reality is that Duncan is in his house as guest, kinsman, and subject; the past fact is that Duncan "Hath borne his faculties" meekly and has been "clear in his great office"; while the future consequence will be that

> his virtues
> Will plead like angels, trumpet-tongu'd, against
> The deep damnation of his taking-off;
> And pity, like a naked new-born babe . . .
> Shall blow the horrid deed in every eye. . . . (12-24)

Here, when Macbeth's awareness of future consequences is about to dissuade him, Lady Macbeth enters; and suddenly time is cemented to the specific, to the chronology of the deed:

MACB.   How now! what news?
LADY M.   He has almost supp'd. Why have you left the chamber?
MACB.   Hath he ask'd for me?
LADY M.   Know you not he has?

Macbeth, however, turns back into another review of the situation. He has been honour'd "of late"; it is "so soon" to cast aside the "golden opinions" he has purchased. Lady Macbeth wonders if his former hope was drunk, or whether it has slept and now awakes, looking on its former action "so green and pale." If so, she will in the same way account his love, "from this time." When he had courage, then he was a man, and that was when time and place did not agree with the event, very unlike their "fitness now." When he mentions the possibility of failure, her famous reply utilizes an image of temporal readiness:

> But screw your courage to the sticking-place,
> And we'll not fail. (60-61)

Murry has described the meaning of Lady Macbeth's image in these words:

When you turn the little wooden screw on a violin—in those days it was a lute or a viol—to tighten a string, your fingers feel delicately for "the sticking-place," where the screw is tight and the string is taut; and you feel for it with a faint and subtle apprehension lest the string should snap.[46]

---

[46] *Shakespeare*, p. 329.

Others have suggested that the reference is to a "soldier screwing up the cord of his cross-bow to the 'sticking-place.'" [47] In either case, the idea is of tension building up to the breaking-point, the moment of release: "One, two," as her mind recalls it later, "why then, 'tis time to do't" (V.i.40).

Her lines now turn again to the specific chronology of the deed. She describes what she will do "when Duncan is asleep," and "when in swinish sleep" his chamberlains lie. Macbeth speaks of how it will be receiv'd "When we have mark'd with blood these sleepy two," and as the plotting is now finished in the most careful detail (that is, as careful as these excited two can make it), the thought turns again to the tension before the moment ("I . . . bend up/Each corporal agent to this terrible feat"—80) and finally the scene is concluded, as it began, on a metaphorical reference to time:

> Away, and mock the time with fairest show;
> False face must hide what the false heart doth know. (81–82)

The next scene begins sharply with a specific reference to chronological time:

> BAN. How goest the night, boy?
> FLE. The moon is down; I have not heard the clock. (II.i.1–2)

The remarkable impression this scene makes depends upon the numerous levels upon which Shakespeare's understanding of time is operating simultaneously. We move back and forth, with great fluidity, between time as fact and time as meaning. Here we have time as the striking of the clock, the setting of the moon, the rhythm of eating and sleeping. Here we have time as that which is bent up or screwed tight toward the opportune moment, as that which "adheres" for the doing of the deed, as that which Macbeth would make it, the present be-all and end-all. And here we have time as that which it must ultimately be, the present moment standing like an island in an eternal sea. But the scene gives us none of these things in isolation from the others. Now one is emphasized, and now another; but there is no sharp line of demarcation; and we perceive that the striking of the clock is not something different from the island in the eternal sea, but is, in fact, one manifestation of it.

The interplay, and interdependence, of time as fact and time as

[47] Muir, *Macbeth*, p. 44.

meaning provides an example of that tension which persists in Judaeo-Christian thought between the event and the interpretation of the event.[48] The facts of time, of this murderous pair's plotting of when and where, are specific, concrete, and irreducible. On the other hand, they cannot be separated from what they mean. If we tried to eliminate the specific, to subsume all under the category of meaning, we would do violence to the writing. This is a play for a theater in which there are hautboys and torches, and servants with dishes, and clocks that strike. In Shakespeare's theater it is sometimes midnight; but that is a matter which has not only prosaic reality, it is a part of the fact that evil appears in the form of "secret, black, and midnight hags!" (IV.i.48).

Finally, the difference between *Macbeth* and the *Oedipus Tyrannus* must be seen in the light of Shakespeare's "time future." It was said above that Shakespeare's view of freedom involves the possibility of the new. Essentially, therefore, the future is open. That does not mean that it is completely uncharted or that it holds an unlimited number of possibilities. It simply means that the anticipation of a not-completely-fixed future is one element which goes to make up the unique moment of the present. This is entirely in line with what has been said (Chap. III) regarding the Judaeo-Christian understanding of the present as being compounded of memory and anticipation.

The future is felt in Macbeth at almost every moment that time is felt. The weird sisters open the play with lines which cause anticipation of the time "When the hurly-burly's done,/When the battle's lost and won," and Malcolm closes it speaking of what he shall do "in measure, time, and place," and of his approaching coronation. Between these two scenes, the technique Shakespeare follows of moving from moment to moment gives at every point the occasion not only for memory of former things, but for anticipation of those yet to be. It is true that Macbeth's future does not turn out as he had hoped, that in a sense, his future is cut off; but the future of Scotland is saved by that very fact. Malcolm's prosaic way of putting it is, "I hope the days are near at hand/That chambers will be safe" (V.iv.1–2). In *Macbeth* everyone lives acutely in the present, and therefore the future is open.

In the *Oedipus Tyrannus* the future is closed. One might almost say that it does not exist. The time significance of the play must be understood entirely in terms of the relation between present and past. The past is dominant. It contains the facts which explain the present,

[48] See Chap. III, pp. 57–58 in this book.

which control the present; and the play, as it moves forward in time through the events of the terrible day, actually moves backward into the completely decisive past.[49] Teiresias' prophecies look no further ahead than the end of the day, and what they reveal is the blackness of the grave or of blindness: "This day shall be thy birth-day, and thy grave" (438). Oedipus has the freedom, therefore, only to discover the past, and as the past is that in which freedom is not even conceivable ("What's done cannot be undone," as Lady Macbeth discovers— V.i.76), he has only the ironical freedom to discover his lack of it. In the end, his blindness is symbolic of our ability to see nothing further than the conclusion of the play.[50] The imagination does not extend into the future, as it does in *Macbeth*, where a line stretches out to the crack of doom (IV.i.117); on the contrary, it turns into the past, where the chain of cause and effect, and the intricate weavings of destiny, stretch backward into the shadow.

The beauty of dramatic structure which *Macbeth* and the *Oedipus Tyrannus* both exhibit would account for their popularity with the critics, but hardly would do so for their popularity with the public through many centuries. To account for the latter it is necessary to realize how the structures of these plays echoed supremely well the fundamental presuppositions of their culture regarding man's place in the cosmos. Time is not a subject on which the ordinary man spends much thought, but it is a basic category of his thinking and a given reality in his existence. When an artist is able to form a work which embodies the culture's unspoken understanding of time, he strikes chords of response in every observer. It was given to Sophocles and Shakespeare to do just that in the *Oedipus Tyrannus* and *Macbeth*. Therefore the two tragedies will excite admiration as long as the cultures of the Greeks and the Christians are known and understood.

---

[49] Cf. what was said here in Chap. II, pp. 29, 35, about the dominance of the past in Greek thought and its relation to the culture's apparently short memory span.

[50] The *Oedipus Tyrannus* does not look forward to the *Oedipus at Colonus*. Whether Sophocles himself did, I do not know. As far as the internal evidence of the *Oedipus Tyrannus* goes, Oedipus' life in exile has no more significance than death, or perhaps one should say as much as death.

VIII

RELEASE AND RECONCILIATION:
THE *ALCESTIS* AND *THE WINTER'S TALE*

After Shakespeare's great tragedies, there appeared in London a new type of drama, prevalent from about the year 1608, of which Shakespeare's last plays are examples. These plays are closer in form to certain Greek dramas than the earlier plays had been. In Athens, the period of high tragedy represented by such plays as Sophocles' *Oedipus Tyrannus* and the *Antigone* also had been followed by a different type of drama, of which Euripides is the surviving exponent, and the *Alcestis* the earliest example. The spirit of many Jacobean dramas is close to that of Euripides. It is the spirit of tragi-comedy.

In spite of this parallel, in spite of the fact that there is an indirect Greek influence on Shakespeare and a consequent change in his dramatic form, Shakespeare's understanding of time and history did not change; and the dramatic form which he developed did not prevent the expression of an essentially Christian, rather than Hellenic, orientation to the temporal world.

Of all dramatic types, tragi-comedy depends least upon analysis in terms of comparison with experience drawn from everyday life, for it depends in such large part upon the sheer wonder of its theatrical effect. The critic must see the work in its proper setting, a child-like world of wonder and miracle. To be sure, tragi-comedy is sophisticated; but its sophistication presupposes the willingness to believe the unbelievable, to revel in the unpredictable. Upon that foundation its meaning is reared. The whole structure crumbles when taken too seriously or when compared too closely (that is, too immediately) to life outside the theater. The meanings of tragi-comedy (when they exist) are such as can be expressed in marvel; they assume in the spectator such a distance from life as will allow tears to burst into laughter upon the instant.

The whole structure is therefore self-contained. With too much light or too much logic, it is gone.

Aside from frank exploitation of wonder, the primary characteristic of tragic-comedy is its unexpected turning of a tragic situation, which normally would lead to death, into a comic one in which victory belongs to life.[1] The simpler and more schematically this is put, the nearer it comes to the heart of the form. Few definitions are better than that put down about 1608 by John Fletcher in the preface to *The Faithful Shepherdess*. Said he:

A tragi-comedy is not so called in respect to mirth and killing, but in respect it wants deaths which is enough to make it no tragedy, yet brings some near it which is enough to make it no comedy.

In other words, it is not that some funny things happen along with some sad, for that was common in English drama, including tragedy, since the Mysteries and Miracles. Rather, it is that death threatens but is at last overwhelmed. If, in these matters, we take death to be a symbol of the most serious defeat which can occur to man, then we are not far from seeing the essential defeat and victory of tragi-comedy.

As tragi-comedy developed in Jacobean times, it assumed a number of recognizable characteristics. Here are those noted by Eugene M. Waith in a representative play, *A King and No King*: (1) the imitation of the manners of the familiar world; (2) remoteness from the familiar world, which reveals that the initial impression of familiarity is in fact deceptive; (3) intricacy of plot; (4) the improbable hypothesis, the situations of the plot being "as unusual as they are sensational"; (5) the atmosphere of evil; (6) Protean characters, meaning either that disguises are assumed, or that "the behavior of some characters is utterly inconsistent with what has gone before," or both; (7) "lively touches of passion"; and (8) the language of emotion, which tends to emphasize "emotion rather than significance," and "to isolate moments of powerful feeling."[2]

All of these characteristics reinforce the notion of artificiality and

---

[1] Richard Wincor, "Shakespeare's Festival Plays," pp. 219–40, emphasizes the importance of seasonal rites and worship as background for the understanding of Shakespeare's last plays. *Pericles*, *Cymbeline*, and *The Winter's Tale*, he notes, have supposed deaths and wonderful rebirths, "the exact pattern of the old Mock Death and Cure" (p. 224). This element is quite important, although Mr. Wincor, to be sure, dwells on it so exclusively that he fails to see the significance of such factors as Time and Grace in Shakespeare's treatment of his subjects.

[2] *The Pattern of Tragicomedy in Beaumont and Fletcher*, pp. 36–40. For a survey of recent literature on Beaumont and Fletcher and various analyses of the formal elements in their plays, see William W. Appleton, *Beaumont and Fletcher: A Critical Study*, pp. 114–19.

marvel in tragi-comedy. They are part of a style which is demanded in order that the sudden reversals essential to the form may be accepted.[3] The elements of the genre which are most important are the love of the marvelous, the threat of death, the sudden reversal, and the sophistication which is willing to acquiesce in a large measure of pretense.

That Shakespeare wrote tragi-comedy needs no argument. Whether he did so because Beaumont and Fletcher had set the popular taste before him, or whether he led the way for them, is the only real debate and may be left to those equipped to wage it. What has been missed is that Euripides wrote tragi-comedy and that the *Alcestis* is a case in point. In all the debate over the interpretation of Euripides, his merits and defects, which has been carried on for the last century or more, no one, as far as I know, mentioned tragi-comedy until Professor Kitto published his *Greek Tragedy* in 1939. Yet to see at least some of the plays as tragi-comedy is the only way of doing Euripides justice as a playwright while attempting to explain the fact that, as Gilbert Murray says, he has "lived through the ages . . . loved by poets and despised by critics." [4] If the critics were looking for high tragedy in the *Alcestis*, or something which resembled the probabilities of life, it is easy to see the reason for their disappointment.[5]

The artificiality of tragi-comedy does not, of course, mean that its author cannot have any ultimate seriousness. It only means that whatever seriousness there is lies on the other side of the frankest theatrical pretense, and that everyone in the theater is party to that pretense. A Shakespeare can make tragi-comedy the vehicle of the most sublime visions of life, and Euripides' skepticism may be added to his artificial creations, not as their whole body, but as what Professor Kitto calls "intellectual stiffening" (p. 335).

Alcestis

In one sense, Euripides comes closer to the "imitation of life" than Aeschylus and Sophocles, and for that reason his imitation of time is

---

[3] Other writers have noticed attributes similar to the eight listed above. F. E. Schelling (*Elizabethan Drama*, p. 192) says that in place of unity the Jacobean tragi-comedy has "multiplicity, surprise, and contrast." T. M. Parrott and R. H. Ball (*A Short View of Elizabethan Drama*, pp. 189–90) say that what distinguishes this drama from its predecessors is sophistication, high flown sentiment, and the deliberate rejection of the old tradition of realism.

[4] *Euripides and His Age*, pp. 7–8.

[5] See Appendix, pp. 216–18 for discussion of *Alcestis* as tragi-comedy.

more realistic and more explicit.[6] On the other hand, references to the specific time of day, establishing the hour as early, late, or what-have-you, do not exist in the *Alcestis*.

The assumption is that the play begins in the morning, yet if one asks what makes him think so, there is very little to substantiate the impression. Verrall said that it was the custom of the dramatists to start the action "in the morning and even with sunrise or before." [7] He assumes that in many plays where the early opening is not stated expressly it is there "by implication." When the Chorus, shortly after its entrance, not finding the signs of death outside the house, says, "Yet surely is this the appointed day" (καὶ μὴν τόδε κύριον ἦμαρ— 107), the spectator probably assumes that the day has already got started but has not progressed very far. It was Verrall's opinion also that when Admetus, returning from the burial of Alcestis, is reminded of that former time when he came to the house on his wedding day (911–25), the suggestion is that it is evening, as it would surely have been when he came to the house with his bride.[8]

Beyond these two sign posts, for what they are worth, there is almost nothing to indicate the passage of time within the day of the action. The play contains only four passages of the kind so numerous in Shakespeare, in which chronological time can be said to be in the least specific. At her entrance, Alcestis addresses the "Sun and the light of day" ("Αλιε καὶ φάος ἀμέρας—244), drawing Admetus' reply that "he sees you and me, two stricken ones" (ὁρᾷ σὲ κἀμέ, δύο κακῶς πεπραγότας—246). These lines suggest that the sun is high, although of course the main point is that Alcestis yet lives and has not passed into darkness. The other passages do not refer to time within the day at all. Admetus promises to mourn for his wife "not for a year . . . but as long as my life will last" (οὐκ ἐτήσιον . . . ἀλλ' ἔστ' ἂν αἰὼν οὑμὸς ἀντέχῃ—336–37). Later he orders that there be no music in the city "while twelve moons complete their circles" (ἔστω σελήνας δώδεκ' ἐκπληρουμένας—431). At the end of the play, Heracles explains that Alcestis will not be able to speak "until the third day comes" (καὶ τρίτον μόλῃ φάος—1146).[9] Incidentally, the absence of specific time

---

[6] Professor Kitto (*Greek Tragedy*, pp. 340–42) has spoken of the naturalism in Euripides' tragi-comedies. That the illusion of familiarity is proper to tragi-comedy has already been noted.

[7] *The Ion of Euripides*, p. li.   [8] *Euripides the Rationalist*, p. 62.

[9] The Chorus' lines (450–51) about Alcestis' fame being sung when the moon rides over Sparta the whole night long is the only other specific chronological reference, but for dating any event it is of even less help than the others cited.

references belies Verrall's attempt to make a cardinal point of what he regarded as the hasty burial of Alcestis.[10] The only passage in the entire play which mentions haste (and surely if it were so important to the meaning of the play, Euripides must have mentioned it some way or other) is in Alcestis' lyric passage where she hears Charon the Ferryman urge her not to linger:

> With his hand upon the pole, Charon
> is now calling me: "Why do you linger?
> Hurry! You are delaying me."

> ἔχων χέρ' ἐπὶ κοντῷ Χάρων
> μ' ἤδη καλεῖ· τί μέλλεις;
> ἐπείγου· σὺ κατείργεις.   (254–56)

It is Death which is in a hurry, not Admetus.

Although in terms of specifics, Euripides has kept his audience ignorant of the passage of time through the day, yet in a general way he manages to represent time as, in the words Aristophanes gives him, "one of the familiar things which we use and live with." [11] There is, for instance, a good bit of talk about the old and the young, as in the dialogue between Apollo and Death, in the Prologue, and in the argument between Admetus and Pheres, his father, whose old age is contrasted with the comparative youth of Admetus (611, 649–50, 669–72). The future, which we found virtually absent from the *Oedipus Tyrannus*, is mentioned rather frequently in this play, although always in quite general terms such as when the Chorus promises Alcestis to loathe Admetus "if ever he chooses a new mate for the marriage-bed" (εἰ δέ τι/καινὸν ἔλοιτο λέχος πόσις—464–65), or when Heracles, urging Admetus to obey him and take the woman he has brought, predicts, "in time, perhaps, you will even praise me" (χρόνῳ δὲ καὶ σύ μ' αἰνέσεις ἴσως—1036).[12] In addition, there are half a dozen generalized speeches on time itself, which are worth examining in detail.

---

[10] "I refer to the haste and precipitancy, irregular and indecent in any case, and in this particular case nothing less than outrageous, with which the corpse of the noble heroine is conveyed to the grave" (Verrall, *Euripides the Rationalist*, p. 44). Verrall objected to what he called the usual view that Time is not important in Greek drama, that we usually are asked not to inquire about the time of day, speed, etc. This "misconception" he thinks is the reason the haste in burying Alcestis has not been seen (pp. 43 ff.). On the contrary, the closer one examines the text, the less one finds to back up Verrall's interpretation of the burial.

[11]   οἰκεῖα πράγματ' εἰσάγων, οἷς χρώμεθ'
       οἷς ξύνεσμεν.   (*Frogs*. 959)

[12] Cf. ll. 244, 374, 390, 394, 651, 1095, 1109, 1120, 1152. The first four all refer to the time after Alcestis is dead; they occur in her death scene. The last four are all in Heracles' final scene of restoration. Hope is mentioned three times (ll. 130, 146, 293) in the negative.

Twice time is spoken of as a healer. When Admetus cries to Alcestis, "Ah me! What shall I do deprived of you?" she replies, "Time will heal you: nothing is one who dies" (χρόνος μαλάξει σ᾽· οὐδέν ἐσθ᾽ ὁ κατθανών—380–81 [lit., time will soften you]). The same expression occurs again in the final scene when Heracles pleads with Admetus to take the woman he has brought and to begin life again: "Time will heal; now your affliction is but young" (χρόνος μαλάξει, νῦν δ᾽ ἔθ᾽ ἡβᾷ σοι κακόν). Here, however, Admetus' reply is thoroughly negative: "You speak indeed of time, if time is to die" (χρόνον λέγοις ἄν, εἰ χρόνος τὸ κατθανεῖν—1085–86). It is to the point to observe that time is here thought of as a continually flowing stream which washes away the sorrowful memory of the past. It is not suggested that time will bring about a new situation; but it will soften, it will ameliorate, the hardness of the present. Admetus is not contradicting the basic idea, he is only stating it pessimistically, when he says that time can really do that only by bringing death, the total oblivion. The other speeches about time are more frankly quantitative in image. Admetus upbraids his aged father Pheres, who would not consent to die for him, by reminding him that the time he had left to live was not long:

The rest of your time of life was at any rate short.
And I, and also she, would have lived through the rest of our time.

βραχὺς δέ σοι
πάντως ὁ λοιπὸς ἦν βιώσιμος χρόνος
κἀγώ τ᾽ ἂν ἔζων χἥδε τὸν λοιπὸν χρόνον.   (649–51)

At the end of the speech he mocks all the aged, who at the approach of death are afraid and cling to life, although formerly they had complained "of age and the long time of life" (γῆρας . . . καὶ μακρὸν χρόνον βίου—670). Pheres is not ashamed of changing his mind:

Indeed, I regard the time down below as long,
and that for living short but nevertheless sweet.

ἦ μὴν πολύν γε τὸν κάτω λογίζομαι
χρόνον, τὸ δὲ ζῆν μικρόν, ἀλλ᾽ ὅμως γλυκύ.   (692–93)

The same sweet shortness of life is the theme of Heracles' speech when he comes out of the house after having drunk so freely of

Admetus' wine-stores. All mortals have to pay the debt of death, he says,

> And there is none of the mortals who knows whether he will live through the coming morrow. . . . Hearing this and learning it from me, enjoy yourself, drink, figure your life from day to day, for all other things are according to chance.
>
> κοὐκ ἔστι θνητῶν ὅστισ ἐξεπίσταται
> τὴν αὔριον μέλλουσαν εἰ βιώσεται . . .
> ταῦτ᾽ οὖν ἀκούσας καὶ μαθὼν ἐμοῦ πάρα
> εὔφραινε σαυτόν, πίνε τὸν καθ᾽ ἡμέραν
> βίον λογίζου σόν, τὰ δ᾽ ἄλλα τῆς τύχης.   (783-84, 787-89)

The play contains four passages which convey the sense of time as an immediate and particular moment. "I must die," says Alcestis,

> And this thing is not tomorrow, nor is this evil coming to me on the third day of the month, but straight-way I shall lie among those who are not.
>
> καὶ τόδ᾽ οὐκ ἐς αὔριον
> οὐδ᾽ εἰς τρίτην μοι μηνὸς ἔρχεται κακόν,
> ἀλλ᾽ αὐτίκ᾽ ἐν τοῖς μηκέτ᾽ οὖσι λέξομαι.   (320-22)

A little later: "O my children, when it is necessary for me to live, I go down below" (ὦ τέκν᾽, ὅτε ζῆν χρῆν μ᾽, ἀπέρχομαι κάτω—379). The servant is incensed with the unfitness of the time for entertaining the boorish Heracles:

> And now I entertain this guest within the house . . . while from out of the house she is borne.
>
> καὶ νῦν ἐγὼ ἐν δόμοισιν ἑστιῶ
> ξένον . . .
> ἡ δ᾽ ἐκ δόμων βέβηκεν.   (765-67)

To Heracles himself a bit later he says, "you did not come to the house in a time fit for welcoming" (οὐκ ἦλθες ἐν δέοντι δέξασθαι δόμοις—817).

These passages show that Euripides does have a sense of time as one of the experiential realities of life. His characters have hope; they live from day to day; they know that life is short; they appreciate the immediacy and fitness of certain hours for specific tasks. All this is part of Euripides' realism. However, the absence of any specific chronology to back up his feeling about time shows that Euripides is not attempting to imitate the passage of time. His references to time are part of his characterization, in which, for striking effect, he excels, but not part of the pattern of the play itself. In Shakespeare, time is always specific, even when for effect he is forced into inconsistency; and time in the general sense is always intertwined with time in the most specific, chronological sense.[13]

I have not yet dealt with the most important use of time in the *Alcestis*, which is the notion that the heroine must die on "the appointed day." Attention to this theme will show where the concept of time finally belongs in the scheme of the play.

In the first five hundred lines, roughly the first half of the play, the theme of the "appointed day" is reiterated with frequency. Nine passages refer specifically to "this day" or to "the appointed day" (9, 19–20, 26–27, 106, 147, 158–59, 178, 233, and 513). Typical are the Chorus' line (106), "Yet surely this is the appointed day" (καὶ μὴν τόδε κύριον ἦμαρ), and that of the handmaid (147), "For the day foredoomed compels her" (πεπρωμένη γὰρ ἡμέρα βιάζεται). Besides these nine, at least two other lines reinforce them by speaking of what is done "for the last time" (πανύστατόν σε προσπίτνουσ᾽ αἰτήσομαι —164; cf. 207). These references to the day foreordained represent the strongest impression of time which the play makes upon the spectator, all the other time-references mentioned being a part of the background. This speech of the handmaid illustrates well the feeling generated:[14]

> But what within she did, hear thou, and marvel.
> For when she knew that the appointed day
> Was come, in river-water her white skin
> She bathed, and from the cedar-chests took forth
> Vesture and jewels, and decked her gloriously,
> And before Vesta's altar stood, and prayed:
> "Queen, for I pass beneath the earth, I fall
> Before thee now, and nevermore, and pray. . . ."   (157–64)

The reiteration of this theme in the first half of the play, and its abandonment in the second half, is of supreme importance for the interpretation of the work. In the first place, the fact that the day has been foreordained for Alcestis' death shows that the act of decision for

---

[13] See Chap. VII in this book.
[14] The translation is that of Arthur S. Way, p. 419.

both Admetus and his wife took place in a former time and is not now
a matter open for choice.[15] If this fact were more carefully attended by
many of the play's interpreters, poor Admetus, whose situation is
mournful enough as it is, would not have to suffer the further castiga-
tions heaped upon him by critics who apparently want him to make a
noble gesture which Euripides has never even hinted that he has the
possibility of making. We are not to ask, as W. N. Bates has reminded
us, why Admetus permits his wife to die for him and does not meet his
own death like a man. "Such questions," he says, "show a misunder-
standing of the dramatic situation which Euripides has undertaken to
set forth. The offer of Alcestis to die for her husband had been made
long before the opening of the play, and when the fatal day arrives
neither he nor anybody else can change the situation." [16] As a matter
of fact, the question of Admetus' rightness or wrongness in letting
Alcestis take his place in death is strictly secondary. It occurs in only
three places, and is not really brought to issue until the play is more
than half finished. The first hint of anything amiss in his action is at
lines 197–98 when the handmaid says,

> Now if he had died, he would have ended; but
> as he escapes he has this sorrow, which he
> never will forget.
>
> καὶ κατθανών τ' ἂν ὤλετ', ἐκφυγὼν δ' ἔχει
> τοσοῦτον ἄλγος, οὗ ποτ' οὐ λελήσεται.

The speech where these lines occur, however, is devoted to Admetus'
woes and those of his house, and far from causing us to blame him, the
lines in their context actually induce sympathy. The first time we are
truly confronted with the nature of what he has done, what any man
does who will not die his own death, is in the dialogue with Pheres,
particularly in its last forty lines (694–733). Here again, I believe the
effect is not one which puts Admetus clearly in the wrong. The scene
is a brilliant exchange between father and son, modeled, as some have
said, on the debates of the law court.[17] Its glory is not in its clear-cut

[15] D. W. Lucas, ed. and trans., *The Alcestis*, pp. 4–5, says that in the original story
Alcestis died immediately after making the bargain. Euripides, he says, changes that feature
deliberately because otherwise he would have had either to include the making of the bargain
in his play, which was beyond the scope of his intention, or else to give the appearance of
beginning in the middle of the action.

[16] *Euripides, A Student of Human Nature*, p. 62.

[17] The rhetorical device of formal debate found its way also into Roman drama and Jacobean
tragi-comedy. See Waith, *Tragicomedy in Beaumont and Fletcher*, pp. 86–98.

moral but rather in its rhetoric, each man holding fast to his own self-truth which he defends with dexterity and fire. It is not clear who has the last word. The scene is best justified, I believe, when it is viewed as a flashing theatrical effect gained from the slightly bizarre spectacle of watching two men who refused death arguing their righteousness over the corpse of the one who did not refuse. And again, the woe of Admetus is increased by the conversation—that on this day he should have to talk to Pheres, of all people! The third place where Admetus' act is questioned is in his own lines at the return from the burial (935–61). Here he himself makes the strongest case against himself, how she in dying is more blessed than he in living, how he will hardly be able to bear the sight of his children, how his enemies will scoff at him. The Chorus' answer to his speech is revealing: they sing a song in which they tell him that he has been gripped by the hands of the goddess Fate (Ἀνάγκη). In short, the question of Admetus' right or wrong action in allowing Alcestis to die for him is used, not to point a moral, but merely to increase the pathos of his situation.

Were it otherwise, Euripides would be obliged to show Admetus in some hour of choice, which, as we have seen, he avoids by throwing choice into the past. The *Alcestis* is not a play about a man who *makes* a mistake; it may be about a man who *made* one. For this reason, the play (until the very end) becomes another example of that essentially Greek situation in which the past dominates the present. Conceptually, this idea is very much like that of the *Oedipus Tyrannus*, where the present but brings to light the deed already committed and the oracle already spoken. To establish such a closed situation, where the hero and heroine are caught in the tragic (or at least pathetic) position, Euripides has utilized the idea of an "appointed day." Time is a trap.

The first half of the play, in which time is most often mentioned, closes in. Euripides is weaving the tragedy in his tragi-comedy. With the arrival of Heracles (477) the basis for the comic release is begun; the imagination begins to move away from the idea of time and into an idea of power, as preparation for the tragi-comic marvel.

After about line 700 the references to time begin to slacken off. There are no references to the "appointed day" after line 513, and very few references to time at all after the scene with Pheres. On the other hand, after line 700 there are more references to the notion of force, strength, and death as a power. The way had been prepared for that in the Prologue, which was an *agon* between Apollo and Death, a

contest in which right is argued against right, and force against force.[18]
At line 419 the Chorus reminds Admetus that death is a debt which
must be paid, the image taken up again by Heracles (782) who warns
that all things lie in fortune's power (789). Admetus mourns for his
helpmeet who has been torn away from his side by Death and given up
to Hades (τοῖον ὅμηρον μ᾽ ἀποσυλήσας "Αιδη θάνατος παρέδωκεν—
870–71). "Death," says the Chorus, "has torn loose many a man from
his wife" (πολλοὺς/ἤδη παρέλυσεν/θάνατος δάμαρτος—931–33).
The Chorus avers that Fate is stronger than anything (κρεῖσσον
οὐδὲν 'Ανάγκας/ηὗρον—965–66); "she has caught you in the in-
escapable bonds of her hands" (καὶ σ᾽ ἐν ἀφύκτοισι χερῶν εἷλε θεὰ
δεσμοῖς—984). As Death has carried off Alcestis bodily, Heracles
recaptures her with athletic prowess. He won the girl, he says, in an
athletic contest (1026–29), and forces Admetus, against his will, to
accept her (ἄναξ, βιάζει μ᾽ οὐ θέλοντα δρᾶν τάδε—1116). When her
veil is removed and she is revealed to be none other than Alcestis,
brought from the shades back to light, Heracles declares that he rescued
her "by closing together in battle with the lord of the spirits" (μάχην
συνάψας δαιμόνων τῷ κυρίῳ—1140).

Heracles' coming upon the scene has nothing to do with time; it
simply happens. It pertains to no ethical issue and it is connected to the
theme of Admetus' curious compulsions regarding hospitality only by
the slenderest thread, as if it were desired merely to give some type of
justice to the miraculous rescue.[19] What is happening is simply that
the tragi-comic miracle of benevolent power is bursting the confines
of enclosing time, conquering death and tragedy. Time is death, as
Alcestis discovered when she greeted the dawn of "the appointed day,"
and as Admetus declared when told that time would heal (1086). The
healing, as it turns out, comes not from time, but from the power of
the demi-god. For time but tightens the web which is wound around
man because of his former choices, choices which we do not see him

---

[18] Ll. 63–76. The prologue, incidentally, mirrors the play. It begins with discussion of
time and ends with threats of force.

[19] The Chorus, by the way, approves of Admetus' behavior toward Heracles. At first it is
astonished and asks what he means by accepting a guest under these circumstances and
concealing the truth from him (551–52, 561–62), but it passes immediately from Admetus'
explanation to a lyric in praise of hospitality. Either we are to accept Admetus' reasoning as
sufficient or the following lines are so satiric as to induce laughter, which is hard to believe.
Verrall (*Euripides the Rationalist*, p. 32) wrote that in Admetus' behavior toward Heracles,
"the substance of friendship is sacrificed to the mere appearance and form of it." Exactly. It
is the way of tragi-comedy to substitute form for substance. The same objection could be
raised to the entire play, if one wished to speak in that way.

make because they are not in the forefront of the author's concern. There is an alliance between Time and Necessity and Death. That alliance is shattered by the mighty son of Zeus, contrary to all expectation, and as a fulfillment, not of the course of things through time, but of the divine power. Here is not to be found the transcendence of history in a more ultimate meaning. Rather, here is the shattering of history by the introduction of another principle altogether.

> And the expected things are not fulfilled,
> And for the unexpected the god has found out a way.
> Such is the result of this thing.

> καὶ τὰ δοκηθέντ' οὐκ ἐτελέσθη,
> τῶν δ' ἀδοκήτων πόρον ηὗρε θεός,
> τοιόνδ' ἀπέβη τόδε πρᾶγμα.   (1161–63)

Such is the tragi-comic vision of the *Alcestis*. How seriously Euripides took it is another question, but there it stands, played for all it is worth in terms of theatrical effect and the shifting delights of poetry. How different it is from the tragi-comic view of Shakespeare we must now inquire.

The Winter's Tale

That Shakespeare, in his late plays, moves toward Greek themes has already been mentioned. If the *Oresteia* and the *Oedipus Tyrannus* are informed by a desire for vision, a poised picture of timeless moral reality, Shakespeare, taking up tragi-comedy, moves in their direction.

The theme of truth opposed to illusion is a natural theme for the theater, which is based upon illusion and pretense as inherent properties in its form. Masks and costumes are the forebears of the drama, a fact which has suggested both to ancient and modern dramatists that the theater is a likely form in which to explore the difference between being and seeming. The theme of truth and illusion is accentuated in tragi-comedy because, according to its convention, it relies so frankly on theatrical pretense and its various types of attendant artificiality.[20] Tragi-comedy arises when the playwrights and other theatrical artists know how to gain theatrical effects and begin to exploit them

---

[20] On the theme of appearance and reality in *The Winter's Tale*, see Theodore Spencer, *Nature of Man*, pp. 192–93.

deliberately. Shakespeare turned to this form at a time when his audience was very sophisticated and when the use of indoor theaters permitted the development of new theatrical legerdemain.[21]

The fashionable turn to tragi-comedy was accompanied, as we have seen, by certain uses of Greek romance, the influence of which can be traced with some detail in *The Winter's Tale*.[22] This leads F. W. Moorman to say that "we are invited by Shakespeare to look upon his *Winter's Tale* as Greek in spirit and atmosphere" (p. xxiv).[23] Yet as a matter of fact, the spirit and atmosphere are far from being Greek; and it must be realized that, however some of the externals changed and however Shakespeare may have used Greek mythology and the names of Greek divinities, it is still Shakespeare who writes, doing so with an orientation to man and the world which is as far from the Hellenic as is the Avon from Olympus. There is, in fact, no thorough break between the tragedies and tragi-comedies. Some recent critics have warned against dividing Shakespeare's work into sharply contrasting periods.[24] Derek Traversi has shown that, although it is quite a jump from *Macbeth* to *The Winter's Tale*, the former in fact prepares the way for the latter in terms of the "more intimate fusion of character and action . . . in their relation to the poetic unity which emerges from the play." [25] Mr. Traversi continues:

In the great tragedies of Shakespeare's maturity, the protagonists and the action which they initiate stand in the closest mutual relationship. The moral drama of the central figure finds full dramatic projection in the external events which he himself has, by an act of the will, set in motion; and the events in turn acquire coherence and meaning through the relationship which binds them at every stage to the tensions which constitute the tragedy of the hero [p. 14].

If this analysis is correct, it means that the root conception in the Shakespearean play is moving toward an expression in which the form, the shape, the complex pattern is more and more important. It was always Shakespeare's way, visible even in an early play such as *Richard III*, to present both the internal and the external patterns of the action.

---

[21] See G. E. Bentley, "Shakespeare and the Blackfriars Theater."

[22] Samuel L. Wolff, *The Greek Romances in Elizabethan Prose Fiction*, pp. 448–50.

[23] Professor Moorman's remarks on the Greek spirit of *The Winter's Tale* have been effectively contraverted by S. L. Bethell, *The Winter's Tale: A Study*, pp. 37–40.

[24] For instance, W. W. Lawrence, *Shakespeare's Problem Comedies*, pp. 175, 223–31.

[25] *Shakespeare: The Last Phase*, p. 12.

Richard III is slung between the two poles of Richard's character and Margaret's historical prophecy. But later the external pattern is more thoroughly fused, as Mr. Traversi says, with the internal drama, with the result that the scheme of the work is more frankly exposed and more fully exploited for the sake of its symbolic meaning. It is a dangerous path of development, which only a poetic genius could follow without sacrificing weight to formality. When Shakespeare retired from the Jacobean stage, the drama began to decline, as in less masterful hands than his the form became everything, the substance nothing.[26]

As an example of the formal conception in *The Winter's Tale*, one may observe that the play from one point of view is built upon an idea of fullness, roundedness, and concentric circles. Mr. Traversi has pointed out that the scheme of the play is expressive of the four seasons, the meaning contained in the full round of the year, beginning in autumn and being complete in the abundance of summer.[27] If we think of the play's structure, imagined simply, we see an early part laid in the court of Sicilia, a middle part in the rustic fields of Bohemia, and a concluding part again with the king in Sicilia.[28] The pattern is circular, with the pastoral scenes enveloped by those of court life. The idea of roundedness and enveloping is suggested early in the play in Hermione's pregnancy. Big with child, she "rounds apace" (16), as her attendant says. In this condition, she is committed by Leontes to prison, where, herself enclosed, she gives birth to the child enclosed in her womb, setting free her own "poor prisoner" (II.ii.28):

> This child was prisoner to the womb and is
> By law and process of great Nature thence
> Freed and enfranchis'd. . . .   (59–61)

[26] Says Waith (*Tragicomedy in Beaumont and Fletcher*, p. 85): "The net effect of the combination of satire and romance upon the pattern of tragicomedy can be described as a major increase in formalization and a corresponding decrease in meaning." It is questionable whether the cause should be laid to satire and romance. Shakespeare reflects both without a "decrease in meaning." But the tendency to move away from meaning to formalization in his successors is clear. Cf. Henri Fluchère, *Shakespeare and the Elizabethans*. Referring to the tragi-comedies of Fletcher, Randolph, and Jonson, he writes, "the substance of the drama, the truth—not logical but human—of the characters counted for less than the form in which it was contained" (p. 69).

[27] *Shakespeare: The Last Phase*, pp. 106–7.

[28] The John Gielgud production of the play, seen in London in 1951, began at Sicilia in subdued colors of grey and wine, set the Whitsun pastoral in outdoor brilliance of straw and sky blue, and returned to the grey and wine of Sicilia, which at the end was lightened by the whiteness of Hermione.

The image of the pregnant circle comes in also through the idea of the blessed island upon which, in a famous mistake in scholarship, Shakespeare places the oracle of Apollo:

> The climate's delicate, the air most sweet,
> Fertile the isle, the temple much surpassing
> The common praise it bears.[29]   (III.i.1–3)

The earth itself is also imagined as a sphere in the center of other spheres (the usual sixteenth-century cosmology), betrayed in such language as that of Leontes when he refers to the earth as "the centre" (II.i.102).[30] Perhaps the most important occasion of the encircling idea, however, is in the famous speech which Polixenes delivers to Perdita when she has scorned the "carnations and streak'd gilly-flowers" (IV.iv.82) as being "Nature's bastards" (83). The lesson which he tries to teach her is the conceptual counterpart of a cosmology of concentric spheres, of the play's symbol of new creation (Perdita) born as a prisoner within a prison, and of the shell-like structure in which the formalities and sins of the court surround the fertile kernel of the pastoral.

> POL.   Wherefore, gentle maiden,
> Do you neglect them?
>
> PER.   For I have heard it said
> There is an art which in their piedness shares
> With great creating Nature.
>
> POL.   Say there be;
> Yet Nature is made better by no mean
> But Nature makes that mean; so, over that art
> Which you say adds to Nature, is an art
> That Nature makes. . . .
>   This is an art
> Which does mend Nature, change it rather, but
> The art itself is Nature.[31]   (85–97)

---

[29] This passage is reminiscent of that in *Macbeth* (I.vi) at the entry of Duncan into Macbeth's castle. See S. L. Bethell, *Winter's Tale*, p. 83, and F. C. Tinkler, "The Winter's Tale," pp. 351–52. Both the Shakespearean passages emphasize the religious tone. That in *The Winter's Tale* adds the idea of "island."

[30] The term is often applied to the earth by Shakespeare. Cf. *T. & C.* (I.iii.85) and *Ham.* (II.ii.159), as well as the significance of "the centre of this isle" (*Rich. III*, V.ii.II), discussed in Chap. V of this book.

[31] It is true that Perdita does not accept Polixenes' argument here, but as Bethell reminds us, "the serious presentation of the argument commends it to our notice" (p. 27). Contrast

Here are Nature and Art, transcending each other as layers of packing, yet the whole which contains all else is Nature. Completeness is that which surrounds all within. How admirably suited this type of thought is to Shakespeare's use of tragi-comic form it is almost impossible to describe. The form of the play contains the meaning, yet the meaning is that which stands above and controls the form. At whichever one looks—symbol or symbolic meaning—the other is revealed as through a transparency; and the whole artistic creation, however much it teaches ultimately about life, is marvelously self-contained.

It might be thought that where we encounter such a structured vision of things and meanings we have gone away from concern with historical existence; for the concept of concentric circles is spatial, and it would seem impossible to present it as vividly as Shakespeare does, and yet in the same work remain faithful to the reality of the temporal process. The task is not, however, impossible; Shakespeare has accomplished it. The historical attitude—that is, the attitude of man in his unique time-situation—remains, although it is in the greatest tension with the completed, circular vision just described. The result is one of Shakespeare's truest creations.

To be sure, the specific chronology of events is less mentioned in *The Winter's Tale* than in the other Shakespearean plays I have discussed. As the action becomes simpler (here there is no double plot, no one group of forces aligned against another, as Claudius against Hamlet or Malcolm against Macbeth), and as we move away from the immediacy of social and political reality (which was retained in the tragedies from the histories), chronology itself becomes correspondingly simplified.[32] But simplification does not mean abandonment. Polixenes' stay at Sicilia is described specifically. He has been away from his throne "Nine changes of the wat'ry star" (I.ii.1), and it would take him as long as that to thank Leontes for his hospitality. He is preparing to leave "tomorrow" (10), but Leontes desires him to stay "One sev'n-night longer" (17), and Hermione desires "The borrow of a week" (39), for which she will exchange permission for

---

Richard Wincor, the essay, "Shakespeare's Festival Plays." He discusses the speech as if Polixenes' reasoning had no validity (p. 233). So also F. David Hoeniger's essay, "The Meaning of *The Winter's Tale*." This failure to see the truth in Polixenes' speech is the only blemish in Professor Hoeniger's otherwise excellent article.

[32] Shakespeare never forsakes the plain realities of life, however. "If the romances are far from the workaday world . . . the workaday world is nevertheless present everywhere through imagery and reference" (Bethell, *Winter's Tale*, p. 28).

Leontes, when he visits Bohemia, to remain "a month behind the gest/ Prefix'd for's parting" (41–42). At her entreaties he agrees to stay, but when Leontes (in the same scene) is seized with his violent jealousy, Polixenes changes his plans and, so that he may "take the urgent hour" (465), sails, his ships being ready and his people having expected his departure "Two days ago" (451).

From the events of the first day to the day of Hermione's trial an interval of twenty-three days passes (II.iii.198), long enough for the journey of the messengers to Delphos and their return, which is accomplished in "good speed" (199). The most important interval in the play is that represented in Act IV. scene i. by "Time, the Chorus," which is to account specifically for the passage of sixteen years. With the exception of these clear intervals, the action moves continuously.[33] The scenes as a whole are much longer than in the earlier plays, so that there is less of a flow through time. Instead, the scenes jump from one day to another, through seven or eight days of action spread over some sixteen years of growth.

To supplement the feeling of time thus generated, Shakespeare has introduced many lines which indicate that the action is taking place in a world of nights and days, circling years, and continuing history. There are, for instance, many conversational references to clocks, days, months, years, and the like. Here is Leontes insisting to Camillo that the behavior of Hermione with Polixenes is amiss:

> Is whispering nothing? . . .
> Skulking in corners? wishing clocks more swift?
> Hours, minutes? noon, midnight? . . .
>   Were my wife's liver
> Infected as her life, she would not live
> The running of one glass.   (I.ii.284–306)

The speech recalls that in which Hermione had told Leontes,

> I love thee not a jar o' th' clock behind
> What lady she her lord.   (I.ii.40)

---

[33] The intervals one must imagine between scenes ii and iii of Act III for Antigonus' voyage to Bohemia and between Acts IV and V for Florizel and Perdita to go to Sicilia do not interrupt the action and contribute little to the feeling of passing time. The journey to Delphos does not interrupt, either, and is mentioned only because Shakespeare has set its length so definitely at twenty-three days.

When Leontes told Hermione that only once before had she spoken to better purpose than now in urging Polixenes to remain with them, he says that former occasion was when

> Three crabbed months had sour'd themselves to death
> Ere I could make thee open thy white hand
> And clap thyself my love. (102–4)

When he looks at his son, he sees himself "twenty-three years" younger (144); and Polixenes' son is so much joy, "He makes a July's day short as December" (169). Leontes' totally unjust action against Polixenes and Hermione robs him, like Macbeth, of sleep. He complains that he has "Nor night nor day no rest" (II.iii.1). Antigonus is bade to take the child Hermione has produced and burn it, bringing word it is done "Within this hour" (136). In the trial scene Paulina chastises Leontes with the words,

> A thousand knees
> Ten thousand years together, naked, fasting,
> Upon a barren mountain, and still winter
> In storm perpetual, could not move the gods
> To look that way thou wert. (III.iii.211–15)

And the repentant Leontes, commanding a common grave prepared for his dead queen and son, declares:

> upon them shall
> The causes of their death appear, unto
> Our shame perpetual. Once a day I'll visit
> The chapel where they lie, and tears shed there
> Shall be my recreation. So long as nature
> Will bear up with this exercise, so long
> I daily vow to use it. (237–43)

Later we learn that Paulina has visited the statue of the queen "twice or thrice a day, ever since the death of Hermione" (V.ii.114–15).

In Act IV the expression of time through the commonplaces of nature becomes more prominent. Autolycus' song at his entrance (IV.iii) is full of references to "the sweet o' the year" (3), of how "the red blood reigns in the winter's pale" (4), of "summer songs" (11) and the pale moon which "shines by night" (16). All this, and the merry heart which "goes all the day" (134), enables him to sleep out the thought of "the life to come" (31). Throughout the act the references

to the seasons are too profuse to bear, or need, cataloguing. But it is to
the point to notice the many allusions to "the day"; that is, to daily life
and to special, eventful days. Florizel bids Perdita,

> Lift up your countenance, as it were the day
> Of celebration of that nuptial which
> We two have sworn shall come.   (IV.iv.49–51)

The Shepherd reminds Perdita,

> when my old wife liv'd upon
> This day she was both pantler, butler, cook,
> Both dame and servant,   (55–57)

whereupon Perdita takes upon herself "The hostess-ship o' th' day"
(72). Among the flowers which she presents to Polixenes is

> The marigold, that goes to bed wi' th' sun
> And with him rises weeping.   (105–6)

And for Florizel she wishes she had "some flowers o' th' spring that
might/Become your time of day" (113–14). Autolycus, Mopsa,
Dorcas, and the Clown bring with them a sense of the every-day. The
Clown complains:

> Is there no manners left among maids? . . . Is there not milking-time,
> when you are going to bed, or kiln-hole, to whistle off these secrets, but you
> must be tittle-tattling before all our guests?   (244–50)

Autolycus has a ballad to sell which is in the latest fashion, being "Very
true, and but a month old" (270). He has another not quite so new,
since, as Dorcas reminds him, "We had the tune on't a month ago"
(300). When Polixenes, revealing himself as the king, vents his anger
upon the old Shepherd, he regrets "that by hanging thee I can/But
shorten thy life one week" (431–32); and the Shepherd, for his part,
desires to "die within this hour" (471). For Autolycus, however, the
sudden change of events which follows is pure joy, for "Sure the gods
do this year connive at us" (690), a statement which in fact is truer
than he knows.

In addition to these passages in which clocks, days, months, and
other measurements of time appear almost as idiomatic expressions,
there are others which reflect a basic assumption of historical existence. Hermione's plea in defense of her innocence, to take a clear

example, reflects an historical understanding in two senses: she not only refers specifically to history as the record of the past against which present occurrences are measured; she also describes her own guiltless life as a history with past, present, and future. Observe that history, as she imagines it, is not merely the passage of time but also the seeing of that time in terms of a meaningful pattern, as in a theater, for which "beholding" she calls upon the gods and implores Leontes (the words expressing the time-sense are here italicized):

> If powers divine
> Behold our human *actions*, as they do,
> I doubt not then but innocence *shall make*
> False accusation blush, and tyranny
> Tremble at *patience*. You, my lord, best know,
> Who least will seem to do so, *my past life*
> *Hath been* as continent, as chaste, as true,
> As I *am now* unhappy; which is more
> Than *history* can pattern, though devis'd
> And play'd to take spectators. . . .
>
> I appeal
> To your own conscience, sir, *before* Polixines
> *Came* to your court, how I *was* in your grace,
> How merited to be so; *since he came*,
> With what encounter so uncurrent I
> *Have strain'd* t' appear thus; if one jot beyond
> The bound of honour, or in act or will
> That way inclining, *hard'ned be* the hearts
> Of all that hear me, and my near'st of kin
> Cry fie upon *my grave*! (III.ii.29–55)

Hermione seems not to be able to imagine human virtue and sin apart from the development of actions through time. No more is the social situation in the play imagined as static or timeless. The old Shepherd, one of many reminders in the play of the difference between youth and old age, is described by the Third Gentleman as one "which stands by like a weather-bitten conduit of many kings' reigns," which line immediately orients the mind to the familiar Shakespearean world of historical succession.

The play is also full of Shakespeare's usual colloquial speech reflecting time as that which develops, brings to birth, hastens, fulfills,

and ripens for immediate action. The following passages will be sufficient to demonstrate the quality conveyed:

> It is in mine authority to command
> The keys of all the posterns. Please your Highness
> To take the urgent hour.   (I.ii.463–65)

1st LADY.	We shall

> Present our services to a fine new prince
> One of these days; and then you'd wanton with us.
> If we would have you.

2nd LADY.	She is spread of late

> Into a goodly bulk. Good time encounter her!   (II.i.16–20)

HER.	Pray you, sit by us,

> And tell's a tale.

MAM.	Merry or sad shall't be?
HER.	As merry as you will.
MAM.	A sad tale's best for winter. (22–25)

> The very thought of my revenges that way
> Recoil upon me: In himself too mighty,
> And in his parties, his alliance. Let him be
> Until a time may serve; for present vengeance,
> Take it on her.   (II.iii.19–23)

> If th' event o' th' journey
> Prove as successful to the Queen,—O be 't so!—
> As it has been to us rare, pleasant, speedy,
> The time is worth the use on't.   (III.i.11–14)

> Ay, my lord; and fear
> We have landed in ill time; the skies look grimly
> And threaten present blusters.   (III.iii.2–4)

> 'Tis a lucky day, boy, and we'll do good deeds on't.   (142)

DOR.	Mopsa must be your mistress; marry, garlic,

> To mend her kissing with!

MOP.	Now, in good time! (IV.iv.163)

> [Leontes] o'er and o'er divides him
> 'Twixt his unkindness and his kindness; the one
> He chides to hell and bids the other grow
> Faster than thought or time.   (561–64)

> So that in this time of lethargy
> I pick'd and cut most of their festival purses.   (625–26)

> You might have spoken a thousand things that would
> Have done the time more benefit and grac'd
> Your kindness better.   (V.i.21–23)

>   O Hermione,
> As every present time doth boast itself
> Above a better gone, so must thy grave
> Give way to what's seen now!   (95–98)

>   Beseech you, sir,
> Remember since you ow'd no more to time
> Than I do now.   (219–20)

It should be clear from this summary that even in tragi-comedy, where, as in *The Winter's Tale*, he is dealing with a cyclical pattern of completion, Shakespeare does not forsake his interest in time. He gives less space to the specific chronology of events than he did in the histories and tragedies, but he does not abandon that subject. On the other hand, the play is full of references to the measurement of time, to historical awareness, and to time in its manifold meanings as the mode of creation, growth, and opportune action. The combination of these factors creates a play in which the spectator is never allowed to forget that, for all the unreal and pastoral elements, the world has not been taken out of history nor given over to the perpetual forms of nature.[34]

The question remains as to what definite role time plays in the picture of reality which *The Winter's Tale* draws.

The reader who looks at *The Winter's Tale* with an eye to its references to time is aware that chronological references are more frequent in the early part of the play. This is because time is made conspicuous in the opening discussion between Polixenes and his hosts over whether he will remain with them a week longer. When that occasion is past, the subject of time appears to recede. The temptation, therefore, is to say that, like the *Alcestis*, *The Winter's Tale* finds its tragi-comic victory by passing beyond the complications of time into some other type of fulfillment. That is not, however, the case. What

---

[34] The production of the play at Stratford, Ontario, in 1958, directed by Douglas Campbell, made fitting use of a giant hourglass which was onstage continuously and was occasionally turned by Time as Chorus.

happens is that time is transmuted from a subject of conscious reflection into what Derek Traversi has called "a persistent base" or "persistent background to the main action."[35]

So little has the importance of time in the scheme of the play been noticed by most that one critic has been led to suggest that the introduction of Time as Chorus at the beginning of Act IV is an unskillful intrusion, illustrating Shakespeare's failure to accomplish in *The Winter's Tale* what he succeeded in doing in *The Tempest*, namely, to bring the idea of *reconcilement* "into accord with dramatic Unity of Time." The commentator goes on:

In this play of ours, having to skip sixteen years after Act 3, he desperately drags in Father Time with an hour-glass, and not only makes him apologize for sliding over the interval, but uses him as prologue to a second intrigue—

> Imagine me,
> Gentle spectators, that I now may be
> In fair Bohemia, and remember well
> I mentioned a son o' th' king's, which Florizel
> I now name to you; and with speed so pace
> To speak of Perdita.

—Which means on interpretation that Shakespeare, having proposed to himself a drama in which a wronged woman has to bear a child, who has to be lost for years and restored to her as a grown girl, simply did not know how to do it, save by invoking some such device. At length, after many essays, in *The Tempest* he did achieve the impossible thing and compress the story into one single, brief movement.[36]

The trouble here is that one is made to feel that it was simply a dramatic inconvenience that sixteen years must pass and a baby grow into a girl. On the contrary, the passage of such time is essential to the idea.

[35] *Shakespeare: The Last Phase*, p. 171. Mr. Traversi is excellent on the importance of time in the play's interpretation. "*The Winter's Tale*," he says, "deals with the divisions created in love and friendship by the passage of time and the action of 'blood' and of the final healing of these divisions" (p. 107). If he seems to reverse himself when he says that time in the play is "not finally valid" (171), he is more nearly correct when he states that "the relation of the time-theme to those of re-birth and reconciliation is . . . retained to the last as a necessary part of the complete effect" (189). The tensions between time and form in this play seem almost to force the critic to inconsistency. Bethell (*Winter's Tale*) says, on the one hand, that the play is "a statement of eternal truth transcending time and place" (p. 31), that it is a "timeless drama" (p. 36), and on the other hand, "We are made to appreciate the significance of time and change . . . and to perceive at the same time, beyond time, a changeless divine order whose redemptive function is providentially effective within the time-process" (p. 44).

[36] Sir Arthur Quiller-Couch, *Winter's Tale*, p. xix.

The personification of Time, which I believe Shakespeare need not have introduced if he had not desired, or at least could have represented simply as Chorus without calling him Time,[37] is a deliberate means of drawing attention to the importance of time in the idea of the work.[38] As for *The Tempest*, Shakespeare's observance of the so-called Unity of Time in that play destroys essentially the force which time carries in the other plays. Not schematically, to be sure, for the time Prospero has spent on the island is stated to be important, and times past, present, and future are carefully laid out; but the prevailing power in that play is precisely that by which Shakespeare has been enabled to bring his action within the compass of one day, namely, the magical abilities of Prospero.[39] While the lover of poetry never ceases to be enamored of *The Tempest*, it is not, I think, what anyone would call typical of Shakespeare, not even the Shakespeare of the earlier histories, comedies, and tragedies raised to a higher power. It is something different. *The Tempest*, although it is superb in its way, does not reflect that orientation of man to a genuine temporal world which Western man understands and which elsewhere Shakespeare has used as the basis and accompaniment of his imaginative creations.[40]

In *The Winter's Tale* the sixteen-year period which passes between the early scenes and the last ones is important not only from the point of view of realism, but also because it carries at least two meanings. For one thing, it is purgatorial. "The motives of hell and purgatory in Leontes are obvious enough," as Professor Tillyard has said.[41] We are not to imagine Leontes as having remained exactly the same for sixteen years. True, he "shuts up himself" (IV.i.19), but that is for the purpose of his penitent acts, which cause Cleomenes to tell him,

---

[37] Remember Gower in *Pericles* and Chorus in *Henry V*.

[38] Cf. Bethell, *Winter's Tale*, p. 47.

[39] Some think that Shakespeare wrote *The Tempest* in conformity with the unities partly to show Ben Jonson he could do it if he liked, although it should be remembered that two earlier plays, *The Comedy of Errors* and *Love's Labor's Lost*, had fulfilled the requirement.

[40] W. H. Auden (*The Portable Greek Reader*) has discussed the Unity of Time in relation to the modern (including Shakespearean) understanding of character:

"Unity of time is not only possible but right and proper in Greek tragedy because the characters do not change, only their situation so that the dramatic time required is simply the time required for the situation to change. In modern tragedy, unity of time is possible as a technical tour-de-force but rarely desirable, since one of the dramatist's principal tasks is to show how his characters not only are changed by changes of situation but also play active parts in creating these situations, and it is almost impossible to show this in a single uninterrupted passage of time" (p. 25).

[41] *Shakespeare's Last Plays*, p. 84. Cf. Knight, *The Crown of Life*, p. 76: "Leontes sins and endures a purgatory of guilt."

> Sir, you have done enough, and have perform'd
> A saint-like sorrow. No fault could you make
> Which you have not redeem'd; indeed, paid down
> More penitence than done trespass.[42]   (V.i.1–4)

Hermione, too, whom all thought dead, has aged. When Leontes see the supposed statue, he objects:

>   But yet, Paulina,
> Hermione was not so much wrinkled, nothing
> So aged as this seems.
> POL.   O, not by much.
> PAUL. So much the more our carver's excellence,
>   Which lets go by some sixteen years and makes her
>   As she liv'd now.   (V.iii.27–32)

We are not allowed to forget the long period of sorrow which intervened since the wrongs Leontes committed. Leontes had a sorrow, says Camillo,

> Which sixteen winters cannot blow away,
> So many summers dry. Scarce any joy
> Did ever so long live; no sorrow
> But kill'd itself much sooner.   (V.iii.50–53)

The theme of purification and repentance which Shakespeare is developing in the character of Leontes is inseparable from "that wide gap" (IV.i.7) which was represented by Time, the Chorus. Leontes' penitence implies memory, which is the more meaningful if it has been carried for many years. "The necessary prelude to reconciliation," Mr. Traversi writes, "is a further projection of the past into the present, a poignant deepening of Leontes' love for Hermione." [43] This projection of the past into present is accomplished by exacting the pledge from Leontes never to remarry until "your first queen's again in breath:/ Never till then" (V.i.83–84), by the introduction and recognition of Perdita, and above all by the visit to the statue, which looks for very life like Hermione herself.

>   O royal piece
> There's magic in thy majesty, which has
> My evils conjur'd to remembrance.   (V.iii.38–40)

---

[42] Other passages suggesting purgatory are Act III, scene iii, lines 211–14, 235–44, and Act IV, scene iv, lines 557–64.
[43] *Shakespeare: The Last Phase*, p. 169.

At the same time that the sixteen-year interval serves the function of purgation and penitence, it also serves that of maturation. Even as Leontes "shuts up himself," Perdita is rescued from death by the Shepherd and begins to grow in a rural setting which later will be suggestive of the bountiful productivity of nature. The language of the fourth act is that of nature bringing itself to flower, even as Perdita, left upon the shore, was addressed as "blossom" (III.iii.46). The rough, wintry weather in which she was exposed gives way to the burgeoning of spring in Autolycus' song:

> When daffodils begin to peer,
>   With heigh! the doxy over the dale,
> Why, then comes in the sweet o' the year;
>   For the red blood reigns in the winter's pale. (IV.iii.1–4)

Perdita is, as the Chorus says, "now grown in grace" (IV.i.24). Mr. Traversi has drawn attention to the importance of the idea of grace in this play.[44] The conception is the spiritual counterpart of the bounty of nature, while it goes beyond nature with that quality which "grace" always conveys, namely, an added dimension of worth and joy which could not be expected in the root thing itself. It is significant that Perdita is born in the moment when Hermione is most out of favor and the evil work of Leontes still rushing toward its acme. That which is redemptive is born, and does not cease to grow, even when evil abounds. The storm symbolizes the same evil raging around the birth of the good. The Shepherd's son describes how he saw all on the ship drowned, whereupon Perdita's discoverer remarks, "Thou met'st with things dying, I with things new-born" (III.iii.116). It is this thing new-born, the seed of Leontes himself, joining with the seed of Polixenes, who in the spring of the play will provide that love and grace which becomes the means whereby Leontes is reconciled with his sorrowing past and ushered into the summer bounty of forgiveness.[45]

Time in *The Winter's Tale* is the means within which reconciliation and fulfillment take place. Reconciliation depends upon repentance,

---

[44] *Shakespeare: The Last Phase*, pp. 119 ff. Cf. F. C. Tinkler, "Winter's Tale," p. 345.

[45] The shipwreck scene, says Mr. Traversi (*Shakespeare: The Last Phase*, p. 106), unites "the idea of birth and death in a single episode" and connects "the tragic past with the happy future in an anticipation of the final reconciliation." Cf. G. Wilson Knight (*Crown of Life*, p. 126) who points out that the evil in the first part of the play is present-past, while the "creative consciousness" in the latter part is present-future. "Hence our poetry plays queer tricks with time. . . ." Shipwrecks are important in three of Shakespeare's last four plays, and in all three they are transition points between the old and the new.

a time of purgation, and the activity of memory, drawing the past into the present. When that is accomplished, time moves to its fulfillment. The indispensable idea here, quite as much as in Shakespeare's histories, is that of continuity. There is no break in time in *The Winter's Tale* for all that there is a "wide gap." The very meaning of the play is the overarching of that gap in a new harmony in which neither present nor past dominates the other, but rather the two are reconciled. In the very opening lines of the play, Camillo had said to Archidamus that when Leontes and Polixenes were separated from each other by distance and royal business, they

shook hands, as over a vast; and embrac'd, as it were, from the ends of opposed winds.   (I.i.34)

The line is prophetic. The play is the explication of a more terrible "vast" which opens between men in the course of their self-assertions as a corollary of historical existence. It is a demonstration of the ruptures which can occur as the result of "opposed winds" blowing through the human heart. The rent which Leontes tears in the fabric of human relations tears apart also the past, present, and future, which would remain severed were it not that grace also grows in time, provided there is penitence. We are reminded of how Leontes and Polixenes once "shook hands, as over a vast" when at the conclusion of the play Leontes requests,

> Good Paulina,
> Lead us from hence, where we may leisurely
> Each one demand and answer to his part
> Perform'd in this wide gap of time since first
> We were dissever'd.   (V.iii.151–55)

In *The Winter's Tale*, continuity, which must be seen to underlie and survive all the ruptures which evil creates, is set forth in the symbol of the family. It is the sustaining means by which events finally are brought to their fulfillment:

The continuity of the family relationship, by which the father is fulfilled in his child, is . . . one of the foundations on which the symbolic structure of *The Winter's Tale* rests.[46]

The play, therefore, reaches its conclusion in a scene in which the families are reunited: Polixenes with his son Florizel, Leontes with

---

[46] Traversi, *Shakespeare: The Last Phase*, p. 115.

his lost daughter and wife as good as returned from the dead, and Paulina, in the manner of comedy, wed to a new husband. This fulfillment of the family unity is matched by a fulfillment in time, carefully built up in the scene with the "statue." After Paulina draws the curtain and "discovers Hermione standing like a statue," [47] the first reaction is marvel, made possible by memory of the Hermione of the past. Some thirty lines are devoted to memory and the past sixteen years. However, as Leontes seems to be transfixed, his heart too heavy burdened, Paulina offers to close the curtain:

> No longer shall you gaze on't, lest your fancy
> May think anon it moves.   (V.iii.60–61)

But Leontes is rapt, and if the statue will make him "think anon it lives" (70) he desires "to think so twenty years together"(71). He would not have her draw the curtain, "No, not these twenty years" (84), and Perdita also says that she could look at it "so long" (84). Rapture thus being drawn out, Paulina offers to make the statue move, tantalizing husband, daughter, and audience with the suggestion. She is deliberate.[48] First mentioning those who may not like her action, as if "it is unlawful business" (96) and then having Leontes' permission to proceed, she brings the slow process to fulfillment with sharp commands:

> > Music, awake her; strike!
> 'Tis time; descend.   (98–99)

'Tis time, indeed. For sixteen years it has been in preparation, the action growing to its hour of ripeness, when memory has fertilized and forgiveness redeemed the now pregnant situation. It is not that there is sufficient power for the tragi-comic miracle, but that the time for it has arrived:

> PAUL. 'Tis time; descend; be stone no more; approach;
> Strike all that look upon with marvel. Come,
> I'll fill your grave up. Stir, nay, come away,
> Bequeath to death your numbness; for from him
> Dear life redeems you. . . .

[47] The statue which is not a statue, incidentally, is surely an excellent stage symbol of "that wide gap" of time which was frozen but not frozen.

[48] Tinkler ("Winter's Tale") has mentioned the slow tempo in the first part of this scene, which increases toward Hermione's reanimation, when "long, weighted enjambments give way to more broken speech" (p. 363).

> Nay, present your hand.
> When she was young you woo'd her; now in age
> Is she become the suitor?
>
> LEON.   O, she's warm!

Such is the use to which Shakespeare puts the tragi-comic form, which revels in the miracle of life bringing to nought the threatened power of death. He turns it into a history of the process of reconciliation.[49] For all the imagery of nature in the play, history is not here sacrificed to nature.[50] On the contrary, nature is made to symbolize the developments in human history, seen internally as the struggle of souls. The seasons in the play are not, in fact, either in themselves or as representatives, the ultimate realities. They are similies of something which is more real than they. "Welcome hither," says Leontes to Florizel, "As is the spring to th' earth" (V.i.151–52), the figure of speech accurately describing the relationship as Shakespeare sees it. If nature were the basic reality, the play should end in the season in which it begins. It does not. It begins in autumn or winter, it ends in the flourishing of summer. And although there is some formal similarity between the harmony of the ending and that of the beginning, they are totally different in character because the one was in a way as innocent and immature as that state Leontes describes when he and Polixenes

> were as twinn'd lambs that did frisk i' th' sun,
> And bleat the one at th' other. What we chang'd
> Was innocence for innocence; we knew not
> The doctrine of ill-doing, no, nor dream'd
> That any did.   (I.ii.68–71)

But the other is a reconciled harmony, full of the memory of ill-doing and existing in the paradox of forgiveness.[51]

[49] The contrast with Greene's *Pandosto: The Triumph of Time* is strong. Greene's work was dominated by the image of the wheel of fortune. See F. D. Hoeniger, "Meaning of *Winter's Tale*," p. 26.

[50] Even within nature history is not ignored. Tinkler ("Winter's Tale") has emphasized the importance of "tradition" in the pastoral life of this play (pp. 350–51).

[51] The beginning and ending are as man's pre- and post-lapsarian states in Christian theology. S. L. Bethell (*Winter's Tale*) speaks of the play's expression "of the Christian scheme from the fall of man to his ultimate restoration in heavenly bliss" (p. 104). Cf. Spencer (*Nature of Man*, p. 201) who says that the last plays, as well as earlier ones, reflect the pattern of the sixteenth-century morality play and interlude: man as he ought to be, man led astray

All that is being said here is a corollary of the internalization of the action in *The Winter's Tale* as compared with Euripides' *Alcestis*. The action of *The Winter's Tale* is inseparable from the sin, pain, and active will of Leontes.[52] It was said here that the play represents developments in human history, seen internally as the struggle of souls. There is no attempt, however, to abstract a vision of what happens in "the soul" from what happens in particular to Leontes, or to remove Leontes from that context of social reality which is suggested by the presence of such people as Autolycus, Mopsa, Dorcas, and "Other Lords and Gentlemen, Ladies, Officers," etc. When we have recognized the artificial conventions of the tragi-comic form and allowed for the suddenness which is inherent in it, Leontes appears before us (not to mention Hermione, Polixenes, and the rest) as the representative of a man who in a particular social and domestic situation committed a sin, not against an inviolable law nor the absolute will of the gods, but against his wife, and his friend, and his son, and his daughter. We are also to take it, I believe, as a sin against whatever ultimate power the play assumes, but not in the abstract. That is why time is essential in the work of reconciliation. For it is at once the province within which the heart comes to itself, and also the common integrator of men in their social relationships.

It was different in the *Alcestis*. If Euripides thought Admetus possessed any internal guilt, he did not dramatize it. Instead, he dramatized the story of a man and wife bound by an external necessity, from which they are released by an equally external benevolence. The only internalization is that of the feelings in a situation from which there seems to be no escape. The state of Admetus and Alcestis at the end is therefore not essentially different from that at the beginning. They are released *from* an imprisonment, but they are not reconciled *to* anything. This means there is an inherent balance in the

---

by the lower part of his nature, and a reconciliation between man and the ruler of the universe. See also F. David Hoeniger ("Meaning of *Winter's Tale*") who speaks in this connection of "man's innocence in childhood, his loss of it through sin, and, after a long period of struggle, sorrow and repentance during which all selfishness is cleansed from his nature, his attainment of permanent peace with the help of grace" (p. 18). At the end of the play, says Professor Hoeniger, Leontes' paradise is not a garden like Perdita's but "a city and a temple, corresponding to the Heavenly City in the New Testament, the Temple of God" (p. 26).

[52] Wolff (*Greek Romances in Elizabethan Prose*, pp. 452–55) has shown that in several instances in the writing of *The Winter's Tale* Shakespeare departed from his sources to substitute natural causation and human motive for what had been the action of Fortune.

work, of which the highly theatrical *agons* with their frequent use of stichomythia are excellent expressions. The result is brilliant theater; but however much we may enjoy it technically or because of its emotion, it can never represent to us what the tragi-comedies of Shakespeare do, which utilize the forms of the stage to body forth images of man's internal history, with its furor, its disseverances, and its reconciliation.

IX

CONCLUSION

If Shakespeare is measured against the criteria proper to the Greek understanding of man and the cosmos, he is found wanting. In that light he must appear barbarian and therefore inferior. By the same token, if the Greek dramatists are measured against a Judaeo-Christian understanding of man, they also appear insufficient. The artistic excellence of each is found only when the harmony is seen between form and intent, the artist in each case making use of the form which best expresses the cultural presuppositions he affirms.

Those who insist that Shakespeare was, after all, Greek in spirit may not realize what a damning judgment they are rendering. It has been stated, for instance, that "the truly tragic spirit is Greek, not Christian, and Shakespearean uniqueness . . . is due to the fact that his spirit is naturally Greek—*anima naturaliter graeca*." [1] If this position were to be taken seriously as a principle of dramatic criticism, it would mean that Shakespeare's plays would have to be examined to see how well his dramatic form expresses that Greek spirit. In such an examination he would fare very badly. The attempt to explain his uniqueness among the Elizabethans (or among Europeans generally) by lifting him out of his time and culture can result only in doing him the greatest injustice. He could not be made to wear the flowing robes of Athens gracefully.

On the other hand, there is no absolute break between the theater of Dionysus and the Globe on Bankside. Shakespeare is still a dramatist, even though he is not a Greek dramatist. The study of comparative literature, although it begins by discovering what is proper and excellent in each separate literature, may proceed to some knowledge of relationships, recognizing both continuities and divergences in the development of a genre. It is from this point of view that we may say

[1] Kathleen Nott, "Small Latin but More Greek?" p. 559.

that Shakespeare fulfills certain aspects of Greek drama which could never have been fully developed on its own soil.

Reinhold Niebuhr has suggested that the Greek dramatists have a feeling for the meaningfulness of historical existence which the Greek philosophers do not have:

> The *dramatis personae* of Greek drama were real persons, engaged in actual history, subject to conflicting claims upon their consciences which were not easily resolved. . . . The persons in Greek drama were not under the illusion that they could bring all the vitalities of life and history into a neat order if only the subrational impulses were subordinated to the order of "mind." These persons were men of spirit, who were betrayed into evil by the same capacity which made their creativity possible: their freedom over natural impulses.[2]

What Professor Niebuhr is pointing to is actually a subordinate strain in the Greek drama. That which he calls the "conflicting claims" is the predominant element. Unlike the claims upon the Shakespearean hero, those upon the Greek are usually between two goods, or two necessities, rather than between a good and an evil. The conflict arises because the Greek tragic flaw is, as W. H. Auden has said of that in Homer's world, "not a flaw in human nature, still less a flaw in an individual character, but a flaw in the nature of existence."[3] The major thrust of the Greek tragedy is toward a way of seeing, if not of understanding, the dichotomies of existence, the relationships between the cosmic powers. When Professor Niebuhr speaks of "real persons engaged in actual history," he points to a subordinate theme which the dramatists came upon through their exploration of character but which they did not develop very far. It is difficult to agree with Professor Niebuhr that the Greeks possessed historical awareness which later philosophy smothered. It appears that consciousness of historical existence was the dimly perceived discovery of the dramatists, who found that in order to represent character they had to show something of what it was like to be caught within a situation. They had, in Collingwood's phrase, to show "the inside of the event," and this impelled them toward a notion of action in an historical setting. But this line of development could not be pursued by the dramatists without abandoning the leading assumptions and questions which they and their audience brought to the stories they told. Therefore they carried

---

[2] *The Self and the Dramas of History*, p. 78.
[3] *The Portable Greek Reader*, p. 20.

it only as far as it aided their demand for verisimilitude, or as far as it added counterpoint to their primary theme. We misread them if we look for a *motif* to be sounded by trumpets which actually is scored for the oboe.

If we were to look at the Greek plays primarily to find "real persons engaged in actual history" we would be at a loss to explain why Xerxes does not appear in *The Persians* until the play is five-sixths completed, although his action is the play's subject; or why Orestes is allowed to depart from the *Oresteia* at the very moment when his dilemma is on the point of being resolved; or why Oedipus is not shown when he makes the decisions which bring about his downfall. It was not the intention of the Greeks to explore "the inside of the events," and we do them an injustice if we hold them to that standard.

At the same time, man is a historical being, whether he knows it or not; and it is perhaps not too much to suggest that the Greek dramatists raised questions about the relation of man to his world for which the Hellenic civilization could not provide satisfactory answers. To put it in terms of art, which seldom deals with "answers," the Greek dramatists stumbled upon the material for questions about man as a historical creature which the culture could not help them to formulate. For the development of this theme, it was necessary to wait until such time as there was a culture historically oriented, a flourishing theater, and an artistic genius the equal of Aeschylus and Sophocles. In Shakespeare, the dramatic question of man's action in a historical situation reached its fulfillment.

If these things are true, we should expect Shakespeare's view of man to be expressed in a dramatic form different from the Greeks, a form which grows out of the culture's historically-minded rituals quite as much as the Greek forms emerged from Hellenic rituals of nature-religion.[4] This is, I believe, the case. The roots of Shakespeare's dramatic form are primarily in the domestic English drama, running back through the chronicle-histories to the Morality plays and the Mysteries based on the universal grandeur of biblical history. This is the drama Shakespeare saw as a boy, in all probability. At any rate, it was the popular drama. If we compare Shakespeare's drama with the

---

[4] As my analysis in Chap. V–VIII has centered on the plays themselves, the argument does not rest on anthropological studies of the origin of Greek drama. However, I believe the argument is not inconsistent with the findings of the Cambridge school.

Mystery plays, we see that the dramatic power is heightened, the artistry much refined, and the situations secularized and universalized. But we do not find that the pattern has changed very much; for that pattern was designed to show the development of historical events in sequence, from the first things to the last, as if man is to be known only through his history.[5] Mable Buland points out that the structure in the play *Mary Magdalene* in the Digby cycle "is exactly that in which Peele cast *Edward I*, and Shakespeare arranged *Henry VI*; it is the method of the chronicle-history, that of showing first the beginning of a story, and then, one after another, its important scenes . . ." [6]

In reminding us that the chronicle play was a very important link between the medieval and the Elizabethan play, W. H. Auden has pointed out that the concern with history committed the playwright to deal with all sorts of situations, ambiguities, and apparent irrelevancies: "he has to take whatever history offers, the humdrum as well as the startling." [7] Here is the basis of Shakespeare's mixture of styles, the failure sharply to separate the comic from the tragic, and the inclusion of many casual details in plot and character which at first appear to be unnecessary.

In addition to seeing man in the sequence of historical events and immersed in a sea of mundane detail, the medieval religious plays also provided an overarching interpretation of history which gave meaning to time and to the apparent trivialities of daily existence. It is this combination of meaning and triviality, event and interpretation, now and eternity, which is the primary key to the understanding of Shakespeare's dramatic form. The problem in understanding Shakespearean form, as in the Christian interpretation of man's existence, is not the quantitative one of relating the parts to the whole, but rather that of relating events in time to a controlling purpose.

What, then, are the specific changes which this understanding of man has wrought in dramatic form between the Greeks and Shakespeare?

If the primary element in dramatic form is the action which it imitates, then the primary change to be noted is in the nature of the action which Shakespeare usually presents, contrasted with the Greek

[5] For the indebtedness of the form of the Elizabethan play to both the Miracles and the Moralities, see Irving Ribner, *The English History Play in the Age of Shakespeare*, pp. 3–32. The Miracles contributed episodic structure, says Professor Ribner, and the Moralities, didacticism and symbolism (pp. 30–31).

[6] *Elizabethan Drama*, p. 29.   [7] *Poets of the English Language*, II, xxviii.

tragedians. In the Greek, the action involves a movement from the temporal to the non-temporal; that is, from event to knowledge. In *The Persians* the movement is from the historical events of Xerxes' expedition against the Greeks to a statement of the law of *hybris*. In the *Oresteia* the theme of the curse upon the house and Orestes' mission as deliverer gives way to the enunciation and celebration of Athenian justice. In the *Oedipus Tyrannus* a skillful arrangement of present and past time is used to demonstrate the inviolable δίκη of the gods. The *Alcestis* shifts from a situation in which time is a prison to one in which divine power brings release.

In Shakespeare, on the other hand, the action is one which moves from knowledge to event, or rather from event to knowledge to new event, and such revelations as there are come about through the power of later events to fulfill and clarify earlier ones.[8] In *Richard III* all the action tends toward a final day of judgment in which a climactic battle reveals the former evil in all its horror and vindicates the good. Here parallels with biblical history and eschatalogical *motifs* give meaning to the history of the English throne. In *Hamlet* the ambiguities and imperatives of a situation where moral action is demanded are resolved in a final denouement which providentially fulfills the original demand, although not according to previous expectation and not without great cost. *Macbeth* reveals the immoral as, among other things, an attempt to usurp time and control the future, the play representing a war between sin and that beneficent power which ultimately controls history. *The Winter's Tale* also focuses upon sin, demonstrating it to be the act of a violent will over which reconciliation triumphs through grace and the fullness of time. In every case, the problems arise in the course of historical existence and the conclusion is a return to orderly succession in the state.

Because the Shakespearean action is one in which the sequence of events supersedes knowledge, it is one in which time is of fundamental importance.[9] The analyses of the plays in the foregoing chapters have shown that the action of the Shakespearean play is expressed through the sense of passing time. The reason for that has not so much to do

[8] In Shakespeare's plays, "there is something at 'the wild heart of life' that insists that the meanings of life are capable of expression in events and that the events of life are capable of expressing the meaning of life" (Roberts, *Theology and Imaginative Literature*, p. 359).

[9] Time, says Fluchère (*Shakespeare and the Elizabethans*, p. 106), "is a dramatic convention ... closely linked not only (as is logical) with space but with the very nature of the play, its object, its chief personage, its message." Later he says that "the haunting theme of Time" is "the most imperative of all to the Elizabethan mind" (p. 223).

with mere "realism" as with the expression of the nature of the action. In moments of crisis and decision, the Shakespearean hero reminds himself and his audience of his history—past, present and anticipated future—because that is the only way he has of seeing the meaning in his act. The moments when the present is most keenly felt are like the "historical present" of biblical thought and like Augustine's reflections on present time: they are compounds of memory and expectation. The past in Shakespeare is very important because it aids in the definition of the present. It is madmen who behave "as the world were now but to begin" (*Ham.* IV.v.103). Yet the past does not, as in the Greek plays, dominate the present and bind it in the grip of necessity. The difference lies in the understanding of the future. In Shakespeare the future is open. It contains the possibility of the new, both as a result of action which man may take and as result of growth and the providential shaping of events which lie outside man's control. The future is open in Shakespeare in the same way that it is in the Bible—not totally uncharted and free for any type of action whatsoever, but full of beneficient promise and tending toward a final culmination which robs the past of its terror and gives significance to the choices of the present. Shakespeare's belief in history is not that of some present day existentialists, to whom the moment of present choice is everything and an order in history nothing except anathema (and who therefore have no notion of history at all); rather he believes in an ordering purpose above the temporal process, indistinguishable in form from the Christian idea of Providence, which imposes the burden of choice upon man without abandoning history to chaos.

In the Greek dramatists we may say that the future either does not exist or is closed and without significance. In *The Persians* and the *Oedipus Tyrannus* the future is unimaginable, as all attention is directed backward to former deeds. In *The Eumenides* the future appears only in the guise of aetiology, and in the *Alcestis* it becomes tolerable only when the bonds of historical necessity are shattered. Past, present, and future do not exist as a meaningful continuum in the plays I have analysed. That is why the action must find its focus in something other than the events of history.

It goes hand in hand with the temporal nature of the Shakespearean action that it should be in some degree internalized. The present which is compounded of memory and anticipation cannot be adequately presented except from "the inside." The importance of time in Judaeo-

Christian thought has accompanied an emphasis upon personal responsibility; for in this view the present is meaningless apart from act,
choice, and will. History, as Collingwood says, is the study of the
"inside" and the "outside" of the event; in the Christian era history
became the history of passion.[10] In line with this tradition, Shakespeare
attempts the fusion of the inner and the outer. The effect on dramatic
form is to be found in the close interdependence of character and
action, in the depiction of moments when decisive choice is made, in
the many ways (of which soliloquy is one) by means of which the in-
terior thought of the character is revealed, and in the sense of involvement and identification which the audience is made to feel for the
people and situations on stage.

The fusion of inner and outer—not only interdependence but also
correspondence between what character experiences and what the
total action reveals—this fusion leads to the adoption of nature into
the realm of the historical. Professor Tillich has reminded us that in
Hebraism and Christianity "history tends to absorb nature into itself,"[11]
and Professor Auerbach has pointed out the New Testament proto-
types for the upheavals in nature which accompany the moral outrages
and spiritual crises of the Shakespearean characters.[12] In Shakespeare
the action is not the result of disturbances in nature, nor is nature in
itself the final arbiter of human action; rather, disturbances in nature
are the result of action taken by men in the course of historical existence. Even in such a nature-drenched play as *The Winter's Tale*,
nature is but a grand metaphor to describe the history of sin and reconciliation in human life. The Shakespearean tragic hero is guilty of sin,
rather than *hybris*,[13] which means his offense originates in the will and
is directed not against nature, but against that unnamed sovereign who
orders nature and against persons actually confronted in the course of
the action. Shakespeare does not believe in a capricious control over
the universe, and therefore the medieval idea of Natural Law may be
used accurately to describe what the plays represent; but the simple
term nature and the word *hybris* are alike too impersonal to do justice
to the reality he presents—a reality which is rooted in a personal center
making choices in a situation defined by its unique history.

In the Shakespearean dramatic action there is a sense of the

[10] See Chap. III, p. 65.   [11] *Ibid.*, p. 61.   [12] *Ibid.*, pp. 62–63.
[13] "Shakespeare's real theme," says Kitto (*Form and Meaning in Drama*, p. 335), "is . . .
the corroding power of sin." Cf. Lewis, "Hamlet, the Prince or the Poem," p. 152; and
Danby, *Doctrine of Nature*, p. 155.

boundlessness of the world and of the dramatic action itself. To the modern mind, trained to think of an expanding universe and infinite galaxies, the Elizabethan world seems small. From our point of view it was a tiny world, and no doubt part of the power of Elizabethan drama comes from the fact that the cosmology of concentric spheres with earth as center (and the Globe Theater as a "wooden O" symbolic of that center) enabled the dramatist to fill up "the wide vessel of the universe" with the dramatic action. The affairs of men loomed large in the Elizabethan cosmos. However, when the Elizabethan world is compared with the Greek, it appears to have infinite reaches. The difference is, once more, the difference between space and time, or between life as a conceptual problem and life as historical existence.[14] Because the tendency of Greek drama is to move from event to knowledge, because it is driven by a desire to envision the order behind the chaotic flux, because its action is predominantly external, and above all because it tends to escape from time into the supposedly firmer realities of law and power, for these reasons its action is depicted as limited and finite. In the Greek tragedy, in contrast to some of the mythological material on which it is based, it is always possible to define clearly the beginning, middle, and end of the situation and therefore the problem it represents. Every detail which we know about theatrical presentation and the written construction of these plays reinforces the impression of clearly defined limits beyond which the imagination is not invited to travel, even though within those limits highly emotional, even ecstatic, lyrics are frequently contained. It is not without reason that the Greek drama is usually regarded as a highly formalized art. By contrast, the Shakespearean play seems ever to reach beyond the limits of the action. As an art form, of course, it does establish the area of its concern, and the critics are correct who emphasize its difference from life and its conventions which seem to hold it in shape. Yet after all that is said there always appears something left over, as if the drama-tist had not quite been able to tie up all the loose ends.[15] There are

---

[14] Stanley Romaine Hopper ("The Future of Religious Symbolism," p. 238) has defined this difference as the "hierarchical context" versus the "dramatic context." "The hierarchical context appropriates the Heraclitean formula of the 'upward and the downward way'. . . . The other context is the dramatic one. As over against the Heraclitean 'upward and downward way,' its motif is that of 'journey and return' after the pattern, the redemptive pattern, of the Prodigal Son."

[15] One remembers how it bothered Mr. Eliot that the Elizabethans would not stay within their conventions but kept running after all sorts of "realism": T. S. Eliot, *Selected Essays*, p. 93.

spurs left jutting into the past and the future which tantalize the mind. If we are not left wondering about such unanswerables as where Hamlet was when his father died, we are left pondering over "tomorrow and tomorrow" or "all our yesterdays." The reason is not difficult to find: it is comparatively easy for the mind to imagine limits to space or to the conceptualized form of a dilemma involving quantitative relationships, but wherever existence in time is taken seriously infinity impinges at every moment.[16]

I shall supplement the foregoing remarks on the nature of the action in Shakespeare and the Greeks with a few observations on the manner of imitation, so that the pertinent differences in dramatic form may be seen more fully. Here are matters of structure, language, theatrical presentation, and the division of acts and scenes.

One of the most fundamental matters of structure is that most often mentioned: the point where the play begins. The Greek procedure is usually, although not always (the *Oresteia* is an exception), to begin near the end and to draw in the antecedent events through some form of recapitulation. The characteristic Shakespearean method is to begin at the beginning and go through the action from start to finish.[17] It would be almost impossible for Shakespeare to communicate the sense of passing time and to portray the moments of decision if this method were not followed.

The question of where one begins is related to the so-called Unity of Time. To represent the action all on one day was not a rule in Greek drama,[18] but it was a definite tendency. The fact indicates that the Unity of Time was not an unbreakable convention but a practice which succeeded in expressing something fundamental about the underlying action and intent. W. H. Auden has suggested that Unity of Time is possible with the Greeks because the characters do not change, and the only time required is for a change in the situation. Unity of Time is not desirable in modern tragedy, he adds, because the dramatist must show not only how character is changed, but also

[16] The reader is referred to Professor Auerbach's analysis of the Abraham and Isaac story (pp. 44–48 of this book), and to Thorlief Boman's discussion of the "borderlessness" in Hebrew thought (p. 48, n. 24 of this book).

[17] There are exceptions, notably *The Tempest* and *The Comedy of Errors*. Very important events are antecedent to the first act of *Hamlet*, but they are fully worked through by the end of the Mouse Trap scene, and from then on the play does not represent a coming to terms with the past, as do the other two mentioned.

[18] Miss Buland (*Elizabethan Drama*) finds four exceptions in the entire canon of tragedies, four more in Aristophanes (pp. 187–197).

how it plays an active part in creating its situation, a demand very difficult to meet in a single uninterrupted passage of time.[19] One should add that Unity of Time is often highly desirable in Greek tragedy because the aim is to minimize the factor of time and to reveal the operation of cosmic laws and powers. In that case, the more compact time is made, the more clearly the other factors stand out. Unity of Time, therefore, is useful as an expression of what I have called the limits of the action.

It has sometimes been thought that Unity of Time was necessitated by the fact of the Chorus' presence in the orchestra, it being unlikely to find the same group of people standing in the same place from day to day.[20] It is better, however, to see the Chorus as another aspect of the same type of concentration which the Unity of Time represents. The Chorus, singing and dancing in formation in its circular or nearly-circular orchestra, is a point of static reference. It tends to minimize movement, not only geographically but also psychologically, for everything must constantly be related to it as to a center, just as in the early drama, the altar of Dionysus was the physical center-point in the orchestra. Shakespeare is not tied down in this way, and it is at least of casual interest that when he does introduce what he calls a chorus, the intention is to pick up the action and move it rapidly through time or space.

Among the many ways in which Shakespeare imitates action in which time is fundamentally important is the technique of anticipation and fulfillment. I have already noted that the action itself is such as reaches its full development and resolution in temporal events— usually in a battle or a duel, or a scene of reconciliation. Shakespeare has not been content to let only the plot represent such action, he also worked into the poetic structure itself a principle whereby early events and lines achieve their full meaning only in later ones. To use examples already analysed, the opening lines of *Richard III*,

> Now is the winter of our discontent
> Made glorious summer by this sun of York,

have an apparent meaning when first spoken, but they are subject to a variety of interpretations as the play progresses and are finally seen to have been prophetic of the play's action, in which England's winter of

[19] See p. 191, n. 40, in this book.
[20] *The Ion of Euripides*, ed. and trans, by Verrall, pp. xlviii–lviii.

discontent is truly dispelled. Similarly, the line in the opening scene of *The Winter's Tale*, "shook hands, as over a vast; and embrac'd, as it were, from the ends of opposed winds" (33), is not fully expounded until the last scene, in which Leontes is shown embracing his friends over the "wide gap" created by sin and time.[21] The nearest equivalent in Greek tragedy is Sophoclean irony, such as Oedipus' pronouncement of the curse which later turns out to have been directed against himself. But here the irony is dependent on a change from ignorance to knowledge, a lifting of a veil, whereas in Shakespeare the full meaning actually does not exist at the beginning but must be brought into being through the events of the play, the process usually being not one in which the later event negates the former but in which early potentialities are deepened, explored, and brought to full fruition. In other words, the later insights of the Shakespearean play often stand in the same relation to its early ones as do the New Testament events to those of the Old Testament in Christian exegesis. The earlier is a "type" of the later, and the full depth of the former is not seen except in the light of the latter, as Moses the deliverer from bondage is a prefiguring "type" of Christ the Redeemer, or the destruction of Jerusalem a prefiguration of the Divine Wrath in the Last Days.

E. E. Stoll has made use of the distinction between "suspense of plot" and "suspense of form" to describe another kind of anticipation and fulfillment that Shakespeare uses. "Suspense of form," characteristic of Shakespeare, is "the excited expectation not of the answer to a puzzle, or of the disclosure of a mystery, but . . . of the rounding out of a harmony, like the rime to come at the end of a verse or the rest tone at the end of a song." [22] Here again, time becomes a part of the very poetic structure, because in time's fullness the early artistic promises are made complete.

When we come to language, two points only need be mentioned. First, Shakespeare's mixture of styles. Shakespeare does not mind moving from poetry to prose and back again when it suits him, or from the most elevated language of the court to the plain speech of porters and gravediggers. The language of his plays more often achieves unity through continuing images and themes than through consistent adherence to a "tone" or "style" throughout. This fact is a reflection of his devotion to concrete reality. At great moments the high and the

---

[21] Cf. the weird sisters' "Fair is foul and foul is fair" (I.i) with Macbeth's "So foul and fair a day I have not seen" (I.ii).   [22] *Shakespeare and Other Masters*, p. 13.

low are bound together in the same events, the drunken Porter with the virtuous Macduff. No more can the comic and tragic be rigidly separated. Shakespeare is in these matters the heir of the medieval religious plays, which had found the most sublime religious events so imbedded in the common stuff of life that the humorous and the momentous played together. The rigid separation of styles depends upon *a priori* principles which cannot be maintained where the starting point is historical reality.

The second linguistic point has to do with the intricate patterns of versification in Greek tragedy. The reader is as much struck by formality in the verse structure as the spectator would be by the sight of the Chorus. Schlegel has described it as simple in over-all plan but of richest variety in poetical ornament.[23] The verse form is another expression of the limits of the action, the shape of the whole being set by convention so that the thought may be both clear and intricate within the frame. In contrast, Shakespeare's iambic pentameter and prose (plus occasional songs) seem almost formless, although in fact they are entirely consonant with the internalized action and the refusal of the action to be contained within arbitrary limits.

Matters affecting theatrical presentation and divisions between the acts and scenes also reflect, ideally in each case, the types of action which they are meant to assist in imitating. The externalized action of the Greek drama can be well expressed by an actor wearing a mask and cothurnus, standing upon a probably shallow stage above a well-trained chorus and in a great open theater before several thousand spectators. The internalized, flowing action of the Shakespearean play could not be represented well in such surroundings. Shakespeare required, in comparison, a more intimate theater where actor and audience were in close rapport, where the mask gave way to the human face, where the actors themselves, instead of a chorus, provided the physical movement, where entrances and exits were facilitated so that action might turn again and again from the reflective word to the immediate event.

The multiplicity of scenes in the Shakespearean play is designed to maintain the flow of events and to be able to show the action from more than one side, as is also the lengthy *dramatis personae* list. It is likely that Shakespeare did not think of act and scene divisions as his editors have impressed them upon our minds; but he certainly thought of a continuous procession of episodes and dialogues so that a freely

[23] *Dramatic Art and Literature*, p. 65.

flowing motion might be maintained, within which a rhythm of acceleration and retardation could be achieved. It is this procession of images that gives the spectator the sense of being on a journey and thus reinforces the notion of movement through time. The Shakespearean play is an account of departure and arrival.

If the division of scenes in the Shakespearean play expresses a principle of motion, the alternation of ode and episode in the Greek play expresses a principle of balance. *Parodos,* when the Chorus enters, balances *exodos,* when it leaves. Between, song and scene follow one another so regularly that there is generated a sense of poise, which corresponds faithfully to the intent of the action, which is to celebrate the fundamental equilibrium of nature.

The roots of popular drama go deep into cultural presuppositions. In addition to entertainment the theater provides enactments which represent to the audience something of the people's deepest understanding of itself. Since the drama is a performed art, portraying actions that take place in time, it will, at its artistic heights, represent the culture's understanding of the temporal world. That is to say, it will reflect the historical consciousness.

The culture of the Greeks, like most of the cultures in the ancient Near East, was oriented toward an understanding of nature in its recurrences, structures, and laws. Its bias was "anti-historical," and its drama reflected the fact with great power. Where the concern of man is with the universal structures of reality, tragedy can reach no greater height nor profundity than it attained in fifth-century Athens.

Another view was possible, however—one which was being prepared in Palestine even before the time of Athens' glory. In Israel there developed a belief, in spite of one national calamity after another, that in history itself there was revealed a divine purpose which would in time be brought to fulfillment. When, in that tradition, the crucifixion and resurrection of Christ was declared to be the very center of history, the story of mankind was turned into an historical drama. This is the tradition which bequeaths to Shakespeare his basic understanding of man. He seldom expresses it in overt religious language. His plays are not to be read as models of Christian doctrine. Yet it is true that the form of his plays is consistent with the biblical interpretation of man and the universe. Shakespearean man is imbedded in the ambiguities and moral demands of history, while the Shakespearean dramatic action seeks its resolution in the fulfilling events of time.

APPENDIX

ON THE CHOICE OF THE PLAYS

The Persians and *Richard III*

Because it is the only play based upon historical subject matter which has survived from classical Greek drama, *The Persians* of Aeschylus becomes the obvious choice among the Greek plays with which to initiate a study of the relation of dramatic form to historical consciousness.[1] The selection from Shakespeare is not so cut and dried. There are, however, reasons for using *Richard III* for comparison and contrast with Aeschylus' play.

The most important consideration is that its subject matter comes the closest of any of the histories to that of *The Persians*. *Richard III* is the only history play of Shakespeare which deals with a strong but sinful king who is justly defeated in battle by a power which represents divine right. It is a matter of some importance to recognize that no Shakespearean play concentrates so exclusively on a central character or event as do most of the Greek plays, including *The Persians*; but comparison is aided if we select a play which comes as close to that as possible.

There is a more basic level of correspondence between the two plays. It is the level on which their contrast is the most marked. In these plays Aeschylus and Shakespeare turn their attention directly upon the realm of history and attempt to find therein patterns of meaning. The quite disparate patterns they discover, which are the patterns that their

[1] It might be argued by some that the stories of the Theban heroes or the house of Atreus were regarded as historical fact by the Greeks, and therefore that *The Seven against Thebes*, the *Oresteia*, *Oedipus the King*, *the Trojan Women*, etc., are history plays. That I feel would be to force the matter. As with Hamlet, Macbeth, and Lear, so with Oedipus, Agamemnon, and Hecuba: their primary meaning for the audience was not their historical reality, but their character as developed by legend, epic, and tragedy. The historical origin is there, but quite remote. The case is different with Xerxes and Richard of Gloucester, who, however they may have been moulded as dramatic figures by their authors, remain in the imagination primarily as historical agents.

cultural presuppositions enable them to discover, are reflected in the contrasting forms of the dramas they produce. My objective was to show how the cultural and ideological background regarding time and history worked itself out in these two plays which take historical events as their theme.

The *Oresteia* and *Hamlet*

Although we have been schooled by the Freudians to think of Hamlet in conjunction with Oedipus,[2] the melancholy Dane actually has more in common with the unhappy son of Clytemnestra and Agamemnon.[3] *Hamlet* and the *Oresteia* are plays [4] "whose common theme/Is death of fathers" (*Ham.* I.ii.103–4). Both heroes are bidden to avenge the death of a father, a mission which raises the question of the rightness of the acts demanded of them. Both plays thus deal with the problem of action compromised.

The concern of both plays is in the moral sphere, rather than the psychological.[5] They consider the nature of moral imperatives. In *Hamlet*, to be sure, the moral question is complicated by the unreadiness of the self to act as demanded; but this amounts, not to a shift of focus to the psychological, but to an enlargement of the moral problem to include the relation of the self to its right course of action. The focus of the *Oresteia* is more objective (that is to say, less concerned with the self), but it is not, for that reason, more moral.

Aside from the similarity in theme, there are more technical reasons for considering these plays together. Both represent their authors at the height of their powers, exhibiting a mature artistry. One may not say that if Aeschylus or Shakespeare had been more in command of his

[2] See particularly Ernest Jones, *Hamlet and Oedipus*.

[3] See Gilbert Murray, "Hamlet and Orestes," in *The Classical Tradition in Poetry*, pp. 204–40. Cf. Florence M. B. Anderson, "The Insanity of the Hero—An Intrinsic Detail of the Orestes Vendetta," *Transactions of the American Philological Association*, pp. 43–62. Miss Anderson notes that previous comparisons of Hamlet and Orestes were made by Herder, Hugo, Ruskin, Henry Mackenzie, and R. G. Latham (pp. 50–51).

[4] I have chosen to regard the *Oresteia* as one play in three parts. The issue raised in the *Agamemnon* is not settled until the end of *The Eumenides*. The *Agamemnon* and *The Libation Bearers* both end inconclusively. Story-line, theme, and character are unified throughout. Whether or not it was the custom to write the trilogy (or tetralogy) as one work, Aeschylus has done so here.

[5] I am aware that many people think of Hamlet in psychological terms. "The modern way of maltreating Hamlet," says Walker, "is to psychologize him" (*Time Is Out of Joint*, pp. ix–x). This pitfall has come with the tendency to study the hero rather than the play.

medium he would have done this or that differently. In addition, both plays are long. The *Oresteia*, being the only trilogy we have intact from the Greeks, is of unique importance in any study of Greek dramatic form. In order to make a point of the compactness, the economy, of the Greek drama, it is necessary to examine the most extensive play which the Greeks have left us. Since the trilogy consists of 3796 lines, it is almost the same length as the modern *Hamlet*, conflated from the shorter Q^2 and F^1 texts, which has 3930 lines.[6] Whereas Chapter VII focuses on *Macbeth* and the *Oedipus Tyrannus*, two short, highly compressed tragedies, in Chapter VI the subject is two long works whose themes are developed at leisure.

The *Winter's Tale* and the *Alcestis*
With a note on the *Alcestis* as tragi-comedy

The *Winter's Tale* and the *Alcestis* have in common not only the fact that they are both tragi-comedies, but also that they have certain similarities in plot. The nineteenth-century critic W. W. Lloyd in his essay on *The Winter's Tale* noted several similarities: the ignoble behavior of the husbands, the quiet virtue of the wives, the silence of both Hermione and Alcestis after their rebirth, and the hasty ending of both plays.[7] F. W. Moorman pointed out that Shakespeare would certainly have had access to the Alcestis story in Chaucer and in the *Petite Palace of Pleasure*.[8] He suggested that Paulina's office in bringing Hermione back to life is similar to that of Heracles in rescuing Alcestis from the arms of Death.[9]

Because of these similarities (to which may be added the fact that in *The Winter's Tale* Shakespeare owes much to influences stemming from the Greek Romances, and also that time in Euripides is treated more realistically than in his predecessors) the contrast between *The Winter's Tale* and the *Alcestis* is illuminating. Their similarities point up their differences. In both, the subject is mythical, fictive, artificial. But Shakespeare uses myth to describe man as a creature of history.

[6] These counts are based on the *Loeb Classics* edition of the *Oresteia*, and the text of Shakespeare's complete plays and poems edited by William A. Neilson and Charles Jarvis Hill.

[7] William Watkiss Lloyd, *Critical Essays on the Plays of Shakespeare*, pp. 161–63. The passage is reprinted in Furness, p. 357, from the 1856 edition of the works of Shakespeare.

[8] *The Winter's Tale*, p. xxxi. Quiller-Couch (*The Winter's Tale*, p. xviii) says, however, that there is no necessity to trace the source back to the *Alcestis*.

[9] Moorman, *Winter's Tale*.

Near the beginning of the nineteenth century Schlegel disparaged Euripides' artistic merit, saying that "he generally sacrifices the whole to the parts." Near the end of the century Verrall attempted to rescue the poet by showing that his interpreters had missed his true intent. This was to be found in a deadly serious attack upon popular superstitions of fifth-century Athens. For "Euripides the fumbler" he substituted *Euripides the Rationalist*. He made of him a "modernist" poet writing for a "fundamentalist" audience.[10]

The trouble was that Verrall's approach was too heavy for the task. He could not imagine that the tragedian was anything but completely earnest.[11] The difficulty becomes apparent when one asks how the audience in the theater was supposed to react. Was it to laugh, or to cry, or to be held in reverent awe? Apparently Verrall thought most of them, believing with pious faith the story of the virtuous wife brought back from death by the semi-divine Heracles, would be held in awe. But what of the others, those who saw a woman who doesn't die at all but merely succumbs to funeral-day hysteria, passes into a trance, and is later found by the uncouth demi-god sitting calmly in her burial-place? That part of the audience must have been highly amused at such a thoroughgoing piece of satire. A work which could divide its audience into two such halves cannot be said to have much artistic integrity; nor would it be likely to survive many generations with the popularity which Euripides enjoyed throughout antiquity.[12]

It did not add much to the understanding of Euripides when Gilbert Murray said that he gives us "sincerity of treatment . . . inside a shell of stiff and elaborate convention," [13] for one still wonders what, if any,

---

[10] "The purpose of the *Alcestis* as a whole, and that which alone connects into a whole its otherwise inharmonious and repugnant elements, is neither to solemnize the legend, as would have been the purpose of Aeschylus, nor to embellish it, as might have been the purpose of Sophocles, but to *criticize* it, to expose it as fundamentally untrue and immoral, before an audience who were well acquainted with the general opinions of the author, well aware that from the circumstances of the case *innuendo* was the only way in which those opinions could be dramatically expressed. . . ." (*Euripides the Rationalist*, pp. 77–78).

[11] Verrall was not really as different from Schegel as one might think. The latter wrote: "We may distinguish in him a two-fold character: the *poet*, whose productions were consecrated to a religious solemnity, who stood under the protection of religion, and who therefore, on his part, was bound to honor it; and the sophist, with his philosophical *dicta*, who endeavoured to insinuate his skeptical opinions and doubts into the fabulous marvels of religion, from which he derived the subjects of his pieces. But while he is shaking the ground-works of religion, he at the same time acts the moralist. . . ." (*Lectures on Dramatic Art*, pp. 116–17).

[12] Verrall has an out. He thinks Euripides wrote for a reading audience more than for the theater. The supposition is open to question; but even if true, there seems to be no indication that the reading public came to Verrall's conclusions.

[13] *Euripides and His Age*, p. 205.

the serious purpose is, and just how it is communicated through the elaborate form.

Following upon much confused ponderosity, Professor Kitto's approach is welcome sanity. He holds that in Euripides' tragi-comedies, among which he includes the *Alcestis*, *Iphigeneia in Tauris*, *Ion*, and *Helen*, high tragic purpose has given way to the desire for theatrical effect. The work has ceased "to be informed, and therefore controlled, by some dominant tragic conception." The first purpose of the dramatist has become "to create an effective stage-piece," and therefore

the dramatist, for the first time, is free to attend entirely to his "form" unhampered by any tragic conception working its imperious will on the play. He can devote himself completely to excellence of workmanship; in fact he must, for this is now his whole "meaning." [14]

Professor Kitto has seen that Euripides is doing something similar to what Shakespeare has done, and that the critic of Euripides must be as flexible as the critic of Shakespeare:

Because these plays have a more limited scope than the tragedies we have entirely to change our critical premises. Alcestis and Antonio are less real than Oedipus and Macbeth; theatrical reality takes the place of tragic, that is to say universal, reality. [15]

As he says later, "the happy ending in fact takes the place of the tragic catharsis" (p. 331).

Once this is seen, a number of the characteristics noted above in reference to Jacobean tragi-comedy appear in Euripides. [16] Let Professor Kitto point them out:

It is to be noticed that all these plays are founded on an impossibility, and that not a "probable impossibility," like the evocation of Darius, but one which is presented as a fiction. By cheating the Fates Apollo prolongs Admetus' life—if he can find a substitute; the *Iphigeneia* and *Helen* start from a miraculous substitution; the *Ion* is based on a divine parentage and miraculous rescue which—told as they are here—nobody would believe (pp. 330–31).

[14] Kitto, *Greek Tragedy*, p. 330. We are the more ready to accept this interpretation, perhaps, if we remember that the *Alcestis* was performed as the satyr-play in the competition. Greenwood (*Aspects of Euripidean Tragedy*) calls it "a tragedy with a satyric prologue and finale. . . ." (p. 12).
[15] *Greek Tragedy*, p. 330.
[16] Of the eight characteristics of tragi-comedy which E. M. Waith found in *A King and No King* (see p. 169 of this book), the *Alcestis* exhibits six. It does not have intricacy of plot nor the atmosphere of evil, but it has all the other features mentioned.

The emotion is limited to the play and to the moment—like our emotion in the presence of Antonio's peril; we feel (if we choose to examine our feelings) that the emotion is temporary because the whole situation is fictive and unreal (p. 331).

As it [tragi-comedy] appeals to our sensations rather than to our apprehensions, it must make its plot continually exciting; in place of the steady development necessary to tragedy it must present sudden changes of mood and unexpected turns of plot (p. 345).

. . . in plays which are essentially plays of incident, characterization cannot be very significant and becomes very largely a mere decoration (p. 346).

One may add, in the words of Paul Decharme, that Euripides' style is "not free from studied elegance." [17]

[17] *Euripides and the Spirit of His Dramas* (New York, 1906), p. 41.

BIBLIOGRAPHY

Aeschylus. Loeb Classical Library ed. 2 vols. Trans. by Herbert Weir Smythe. Cambridge, Mass., 1952.

———— Aeschyli, Septem Quae Supersunt Tragoediae. Ed. by Gilbert Murray. Oxford, 1952

———— The Oresteia. Trans. and Introduction by Richmond Lattimore. Chicago, 1953.

Alexander, Hartley B. God and Man's Destiny. New York, 1936.

Allen, Don Cameron. "Shakespeare's Hamlet," Literary Masterpieces of the Western World. Ed. by Francis H. Horn. Baltimore, 1953.

Anderson, Florence M. B. "The Insanity of the Hero: An Intrinsic Detail of the Orestes Vendetta," in Transactions of the American Philological Association, LVIII (1927), 43–62.

Appleton, William Worthen. Beaumont and Fletcher: A Critical Study. London, 1956.

Aristophanes. Loeb Classical Library ed., 3 vols. Trans. by Benjamin B. Rogers. Cambridge, Mass., 1946–50.

Aristotle. On the Art of Poetry. Introduction, trans. and ed. by Ingram Bywater. Oxford, 1909.

———— Physica. Trans. by R. P. Hardie and R. K Gaye, in The Works of Aristotle. Ed. by W. D. Ross. 12 vols. Oxford, 1908–52.

Auden, W. H. (ed.). The Portable Greek Reader. New York, 1948.

Auden, W. H., and Norman Holmes Pearson (eds.). Poets of the English Language. 5 vols. New York, 1950.

Auerbach, Erich. Mimesis: The Representation of Reality in Western Literature. Trans. by Willard R. Trask. Princeton, 1953.

Augustine. The Confessions. Trans. by Edward B. Pusey. New York, 1949.

Baldwin, Thomas Whitfield. Shakespeare's Five-Act Structure. Urbana, 1947.

Bates, William Nickerson. Euripides: A Student of Human Nature. Philadelphia, 1930.

Bentley, Eric. In Search of Theater. New York, 1954.

———— The Playwright as Thinker. New York, 1955.

Bentley, Gerald E. "Shakespeare and the Blackfriars Theater," in *Shakespeare Survey*, I (1948), 38–50.

Bethell, Samuel Leslie. Shakespeare and the Popular Dramatic Tradition. Durham, N. C., 1944.

———— The Winter's Tale: A Study. London, n.d.

Boman, Thorlief. Das hebräische Denken im Vergleich mit dem griechischen. Göttingen, 1952.

Bowra, C. M. Sophoclean Tragedy. Oxford, 1944.

Bradbrook, M. C. Shakespeare and Elizabethan Poetry. London, 1951.

Bradley, A. C. Shakespearean Tragedy. 2d ed. London, 1905; reprinted 1952.

Brock, F. H. C. "Oedipus, Macbeth, and the Christian Tradition," in Contemporary Review, CLXXVII (March, 1950), 176–81.

Brooks, Cleanth. The Well Wrought Urn. New York, 1947.

Buland, Mable. The Presentation of Time in the Elizabethan Drama. New York, 1912.

Butcher, S. H. Some Aspects of the Greek Genius. London, 1891.

Buttrick, George Arthur, et al. (eds.). The Interpreter's Bible. 12 vols. New York, 1952–57.

Bywater, Ingram (ed.). See under Aristotle, On the Art of Poetry.

Campbell, Lewis. Tragic Drama in Aeschylus, Sophocles, and Shakespeare. New York, 1904.

Campbell, Lily B. Shakespeare's Histories. San Marino, Calif., 1947.

Chickering, Edward Conner. An Introduction to Octavia Praetexta. New York, 1910.

Clark, Barrett H. European Theories of the Drama. New York, 1947.

Clemen, W. H. The Development of Shakespeare's Imagery. Cambridge, Mass., 1951.

Coleridge, Samuel Taylor. Lectures and Notes on Shakespeare. London, 1884.

Collingwood, R. G. The Idea of History. Oxford, 1946.

Cornford, F. M. From Religion to Philosophy. London, 1912.

———— Greek Religious Thought from Homer to the Age of Alexander. Boston, 1950.

———— Thucydides Mythistoricus. London, 1907.

Crane, R. S. (ed.). Critics and Criticism: Ancient and Modern. Chicago, 1952.

Cullmann, Oscar. Christ and Time. Trans. by Floyd F. Filson. Philadelphia, 1950.

Cunningham, James Vincent. Woe or Wonder. Denver, 1951.

Danby, John F. Shakespeare's Doctrine of Nature. London, 1949.

Decharme, Paul. Euripides and the Spirit of his Dramas. Trans. by James Loeb. New York, 1906.

Dodd, Charles Harold. History and the Gospel. New York, 1938.

Duckworth, George Eckel (ed.). See under Seneca.

Eliade, Mircea. The Myth of the Eternal Return. New York, 1954.

Eliot, T. S. Selected Essays. New York, 1950.

Elliott, G. R. Scourge and Minister. Durham, N. C., 1951.

Empson, William. "Hamlet When New," in *Sewanee Review*, LXI (1953), 15–42 and 185–205.

Euripides. Alcestis. Trans. and Introduction by D. W. Lucas. London, 1951.

Euripides. The Ion of Euripides. Ed. and trans. by A. W. Verrall. Cambridge, Eng., 1890.

———— Ion, Hippolytus, Medea, Alcestis. Vol. IV of Euripides. Loeb Classical Library ed. 4 vols. Trans. by Arthur S. Way. Cambridge, Mass., 1946.

Farnham, Willard. The Medieval Heritage of Elizabethan Tragedy. Berkeley, 1936.

———— Shakespeare's Tragic Frontier. Berkeley, 1950.

Fergusson, Francis. The Idea of a Theater. Garden City, N.Y., 1953.

Feuillerat, Albert (ed.). See under Sidney, Sir Philip.

Fletcher, John. The Faithful Shepherdess. Ed. by F. W. Moorman. London, 1922.

Fluchère, Henri. Shakespeare and the Elizabethans. Trans. by Guy Hamilton. New York, 1956.

Frank, Erich. Philosophical Understanding and Religious Truth. New York, 1945.

Frankfort, Henri, *et al.* Before Philosophy. Harmondsworth, Eng., 1951.

Frazer, Sir James George. The Golden Bough: A Study in Magic and Religion. 13 vols. 3d ed. New York, 1951.

Freytag, Gustav. The Technique of the Drama. Trans. by Elias J. MacEwan. Chicago, 1900.

Frye, Roland M. " 'Out, out, brief candle' and the Jacobean Understanding," in *Notes and Queries* (New Series), II, 4 (April, 1955), 143–54.

Furness, Horace Howard. See under Shakespeare, A New Variorum.

Galloway, Marion. Constructing a Play. New York, 1950.

Gaster, T. H. Thespis: Ritual, Myth, and Drama in the Ancient Near East. New York, 1950.

Godley, A. D. (ed.). See under Herodotus.

Gomme, Arnold Wycombe. The Greek Attitude to Poetry and History. Berkeley, 1954.

Granville-Barker, Harley. On Dramatic Method. London, 1931.

Greene, William Chase. Moira. Cambridge, Mass., 1944.

Greenwood, Leonard Hugh Graham. Aspects of Euripidean Tragedy. Cambridge, Eng., 1953.

Greenwood, Ormerod. The Playwright: A Study of Form, Method, and Tradition in the Theatre. London, 1950.

Grene, David. See under Sophocles, Oedipus the King.

Hadas, Moses. A History of Greek Literature. New York, 1950.

Harrison, Jane. Themis. 2d ed. Cambridge, Eng., 1927.

Hazlitt, William. Lectures on the Literature of the Age of Elizabeth. London, 1909.

Hegel, G. F. W. The Philosophy of Fine Art. London, 1920.

Hernried, Erwin. "Weltanschaung und Kunstform von Shakespeares Drama," in *Zeitschrift Ästhetik und allegemeine Kunstwissenschaft*, Bd. 9 (1914), 502–34.

Herodotus. Loeb Classical Library ed. Trans. by A. D. Godley New York, 1921–24

Hoeniger, F. David. "The Meaning of The Winter's Tale," in *University of Toronto Quarterly*, XX (1950–51), 11–26.

Hooke, Samuel Henry (ed.). The Labyrinth. New York, 1935.

——— Myth and Ritual. London, 1933.

Hopper, Stanley Romaine. "The Future of Religious Symbolism: A Protestant View," in Religious Symbolism. Ed. by F. Ernest Johnson. New York, 1955.

Jaeger, Werner. Paideia: The Ideals of Greek Culture. Trans. by Gilbert Highet. New York, 1939.

James, E. O. The Beginnings of Religion. New York, 1952.

——— Christian Myth and Ritual. London, 1933.

——— Origins of Sacrifice. London, 1933.

Johnson, S. F. "Critics and Criticism: A Discussion of the Chicago Manifesto," in *Journal of Aesthetics*, XII, 2 (December, 1953), 248–57.

——— "The Regeneration of Hamlet," in *Shakespeare Quarterly*, III, 3 (July, 1952), 187–207.

Jones, Ernest. Hamlet and Oedipus. London, 1949.

Joseph, Bertram. Conscience and the King. London, 1953.

Kemble, John Philip. Macbeth and King Richard the Third. London, 1817.

Kent, Roland Grubb. "The Time-Element in the Greek Drama," in *Transactions and Proceedings of the American Philological Association*, XXXVII (1906), 39–52.

Kitto, H. D. F. Form and Meaning in Drama. London, 1956.

——— Greek Tragedy: A Literary Study. Garden City, N.Y., 1954.

Klausner, Joseph. The Messianic Idea in Israel. Trans. by W. F. Stinespring. New York, 1955.

Knight, G. Wilson. The Crown of Life. London, 1947.

Lattimore, Richmond. See under Aeschylus, Oresteia.

Laue, Theodore H. Von. Leopold Ranke: The Formative Years. Princeton, 1950.

Lawrence, William Witherle. Shakespeare's Problem Comedies. New York, 1931.

Lewis, C. S. "Hamlet, the Prince or the Poem?" in *Proceedings of the British Academy*, XXVIII (1942), 139–54.
——— Preface to Paradise Lost. London, 1942.
Lloyd, William Watkiss. Critical Essays on the Plays of Shakespeare. London. 1909.
Lounsbury, Thomas R. Shakespeare as a Dramatic Artist. Vol. I of Shakespearean Wars. 3 vols. New York, 1901–6.
Lucas, D. W. See under Euripides, Alcestis.
Mack, Maynard. "The World of Hamlet," in *Yale Review*, XLI (1952), 502–23.
Marsh, John. The Fulness of Time. New York, 1952.
Matthews, Brander. A Book about the Theatre. New York, 1916.
——— A Study of the Drama. New York, 1910.
Milburn, R. L. P. Early Christian Interpretations of History. New York, 1954.
Miller, Frank J. The Tragedies of Seneca. Chicago, 1907.
Moorman, F. W. (ed.). See under Fletcher, John; also under Shakespeare, The Winter's Tale.
Morgann, Maurice. "Essay on the Dramatic Character of Sir John Falstaff" (1777), reprinted in Eighteenth Century Essays on Shakespeare. Ed. by D. Nichol Smith. Glasgow, 1903.
Moulton, Richard G. Shakespeare as a Dramatic Artist. Rev. ed. Oxford, 1929.
Muilenburg, James. "The Faith of Ancient Israel," in The Vitality of the Christian Tradition. Ed. by George F. Thomas. New York, 1944.
——— "The History of the Religions of Israel," in The Interpreter's Bible, Vol. I. 12 vols. New York, 1952–57.
Muir, Kenneth (ed.). See under Shakespeare, Macbeth.
Murray, Gilbert. Aeschylus, the Creator of Tragedy. Oxford, 1940.
——— The Classical Tradition in Poetry. Cambridge Mass., 1927.
——— Euripides and His Age. New York, 1946.
——— (ed.). See under Aeschylus.
Murry, John Middleton. Shakespeare. London, 1948.
Nicoll, Allardyce. Masks, Mimes, and Miracles. London, 1931.
Niebuhr, Reinhold. Faith and History. London, 1949.
——— The Self and the Dramas of History. New York, 1955.
Nott, Kathleen. "Small Latin but More Greek?" *Partisan Review*, XXII, 4 (Fall, 1955), 556–60.
Oates, Whitney J., and Eugene O'Neill, Jr. (eds.). The Complete Greek Drama. 2 vols. New York, 1938.
Oesterley, William Oscar Emil. "Early Hebrew Festival Rituals," in Myth and Ritual. Ed. by S. H. Hooke. London, 1933.
Oesterley, William Oscar Emil, and Theodore H. Robinson. Hebrew Religion: Its Origin and Development. 2d ed. New York, 1937.

Otto, Rudolf. The Idea of the Holy. Trans. by John W. Harvey. London, 1950.

Pack, Robert. "Macbeth: The Anatomy of Loss," in *Yale Review*, XLV, 4 (June, 1956), 533–48.

Palmer, John. Political Characters of Shakespeare. London, 1948.

Parrott, Thomas Marc, and R. H. Ball. A Short View of Elizabethan Drama. New York, 1943.

Paul, Henry Neill. The Royal Play of Macbeth. New York, 1950.

Pedersen, Johannes. Israel, Its Life and Culture. 2 vols. London, 1926–47.

Pfeiffer, Robert H. Introduction to the Old Testament. New York, 1948.

Pickard-Cambridge, Sir Arthur Wallace. Dithyramb, Tragedy, and Comedy. Oxford, 1927.

——— The Dramatic Festivals of Athens. Oxford, 1953.

Porter, Charlotte (ed.). See under Shakespeare, The Tragedy of Richard the Third.

Price, H. T. Construction in Shakespeare. Ann Arbor, Mich., 1951.

Quiller-Couch, Sir Arthur (ed.). See under Shakespeare, The Winter's Tale.

Ribner, Irving. The English History Play in the Age of Shakespeare. Princeton, 1957.

——— "Political Doctrine in Macbeth," in *Shakespeare Quarterly*, IV (April, 1953), 202–5.

Richardson, Alan. Christian Apologetics. New York, 1947.

Roberts, Preston Thomas. Theology and Imaginative Literature. Doctoral dissertation, microfilm. Chicago, 1950.

Robinson, H. Wheeler. The Religious Ideas of the Old Testament. New York, 1913.

Robinson, Theodore H. "Hebrew Myths," in Myth and Ritual. Ed. by S. H. Hooke. London, 1933.

Rogers, Benjamin B. (trans.) See under Aristophanes.

Schelling, Felix Emmanuel. Elizabethan Drama. New York, 1908.

Schlegel, Augustus W. A Course of Lectures on Dramatic Art and Literature. Trans. by John Black. 2d ed. London, 1892.

Schmid, Wilhelm, and Otto Stählin. Geschichte der griechischen Literatur. Teil I, Band 2. Munich, 1934.

Seneca. Thyestes, in The Complete Roman Drama. Ed. by George Eckel Duckworth. 2 vols. New York, 1942.

Shakespeare, William. Complete Plays and Poems. Ed. by William A Neilson and Charles J. Hill. Cambridge, Mass., 1942.

——— Macbeth. Ed. by Kenneth Muir. New Arden Ed. London, 1951.

——— Macbeth. Ed. by John Dover Wilson. Cambridge, Eng., 1947.

——— A New Variorum Edition of Shakespeare. Ed. by Horace H. Furness. 26 vols. Philadelphia, 1871–1953.

Shakespeare, William. The Tragedy of Richard the Third. Ed. by Charlotte Porter. NewYork, 1903.
———— The Winter's Tale. Ed. by F. W. Moorman. Arden ed. London, 1912.
———— The Winter's Tale. Ed. by Sir Arthur Quiller-Couch. Cambridge, Eng., 1931.
Sidney, Sir Philip. Complete Works. Ed. by Albert Feuillerat. 3 vols. Cambridge, Eng., 1912–23.
Siegel, Paul N. "Echoes of the Bible Story in Macbeth," in Notes and Queries (New Series), II, 4 (April, 1955), 142–43.
Simpson, Cuthbert A. Introduction to and exegesis of the book of Genesis. The Interpreter's Bible. Ed. by George A. Buttrick, et al. 12 vols. New York, 1952–57.
Smith, C. Forster (trans.). See under Thucydides.
Smyth, Herbert Weir. Aeschylean Tragedy. Berkeley, 1924.
———— (trans.). See under Aeschylus.
Sophocles. Oedipus the King. Trans. and Introduction by David Grene. Chicago, 1954.
———— Oedipus the King, Oedipus at Colonus, Antigone. Vol. I of Sophocles. Loeb Classical Library ed., 2 vols. Trans. by F. Storr.
Spencer, Theodore. Shakespeare and the Nature of Man. 2d ed. New York, 1951.
Spender, Stephen. "Time, Violence, and Macbeth," in The Penguin New Writing 3. Ed. by John Lehmann. February, 1941.
Spurgeon, Caroline F. E. Shakespeare's Imagery. Cambridge, Eng., 1952.
Stoll, Elmer Edgar. Art and Artifice in Shakespeare. Cambridge, Eng., 1934.
———— Shakespeare and Other Masters. Cambridge, Mass., 1940.
Storr, F. (trans.). See under Sophocles.
Thomson, George. Aeschylus and Athens. 2d ed. London, 1946.
Thucydides. Loeb Classical Library ed., 4 vols. Trans. by C. Forster Smith. New York, 1919–23.
Tillich, Paul. Biblical Religion and the Search for Ultimate Reality. Chicago, 1955.
———— The Interpretation of History. New York, 1936.
———— Theology of Culture. New York, 1959.
Tillyard, E. M. W. The Elizabethan World Picture. London, 1952.
———— Shakespeare's History Plays. New York, 1946.
———— Shakespeare's Last Plays. London, 1951.
Tinkler, F. C. "The Winter's Tale," in Scrutiny, V, 4 (March, 1937), 344–64.
Traversi, Derek. Shakespeare: The Last Phase. London, 1954.
Tynan, Kenneth. He That Plays the King. London, 1950.
Verrall, A. W. Euripides the Rationalist. Cambridge, Eng., 1895.

Verrall, A. W. (ed. and trans.). See under Euripides, Ion.
Visser't Hooft, Willem Adolph. The Kingship of Christ. New York, 1948.
Vollborn, Werner. Studien zum Zeitverständnis des Altentestamentums. Microfilm. Göttingen, 1951.
Waith, Eugene M. The Pattern of Tragi-Comedy in Beaumont and Fletcher, New Haven, 1952.
Walker, Roy. The Time Is Free. London, 1949.
——— The Time Is Out of Joint. London, 1948
Way, Arthur S. (trans.). See under Euripides.
Weiser, Artur. Glaube und Geschichte im alten Testament. Stuttgart, 1931.
Weisinger, Herbert. Tragedy and the Paradox of the Fortunate Fall. East Lansing, Mich., 1953.
Welch, Adam C. Prophet and Priest in Old Israel. London, 1936.
Whatley, Thomas. Remarks on Some of the Characters of Shakespeare. London, 1770.
Whitman, Cedric. Sophocles: A Study of Heroic Humanism. Cambridge, Mass., 1951.
Wilson, Edmund. "On First Reading Genesis," in New Yorker, May 15, 1954, 30 : 130–40.
Wilson, John Dover (ed.). See under Shakespeare, Macbeth.
Wincor, Richard. "Shakespeare's Festival Plays," in Shakespeare Quarterly, I, 4 (October, 1950), 219–40.
Wolff, Max J. "Shakespeares Form," in Germanisch-romanische Monatschrift, Jg. 13 (1925), 382–90.
Wolff, Samuel Lee. The Greek Romances in Elizabethan Prose Fiction. New York, 1912.
Wright, G. Ernest. "Faith of Israel," in The Interpreter's Bible, Vol. I. Ed. by George A. Buttrick, et al. 12 vols. New York, 1952–57.
——— God Who Acts. Chicago, 1952.
——— Introduction to the book of Deuteronomy. The Interpreter's Bible. Vol. II. Ed. by George A. Buttrick, et al. 12 vols. New York, 1952–57.
Yaker, Henri Marc. "Motifs of the Biblical View of Time." Unpublished doctoral dissertation, Columbia University, 1956.

INDEX

Printed in Great Britain by
Richard Clay & Company, Ltd.,
Bungay, Suffolk

2